Winding Round
the Square

Winding Round the Square

Fall in love with a small mountain
town as you travel back with her
to another time and place

Betty Benedict

Library of Congress Control Number: 2009913423
ISBN: Hardcover   978-1-4415-9911-7
                  Softcover   978-1-4415-9910-0

To order additional copies of this book, contact:
Xlibris Corporation
1-888-795-4274
www.Xlibris.com
Orders@Xlibris.com
69767

DEDICATION

In memory of my parents

Fred and Carrie Benedict

With love to my children

Alisa Ann Lyon, daughter

Matt Sullins, Grandson

Shelby E. Sullins Puckett, Granddaughter

Chatham Michael Sullins, Great-Grandson

INTRODUCTION

Betty Ray Benedict at Four

This is the true life story of a little girl who grew up in a small mountain town during the Depression and World War II. She was sometimes conniving and often in one kind of mischievous trouble or another. From the age of four, she had no relatives in the area except her mom and dad, and yet she captivated an entire community with her comic and precocious antics. You will fall in love with this little girl, and feel you have lived these times with her as you go with her to meet the people she loved.

You will travel back to another time and place. It was the hardest of times, and yet the best of times, because the spirit of the mountain people made it so.

Many of the poems inserted throughout the book were composed by her before she was twelve years old. Most of these poems were written on table napkins while she was in her mother's restaurant.

Many of her antics seem unbelievable, but they are true. There was never a dull moment in Hayesville, North Carolina, when this little pixie was *Winding Round the Square.*

Each family home or business that she visited each day had something that held an interest for her. Most of all, she loved the people, and they returned her love.

The town of Hayesville is located in the westernmost part of the state in the middle of the beautiful North Carolina Mountains. The center of the town square has the historic Clay County Courthouse built in 1890. This story is the life experiences of Betty Benedict from birth through her high school graduation.

WITH GRATITUDE

CHARLES THOMPSON

Without the knowledge, help, work, and encouragement of my friend Charles Thompson, there would be no book. I talked, and he entered all the data into the computer. He spent many hours typing, researching, arranging pictures, and prodding me. His work on formatting the book was no small task. I pay tribute to him, and give him credit for the existence of *Winding Round the Square*.

NO USE OF MY BRAIN

Betty Benedict

I write well and have such a play with words
But I refuse to learn to spell
I also refuse to learn to punctuate or to type very well
I thought someone else could do it for me
I'm so above these mundane things
Just let me create and be rich and famous
Without any use of my brain

(Written in ninth grade, 1949)

ACKNOWLEDGMENTS

I met May Ferguson several years ago in Tucker, Georgia, and we have been close friends for over twenty years. We have helped each other with many changes in both our lives. It was a great surprise when May met and married Bill Atkinson, and moved to my hometown of Hayesville, North Carolina. I believe she has come to love Hayesville as much as a natural native. She and Bill live on Cold Branch in the community of Tusquittee that is mentioned so often in my book. She has two Master's Degrees in Education. She spent years in the Fulton County School system in Georgia. Any success of my book will be due in part to the work of May and Charles Thompson. We have labored over this book many, many long hours. You have read my poem in the beginning of this book, "No Use of My Brain." She and Charles have worked together diligently to get this book punctuated and worded as it should be. At times like these, when I need special help and expertise, I am fortunate to have a friend like May. She has given of herself, her time, talent, and energy for no other reason than caring and friendship. If all of my Ts are crossed and all of my Is are dotted, I owe it to my special friend May Ferguson Atkinson.

To Rob Tiger, grandson of my friend Mr. Bob Tiger, for his generous loan of his collection of Vintage Hayesville pictures featured in this book.

To Joy Padgett Loggins, for her generous contribution of the many pictures of our Gang. These pictures are scattered through the book.

Contents

PROLOGUE

Benedict Family
Moves to Clay County
1929

RED BENEDICT

My dad, Frederick Russell "Red" Benedict, was born on April 18, 1886, near Lexington, Kentucky. Horses were his most important interest and remained so throughout his life. He always considered his business opportunities a sideline. He took advantage of the times and the opportunities that came his way. He always kept horses as a constant in his life. As a young man, he worked on many of the large horse farms around Lexington, Kentucky. He also managed the racing stables and riding school owned by the Mashburn family in Louisville, Kentucky.

He and his brother, Robert Ellis Benedict, were the youngest children in the Benedict family. They were very close and were partners in most of the business ventures throughout the years. Once, they bought a candy factory that was going broke, revived it, and later sold it at a good profit. Between their business ventures, they would trade horses. Since there were no cars at the time, horses were the mode of transportation, and very much in demand. They would go into towns with a herd of horses and find a shady area for them. To attract people, they had a banjo player and singer named Bailey Brisco. He would entertain the crowd, while they paraded their horses for sale. Dad would also work as an auctioneer for tobacco sales in warehouses.

My dad was married three times. His first marriage ended in divorce shortly after my brother Ray Clyde was born. My brother Edwin was born before the second marriage ended. Edwin was raised by his maternal grandparents, the James family, near Lexington, Kentucky.

Ray lived with Grannie Benedict in Kentucky. Dad's brother, Robert Ellis, married Mattie Yates. Mattie Yates and Robert had a son J. Paul Benedict. Mattie died when J. Paul was only four years old. Grannie and Granddad Benedict brought J. Paul to live with them. J. Paul and Ray grew up together and were like brothers. Dad and Uncle Bob were home at Grannie's as much as they could be. Grannie and Granddad Benedict both died when the boys were less than eight years old. Dad and Uncle Bob had no choice, but to take the boys wherever their business opportunities led them. The two boys continued their education wherever they traveled.

When the stock market crashed in the late twenties, many large businesses failed. Dad and Uncle Bob seized the opportunity to buy merchandise from large bankrupt department stores throughout the country. They found that they could rent warehouses for very little money to store their merchandise. They rented store buildings in small towns in Kentucky, Georgia, Tennessee, and North Carolina to sell their merchandise. Dad managed the store in Murphy, North Carolina, and Russell Yates, J. Paul's uncle, managed the one in Hayesville, North Carolina.

Dad lived at the Dickey Hotel in Murphy, and ate his meals at a nearby restaurant. My great uncle, Luther Cearley, owned and operated this restaurant which included a bakery. The bakery was large and had trucks to deliver bread to grocery stores throughout the area.

(At that time, there was no sliced bread.)

CARRIE CEARLEY BENEDICT

My mother, Carrie Cearley, came from her home in Athens, Georgia, to Murphy to work for her Uncle Luther.

As she came into Murphy, she saw a large sign that said, "Visit Shields Service Station, the Only Indoor Restroom in Town." Seeing this, she said she wondered what in the world she was getting into. She started working in the restaurant and bakery for her uncle.

Carrie Benedict

Murphy was a major hub in western North Carolina. Two railroads, Southern and L & N, tied Murphy with Atlanta, Georgia, and Asheville, North Carolina. At this time, most freight was brought into the area by railroad. Freight was then delivered locally by horse and wagon.

One local freight line was owned by my friend Frances Beal's grandfather, Lawrence Francis Beal, in Murphy. He had four sons who worked for his freight line, and Frances's father, Ralph, had the route from Murphy to Hayesville. He would stop in Hayesville at the Commercial Hotel, owned by Frances's grandfather John O. Scroggs, spend the night there, and change horses at the Hayesville Livery Stable. He would then go on to Franklin, North Carolina. Halfway to Franklin, he would stop at a campsite to spend the night. His route back to Murphy was by way of Clayton, Hiawassee, Young Harris and Blairsville, Georgia.

Mother met Dad while working at the restaurant, and they started dating. They were married a year later, in March 1932. Dad said that he was sure she thought he was filthy rich. Dad thought Mother was beautiful. She had very black hair and blue eyes. He would often say she was as beautiful on the inside as she was on the outside. His favorite name for her was *The Good Woman*. He would often tell me The Good Woman changed his life.

Soon after Mother and Dad married, Russell Yates's wife became ill in Kentucky. Russell had to leave Hayesville to go back home. Dad, Mother, and Ray came to Hayesville to manage the Hayesville store. At this time, Uncle Bob came to manage the Murphy store. J. Paul stayed with his father, Uncle Bob, and later graduated from Murphy High School.

Mother, Dad, and Ray lived at Kate Passes Hotel in Hayesville. Ray was fourteen years old and very happy to have a mother; they became very close. Mother and Ray wanted to move into a home of their own, but Dad didn't seem interested. They would all go down and eat in the hotel dining room, and Mother said the food was very good.

Several months later, Dad went to Philadelphia to get stock for the stores that were running low on merchandise. While he was gone, Mother and Ray hired Didley Bryan to build living quarters in the back of the store. They moved in before Didley got the electricity connected. They used oil lamps and cooked their meals on a wood-burning stove. Mother and Ray had a great time making a home in the back of the store. When Dad came back to Hayesville and went to the hotel, Kate Pass told him his family had moved out. She said he would find them in the back of their store. He went there and was pleased with the job they had done. Mother and Ray had been worried that he would be upset with the move.

Across from my Dad's store on Tusquittee Street was the Blue Goose Restaurant, owned and operated by Pansy Bradshaw. Eventually, Pansy closed it, and then Bertha and Boss Cothern operated a restaurant there. This building later became the Duckworth home, and is now Friends of the Library Book Store.

The Depression had a very strange effect on the families in Hayesville. When Mother came to Hayesville, she was astounded to see so many pregnant women walking all over town. These women were pregnant with my friends—Bill and Earl Standridge had Amelia, Avis and Wilbur Mingus had Gay Nell, Neva and Ruel White had Mary Janice, Bonnie and Ralph Beal had Frances, Mattie Lou and Robert Penland had Jo Ann, Ethel and Harley Thompson had Charles, Minnie and Grady Palmer had Worth, Myrtle and Marvin Alexander had Patsy, Blanche and Horace Lyon had Quenton, Eva and Andy Padgett had Jerry, Mary and Bob Mease had Jane, Betty and Taft Wimpey had Howard, Edith and Claude Winchester had Evelyn, and Carrie Hope Johnston and Herbert McGlamery had Willa Jean. These children were all born in 1932. It wasn't long until Mother was pregnant with me.

I was born on May 6, 1933. Dad was thrilled; he had a baby girl born on the first Saturday in May, Kentucky Derby Day. Don Meade riding Brokers won the 57th Kentucky Derby. Postage stamps were three cents, bread, seven cents a loaf, gas, eighteen cents a gallon, cars, five-hundred-fifty dollars, and the DOW Index was one hundred.

Dr. May came to deliver me in our home in the back of our store. He gave me a whack on the butt.

I started crying, and he said, "My God, she looks just like old man Amos." Mr. Amos owned a shoe shop in town and was not a handsome man.

Grannie White came across the street from her house and gave me my first bath.

RAY BENEDICT

My teenage brother Ray was very excited to have a baby sister. All of his buddies in town gathered to see me. Ray wanted to name me. The other boys started suggesting names they would like. It was decided they would have a drawing. Ray made the rules. Each of his friends could put their favorite name in a box to draw. Ray said they could do this, but he wanted his name on every name that went into the box, thus every entry had to include Ray or Clyde.

Betty six months

**Nannie Belle Lyon
With Silk Dress from
Red Benedict's Store
holding Quenton Lyon**

Mother gave them a cigar box, and each wrote their favorite name on a strip of paper. They put them in the box and shook it up. They asked Dad to draw the name from the box. This was how I became Betty Ray. Hoover Anderson said he put in the name Margaret Clyde. I wished they had saved all the names. It would have been fun to see what my name might have been.

Mother was thirty-four years old when I was born. I was her only child. Grandmother Cearley could not imagine that a mother would allow a bunch of teenage boys to name her child. Mother loved Ray very much, and she knew this would make me very special to him.

Years later, I could not understand why I only had the name Betty. All of the other Bettys I knew have their real name Elizabeth.

I would question Ray and say, "Why didn't you have them call me Elizabeth?"

I was about thirteen years old. Ray was home, and he told me, "Your full name is Elizabeth Raymond."

I said, "Ray, it is not."

He said, "Go ask Mom if you don't believe me."

I went to the kitchen and asked her if my name was Elizabeth Raymond, because Ray said it was. Mother said, "Ray knows because he supervised the drawing."

I knew better. I went out and told everyone that I was Elizabeth Raymond, and wrote my name that way for a long time. Years later, I formed a corporation and named it Elizabeth Raymond Limited. Ray got a great charge out of this.

Joy Padgett at six Months

When I was two months old, Mother dressed me up, put on my little kid leather button shoes, and took me down to meet my little newborn friend, Joy Padgett. During the trip, I kicked off one of my shoes, and we never saw it again. I don't know when I first met any of my other friends, but Joy and I know. Mother took me to Willa Jean McGlamery's first birthday party on June 5, 1933, when she was only one. I was only one month old. Willa Jean is the daughter of Carrie Hope Johnston and Herbert McGlamery. They soon moved to Asheville, North Carolina. I would see Willa Jean when she came back to Hayesville to visit her Grandmother Carrie Johnston, and her first cousin, my friend, Regina Johnston.

Mother often talked about the high-fashioned clothes Dad had in his stores in small towns. This merchandise was from leading department stores all over the country. One of my first memories is sitting on the floor, on a blanket surrounded by loads of jewelry that would not sell during the Depression.

Blanche Mease Lyon told me years later, as she walked from Qualla community to town, that she found a fifty-cent piece on the sidewalk. She went into Dad's store and bought the most beautiful silk dress she had ever seen for only fifty cents.

Dad had wonderful fur coats that were very lightweight for sale in his stores. Many of the pretty ladies in town bought them, and said they were the warmest coats imaginable. I would sometimes put a fur coat over my feet at night when I was cold.

F. R. Benedict
Bargain Cash Store

"Where Your Dollars Have More Cents"

We have received a new line of men's wo-men's and children's shoes

Children's $1.10 to $1.29   Women's $1.49 to $1.95
Men's and Boy's $1.50 to $2.25

We also have men's odd coats at a bargain, all sizes, colors

Sweaters from .50c to $1.29

All underwear at a reasonable price

Outing, per yard 10c.   Sheeting, per yard 8c. and 10c.
Ladies's hose 15c. All other dry-goods at a BARGAIN

GROCERIES

Sugar per lb.   5c.   Guaranteed Flour, Plain
Coffee 2 lbs.   25c.   and Self-rising $1.00 to $1.10
Cotton Seed meal $1.35 .   Cotton Seed hulls   75c.

We pay market price for chickens, eggs, dried fruit, clay peas, rye, corn and irish potatoes

Red Benedict sale sheet

Mother has told me about wondering where Dad, Ray, J. Paul, and Uncle Bob put their dirty clothes. She said she would never have a washing load for anyone except herself. She asked Dad what they did with them. Dad explained to her that they just threw their dirty ones away, and got new ones at the store. Mother was horrified, and said she would wash and iron them. Apparently, Dad had plenty of stock in the stores and warehouses. He got these clothes for almost nothing, and said the laundry bill would be more than he paid for a new item. Mother told Dad that it seemed like she had married into a bunch of Gypsies. She said she had never heard of anything like it.

Before Dad opened his stores in North Carolina, he was trying to find a location in Hayesville, while staying at the Kate Pass hotel. Mr. Bob Tiger owned the most prosperous department store in Hayesville. Dad got word that Mr. Tiger was upset about another department store coming to town. He visited Mr. Tiger and explained to him that he would only be in business until his merchandise ran out. They became good friends, and the friendship lasted until Dad passed away in 1965.

As the store merchandise dwindled and after much discussion, Mom and Dad decided a restaurant was needed in Hayesville. They rented a building near Dr. May's office on the square, and Mother used her previous experience to open the restaurant and prepare the food. The location was small, and they soon needed more dining room space. Silvey Penland built a restaurant building for them to rent. A garage was built on one side, and was rented to another tenant. Dad had Gulf Oil gas pumps added at the front of the restaurant.

Later a dime store was built in the garage space for Leonard (Shorty) Crawford. An apartment was made in the back of the dime store where Catherine and Frank Crawford, Leonard's brother, lived with their daughter Betsy Jane. Betsy was two years younger than me, and we would often play together. They had lived in Christine Anderson's house before moving into the apartment, and Frank taught and coached football at Hayesville High School.

Mr. Leonard Crawford was married to Eva Woodring. They lived on the highway to Murphy, near Warne, North Carolina. Their son, James, was their only child; sometimes he would come to the store, and we became friends. Mr. and Mrs. Crawford and James later moved to a house on Riverside Drive where Allen Bell's family had once lived. This house was next-door to Joy Padgett's house.

Dad bought the Sanderson house on the courthouse square from Ed Curtis. It is just across the street from our restaurant. We moved from the back of Dad's store to this house shortly before his merchandise ran out, and he closed the store.

We had more room in the two-storey house than we did in the back of the store. On the first floor, Ray and I had our own bedrooms. Mother and Dad used the kitchen for their bedroom. We didn't need a kitchen because we ate all our meals at the restaurant.

HHS 1937

Rays Hayesville High Football Team, 1937

We also temporarily rented rooms to other families. Claude and Edith Winchester, with their children Billy and Evelyn, moved into the dining room and the second parlor to the right of the stairs on the first floor. Upstairs was rented to Martha Herbert Campbell and her husband Percy. This made three families in our large new home on the square.

Mother and Dad would go across the street to open the restaurant every morning and leave Ray and me in bed. When I got up, I would go to Ray's room and wake him up. He would put my bathrobe on and carry me across the street on his shoulders to have breakfast at the restaurant. We ordered our eggs over medium; this worked out greatly for me. I would eat all of the yellows, and Ray would eat all of the whites. We continued to divide our eggs this way for years when we were both home.

In the evenings, Ray would take me with him to milk Dad's cows. They were kept in a pasture below Mrs. Flora Davis's house and the jail house in town. I would carry an olive jar with holes punched in the lid to catch lighting bugs. Many of my little books had stories of pretty little fairies that live in pastures. Each evening, I spent some time looking for them in the grass and under leaves. At night after I went to bed, I would often think of the fairies, and how they must look as they play in pastures among the flowers.

Mom and Dad were busy, but Ray was very good to take care of me. Once, I remember Ray and his friends taking me to a place where there had been a cloud burst. I remember climbing a steep bank on the side of the road. This event had the town's people excited.

One night, Ray took me to the school. They had a country-music show in the high school auditorium. He got us seats on the aisle so I could see well. The stars of the show were James and Martha. All of a sudden, they announced that Hot Shot Elmer, a country comedian, was there. He came down the aisle yelling loudly, hopping and jumping and carrying on. Frightened, I grabbed Ray around the neck, and I remember he had to hold me in his lap for the rest of the show. Many country music shows came to town, but I never wanted to go to another.

Ray Benedict

When I was four in 1937, Ray graduated from Hayesville High School. Mother, Dad, and I sat together and watched Ray in his cap and gown receive his diploma. We were very proud. I didn't know that this night would be near the end for my brother, being a part of our every day family life. Within a few weeks, Ray and several of his buddies joined the U.S. Navy to see the world.

At four years old, I didn't understand what this meant. I remember when he put a cigar box on one of the stools in our restaurant. He put his shaving things into the box, and placed it in a small valise with some of his clothes. He picked me up and held me and told me to be a good girl. He hugged Mom and Dad, and they had tears in their eyes. The next thing I knew, he was gone. I went into a deep grieving time. Mother could not get me to eat. I sat in my rocking chair and rocked and rocked.

I would say, "Come back, Ray. Come back, Ray" over and over again.

Everyone tried hard to be good to me and make me laugh. I remember wanting to be left alone.

We soon got a letter from Ray and mother read it to me. I had her read it over and over in the part where he said he missed me and to tell me that he would be home in a few weeks. This lifted my spirits, and I felt happy again. Ray would be coming home soon. I carried that letter around with me, and slept with it under my pillow.

The next thing I knew, Dad came from the post office with a large package. They had sent home the clothes my brother wore on the day he left. I just fell down on the clothes and cried and cried. I thought that my brother, my Ray, was dead, since no one explained that the Navy sent your clothes home when you enter boot camp. It seemed that I grieved for many weeks. I have never forgotten the way I felt.

The leather jacket that he had worn in high school was in the clothes returned from the Navy. I grabbed the jacket, went to my rocking chair, and I rocked holding the jacket close to me. Sometime later, Mother wanted the jacket to be put with Ray's other things, but I held on to it day and night. I slept with it, and carried it everywhere I went. I wore it when it was cool, making me a full-length coat. Mother would try to take it from me.

Dad said, "Carrie, let her keep it, it is already ruined and will never be worn again."

I have to admit it looked pretty ragged, and I had worn it out.

Mother and Dad became very worried about me. Mother later told me that she had no idea that I thought Ray was dead. I lost a lot of weight, and they became concerned that I was going to be seriously ill. They talked to Dr. May; he had them give me cod liver oil and a terrible-tasting powder stirred up in milk. I would take the cod liver oil and almost be sick. Then, here they came with the milk and stuff stirred up in it. Someone would always sit with me until I drank it all. It was terrible.

One day, I was on the porch of our house lying on a blanket. I looked up and saw a sailor way up the sidewalk. He had a large box about the size of a trunk upon his shoulder. As he came closer I realized it was Ray. I have never moved so fast. I ran to meet him; he dropped the big box and his duffle bag on the sidewalk. He grabbed me, and threw me up in the air. I put my arms around his neck, and he could not get me loose.

He kept saying, "Whoa, whoa, let me get my things so we can go see Mom and Dad."

I had dragged his leather jacket up the street to meet him.

Looking at his jacket, he said, "Buddy, (my nickname by Ray) what on earth have you done to my jacket?"

I just grabbed it and ran screaming "Ray is back, Ray is back" over and over again. Someone had gone to the restaurant to tell Dad and Mom because they came running to meet us.

He took the big box over to the house and told me to open it. It was full of toys. There was a monkey that climbed a stick, a bolo paddle and ball, a yo-yo, a little sink with a faucet that turned. You filled a tray on the back with water, turned on the faucet, and it would run just like a real sink. There was a stove, a tea set, pots and pans, a doll with two front teeth, hair, eyes that opened and closed. I named her Shirley. There was a dust pan with a handle long enough to stand and sweep into. Mother used it for years. Included was a little feather duster for cleaning the house, and an upright vacuum cleaner with a bag on it. I later took all of these presents over to the restaurant to display them to all our friends and guests who came in. Ray said that he had a layover in Franklin, North Carolina, where he went to a dime store and bought all these things for me. He then caught the bus to Hayesville; we did have buses coming to our town at that time in 1937.

Mother told Ray about the problems they were having with me. She told him she had known all the time that it was grief over him leaving. He talked to me before he left to go back to the service. He said, "I will never leave you, forever. I will always come back home." It was many years later when I told him that I thought he was dead when his clothes came back.

I was relieved and felt that he would be back. Although I missed him, I never had the terrible lonesome feeling again. Little did I realize that we had some horrible times ahead of us when World War II came four years later, on December 7, 1941.

PART ONE

1937-1947

WINDING ROUND THE SQUARE

I am having such a wonderful time winding round the square. There are many fun things to do and interesting people here. The Square is my playground and the people are my friends. If you would like, I'll take you there and introduce you to them. We will start at Mother's Restaurant, where she is very busy and doesn't have time to talk. Then, we will go down to the knoll where the circus comes in spring, and then across to Dad's town stable, where he hangs out with half of the men in town. It's lots of fun there; they tell jokes, some I don't understand.

GRANNIE WHITE

Grannie Whites Home

I go around to visit Grannie White. Remember, she gave me my first bath when I was born. She has a well right in the middle of her kitchen. It's the only well in a kitchen that I know of. Her name was Lena McCracken before she married Mr. John White. When Mr. John was the Clay County Sheriff, he and Grannie lived in the jail. Her son, McCracken, (Mac), was born while they lived there.

Grannie said, "He's the only baby ever born in that jail."

Her sons Ray and David are at home, and they are a lot bigger than me. She has other children who have left home, and some are married and have children of their own. Her sons are: Garland, Ruel, Ray, Mac, Fred, Joe, and David.

Juanita Crisp

Grannie lost her second son, little Magellan, when he was only six years old. Grannie's heart was broken again when her teenage son Joe ran off from home. Grannie worries and talks about Joe almost every day that I visit her. She loves Joe and wants him to come home. My friend Mary Janice is Ruel's daughter. I have always known her, and she plays with me at the Square. Grannie loves all of her children and grand children, and she talks about them almost every day.

Sidney Crisp

We have a library in our courthouse at the Square. Everyone says that any book they check out has Lena White's (Grannie White) name in it. Reading has made her very wise. She knows just about everything there is to know about anything.

Gengie Jones

She belongs to the Hayesville Baptist Church, a little white, wooden church in town. She teaches Sunday school there. Grannie speaks often of Gengie Jones being so bright and knowing the Bible so well. She talks about Mr. Martin Crisp's daughters, Sidney and Juanita. She says, "Oh, they are such lovely girls." I also think they are very pretty. Mr. Crisp is superintendent of the Sunday school.

Grannie makes beautiful quilts for people who don't want to make their own. She has these big wooden quilt frames that hang from her ceiling in the front room of her house. She rolls the frames up as she quilts, and the smaller they get, the nearer the quilt is to being finished. I sit with her at the quilt frame and watch her take very tiny stitches. She tells me many stories of her childhood and the way things have changed in her lifetime. A highlight of her life was when her son Mac took her to Florida's Silver Springs to ride in a glass-bottom boat. She describes so vividly the beautiful colorful fish she could see through the bottom of the boat. I often close my eyes at night and picture the beautiful fish swimming deep in the water until I go to sleep.

Grannie will not let me quilt on any of the quilts she makes for other people. She told me I could quilt when she makes some for herself. I have now quilted on several. Her sons Ray and David have quilts on their beds I helped quilt.

(Ray told me years later that he has the quilts that I helped quilt, and he said he wanted me to have them. I don't know what happened to them, but I never got one.)

Ray said, "They are special quilts because you helped quilt them."

John White

Sometimes, people who pass on the street knock on Grannie's door and ask for a cold drink of water from her well. Sometimes, this interrupts her work. So now, she fills a bucket with water several times a day. She puts it out near the street with a metal dipper. People can help themselves to the well water and not bother her work.

If I stay the whole day with Grannie, we stop around lunchtime and sometimes have a picnic. We take a little wash pan of water to wash the vegetables. We take a basket that has salt, pepper, cornbread, and a knife. When we get to the garden, we pick lettuce, radishes, tomatoes, cucumbers, and onions. We peel our vegetables and wash them in the water. The corn bread and vegetables are the best food. Our picnic at the side of the garden is the most fun I can think of.

If I stay at Grannie's till late afternoon, Mr. John, Ray, David, Grannie, and I sit around the dining room table and have something good to eat. We call this our supper. Mother is from Athens, Georgia, and she calls it dinner. Mother often sends someone from her restaurant with food and a desert because she knows Grannie is very busy. Mother always worries that I will be trouble for Grannie. Grannie says I am never trouble to her.

Before I leave Grannie's house to go home, I thread a bunch of needles for her, and stick them in the quilt at one end of the frame. Grannie says this helps her more than I can ever know because she has poor eyesight. She also tells Mother what a great help this is to her. Grannie taught me how to knot the end of the thread on each needle.

Sometimes, I spend the night at Grannie's. I have a black leather suitcase that really belongs to my dad. I put one of his belts through the handle so I can drag it down the street. It is too heavy for me to carry. I fill it with my night clothes, my doll, Homer Gene, my coloring books, crayons, and story books. If I am lucky, Ray or David will read one of my books to me. I like to look at the pictures, but I cannot read many of the words myself.

Grannie named my rubber doll Homer Gene, after a little boy that is akin to her. His family lives out west somewhere. Homer Gene's family came to visit Grannie. We were really excited to have them come. Grannie said that I could come to stay and play with Homer Gene while he was there. I was really disappointed because Homer Gene turned out to be a great big boy, and he wanted nothing to do with me. Even though it turned out that way, we still call my rubber doll Homer Gene. When I spend the night at Grannies, I sleep in a tiny room off the dining room. I think of this room as my own. I am very fortunate to have Grannie, Mr. John, Ray and David as my special friends.

MY HOUSE

Let's go up to my house setting on the square. We have a great big backyard, but no front yard there. The big upstairs and downstairs porches give us plenty of room to play. Our house is called the Sanderson House. Mrs. Pearl Herbert was a Sanderson, and she grew up there. The house has a kitchen that is just one big room. The only way you would know it is a kitchen is the great big fireplace with metal arms swinging out to hang your cooking pots on. We use this room for a bedroom because we don't need to cook at our house on the square. We eat our meals at Mother's restaurant across the street.

Betty's home today in Social Circle, Georgia.
Same plan as the one in Hayesville.

OUR BACKYARD

Our house faces the courthouse. We have a big gazebo in our backyard that has an old well. We sometimes draw water from the well. The Sanderson family used this well before the town had city water. My dad partitioned the gazebo to make me a playhouse. My friends and I made a garden in our backyard. Dad had it plowed; he gave us corn seeds and tomato plants. We worked very hard. All of our plants grew way above our heads. We were so excited, but our corn never had any corn on it, and our tomato plants never had a tomato.

We told Dad, "We have done all our work for nothing."

Dad said, "Oh, I don't believe so. If someone was having a garden contest, I think this garden would win the prize for the largest corn and tomato plants ever seen anywhere."

We don't know where we can find a contest, but I don't think we will try another garden next year because people can't eat corn stalks or tomato plants.

SKATING THROUGH THE COURTHOUSE

Sanderson—Benedict House

My yard is a gathering place for me and my friends. If we want to roller skate, we go to the courthouse square and skate on all the sidewalks there. The courthouse has a big hall running through the middle of it, from one end to the other. The floor is concrete, and we can skate through there. We jump over the steps at the other end, land on the sidewalk, and just keep going. The people working in the courthouse told Dad what we are doing, and he told us not do it anymore. We didn't do it for a while, but then it got too tempting, and we skated through it again. If the workers in the courthouse are busy, we get by for a while.

Betty Frances Cherry

Our skates are not the kind they have in big-city indoor skating rinks. Our skates fasten on our shoes with a key that turns to tighten them on the shoe. The wider the sole of the shoe sticks out, the easier they are to fasten. Most of us have a pair of shoes that look like winter shoes, and we use these to skate with year-round.

Mr. Glover Ledford works in the courthouse. He came to my dad, and said, "Red, these children are taking over this town."

Since I live near the courthouse, this makes it easy for people to complain to Dad about every little thing we do. My friends are lucky because they live further away and never get in the kind of trouble I do.

GRADY PALMER'S BARBERSHOP

Amelia and Betty

On the right hand side of our house, facing the courthouse, there is a side yard where we sometimes play. Between this yard and Thompson's store is a small barbershop. Grady Palmer works there. He cuts the men's hair and gives some of them a shave if they don't want to shave themselves.

Dad gets up every morning, takes his bath under the stairs at our house, and then walks next door to the barbershop. He gets up in the barber chair; he doesn't have to say a word. Grady lathers up his face, puts a hot wet towel over it to soften up his beard. He takes a straight razor and gives it a swarp or two on a leather thing they call a "strop," then he shaves my dad. Dad gets up and splashes Old Spice, his own favorite shaving lotion, on his face and pats it until it is dry.

When Dad needs his haircut, he will go to the barbershop first thing in the morning. Grady gives him a haircut and shave, then Grady puts powder on a brush and tries to get all the hair off his neck. Dad goes back to the house, takes his bath and shampoos to get all the loose hair off.

Amelia Standridge

Mentory, our housekeeper, fusses under her breath because she says that Dad leaves hair in the bathtub. We are used to her fussing, and the grown people pay no attention to her at all. I don't understand it, but Mother tells me I have to listen to her, and do everything she says. I guess it doesn't surprise anyone that I sometimes don't listen.

Grady cuts my hair and all of my friends'. My friend Amelia Standridge stays at my house most of the time. We have watched Grady shave so many men that we often play barbershop in the front room of my house. We have a sofa and a matching large chair. We are small, but we work until we get the front of the chair tilted back on two Sears Roebuck catalogs. It leans back, and makes a fine barber chair. My dad has everything we need to shave and play barbershop. He often brags about his straight razor having a real ivory handle. Amelia found out that ivory is made from elephant tusks.

While playing barber, we hooked my dad's leather strop on the arm of the big chair so many times it finally made a hole in it.

One day, Mother asked, "What on earth made this hole in my chair?"

Mentory, Teddie, and Tish, our housekeepers, knew why the hole was there, but they did not tell on us. They threaten to tell on me every time they ask me to do something that I don't want to do. This is what you call blackmail. I told Amelia we had better not call them blackmailers to their face, because they would tell Mother on us. They all know that we are lathering up, and shaving each other with a straight razor.

While the housekeepers work doing laundry and ironing for our home and restaurant, they are also supposed to look after me. Mother has white linens on all the tables and chair backs in the restaurant that they wash and iron. This keeps them very busy.

(Many years later I told Dad about us using his straight razor and the house keepers not telling on us.

He said, "Lord have mercy, what about them letting you all do something so dangerous. They probably were hoping you would cut your throats."

Mother said, "I was so busy working at the restaurant; it was a great wonder that you ever survived it all.)

DRESSING UP

We play a lot in the side yard between our house and the barbershop. I have two neat tables made out of wooden baking soda boxes. Didley Bryan put legs up in the corners of each box to make the tables. I use these tables for many different things.

We have a big fish bowl where Mother kept her goldfish. They died, and we now play with the big goldfish bowl. We put some tablecloths on our tables to make them look good. When we play dress-up, we have our goldfish bowl on a table with different sizes of paper wadded up into round balls. Sometimes we play like we are grown-ups. I have dresses, high-heeled shoes, hoses, pocketbooks, gloves, hats, and loads of pretty jewelry. These are things that did not sell in Dad's stores. Dad says there was little demand for evening dresses in the little towns where his stores were located. When my friends come over to play dress-up, they can pick the outfit they want to wear. After we dress, we can go to the fish bowl and pick out two of the wadded-up paper balls, the size we want our boobs to be. We put them down in our dress, and tie a string under them so they will not fall out.

Mentory says, "You girls are a sight for sore eyes. What will people think, seeing you girls strutting around with your chest stuck out?"

No one else has ever said a word about it even though we sometimes strut around the Square.

Mother will often let us have food from the restaurant. We set the other table with my tea sets and have a grown-up party. We either roll up white paper, or have candy cigarettes to pretend we are ladies smoking. We want to look like the beautiful ladies we see in the movies or on the billboards advertising cigarettes.

(We had never heard that cigarettes were harmful. All of the movies showed beautiful ladies smoking. We thought that in order to be very glamorous, we had to have a cigarette.)

ALL ABOUT SEX

Often, when we are playing with our dolls and playing house, we try to figure out how babies are born. We know that there is something called sex, and we know this has something to do with babies being born. We have discovered that each of us has a little faint line that goes down the middle of our stomach. We have decided that this must be where the baby comes out. We think this is like a zipper, that it comes open, the baby comes out, and then it closes back up. We have figured this out, and we are pretty sure that this is the way it is.

We also know that in order to make a baby, you have to be married. After you are married, the two people sleep together. If they decide they want a baby, they can make a baby while they are in bed. This is done by lying on top of each other. If they want the baby to be a girl, the wife lays down on top of the man. If they want a boy, the man lays on top of the woman. We don't know how long they have to lie there like that, but we think that this happens almost immediately.

When we play like we are making babies, we lie down on each other and then get up immediately. We pretend our zipper opens and the baby comes out. We always have our doll handy.

I was in mom's restaurant one evening and a man came in, and everyone congratulated him on his wife just having a baby boy.

The man said, "Well, it was an accident this time."

I got real confused thinking about how anyone could have a baby if they didn't plan to. My friends and I have discussed it, and are quite sure the man must have rolled over on the lady without intending to while he was asleep. That's all we could figure out, and it does make sense. I bet they will be more careful from now on, because he didn't sound very pleased.

One thing we know for certain is that the woman always has the baby, and she has to take care of it and feed it. We see some of the women who come to town from out in the country feeding their babies. They have milk in their boobs. We don't pretend to feed our babies this way. Homer Gene has a bottle. We feed him, and he wets his diaper, and we have to change it. Homer Gene is just the right size to be a newborn baby; he has been born over and over.

AUNT NANNIE BENEDICT BOWLES

Betty Benedict

My tongue is loose on both ends
That's what my Daddy said
I'm just like his sister Nannie
And that can't be so bad
Because she has people around her

Wanting to be her friend
I hope I'm really like her
But I sure wouldn't want her name
She isn't pretty really
But most people don't know that
They just see a marvelous creature
Who knows how to talk and laugh
She also knows how to listen
And that is most important
I need to learn to do that too
I am sure some people doubt it
I am going to dye my hair black
When I am too old to spank
I am going to smoke cigarettes in a holder
And travel all over the world
I can't wait to do all this
It will sure be lots of fun
Not to have to slip and smoke down behind the barn

COURTHOUSE STORE

We sometimes stroll across the street to buy candy from Mr. Frank Curtis. He has a little room in the courthouse where he sells his candy. We like to have some money to spend with Mr. Curtis because he has only one arm and needs money to take care of his family. It's good of whoever runs our courthouse to let him have his little store there. Mr. Curtis is always very glad to see us. We always enjoy our visits and buying his candy. He tells my dad that he appreciates us buying candy from him because he knows we have plenty of candy at the restaurant.

BIRTHDAYS ON THE SQUARE

I have always had my birthday parties on the Square. Mother sets up the two soda box tables and another big table. She puts very pretty table clothes on each table. I ask her to make angel food cake for my birthday because this is my favorite. She actually makes two cakes and puts lots of white icing that she calls "seven minutes" on one, and lots of chocolate fudge icing on the other one. I have birthday candles on both of them. I have candles for each year of my life and one to grow on. I get to make a wish on the white cake first, and if I don't get them all blown out, I get another chance on the chocolate cake. I usually blow real hard and blow out the candles on both cakes. That way, I get two wishes that are supposed to come true.

The first time I ever had a birthday party, I was two years old. Mother said I didn't understand exactly what a birthday party was. She said I woke them up very early that morning and said, "Let's go see if my party is out on the Square."

All of my friends have birthday parties, too. We take presents to the parties. We usually have a dime or spend up to a quarter on each gift. We can get some neat gifts at the dime store for a dime. You have splurged if you spend a quarter. Some of the things that my friends give to me are little bottles of Prell or Halo shampoo, hair bows, socks, and all kinds of toys. One birthday, two different people gave me a white dish that had a lid on it that looked like a hen sitting on a nest. They cost a quarter each at the dime store. I put them on each end of the mantel in my room, and I intend to keep them forever.

Sometimes we get perfume. At my last birthday party, Tommy Gray gave me a grown-up bottle of cologne. It is Richard Hudnut, Yankee Clover Toilet Water, from New York/Paris. It is sold at Booth's Rexall Drug Store on the Square. I am sure that Tommy's mother, Viola Gray, picked it out for me. I also got a bottle of perfume shaped like a tiny oil lamp. The perfume in the bottom looks like the oil for the lamp. You can buy them at the dime store for a dime.

SMOKING

One birthday, Mother's friend Katherine Eller gave me a pretty red jewelry box that looked like a little red suitcase. It has a compartment at the top that lifts out, has a lady pearl necklace, and big pearl earrings in it. These are for playing dress-up. When you lift the top tray out, there is a good-sized space underneath.

The housekeepers who work at our house smoke cigarettes. Sometimes they ask me to go over to Mom's restaurant and get them a pack of cigarettes and a dope, without letting anyone see me.

(Softdrinks of all kinds were called "dopes" in this area.)

I take my rubber doll Homer Gene across the street to the restaurant because I can snap off his head and snap it back on. I can put a dope and two packs of cigarettes inside Homer Gene, snap his head back on, and carry him back across the street. I soon got tired of making so many trips. I took Homer Gene across the street, and when everyone was in the kitchen and no one was in the restaurant, I filled him with one pack of every kind of cigarette Mother had, and a cloth bag of Bull Durham smoking tobacco. I also got a pack of paper to roll your own cigarettes on. I want to put the bag of Bull Durham in my flannel shirt pocket so I can play cowboy and roll my own cigarettes. I had to go back later to get Bull Durham for the rest of my friends.

(There were only a few brands back then—Camel, Lucky Strike, Chesterfield, and Phillip Morris.)

I put all of these cigarettes in the bottom of my red jewelry box. I put the tray with my pearls and earrings on top. If anyone opens my box, they won't see my cigarettes, unless they lift the tray. I hide the red box under my bed to keep it hidden from the workers.

Now, when a worker asks me to get cigarettes, I take a pack out of the bottom of my jewelry box. I walk around a while outside, and then bring them in, and give the cigarettes to them. Later, when no one is around the front register, I replace the pack I gave away. Sometimes, my girlfriends and I go into my bedroom, sit on the floor with our backs against the bed, and smoke cigarettes.

There is a little girl who lives in town whose mother will not let her play with us. She did come over one day, and we asked her if she wanted to smoke.

She said, "I guess so."

We lit up our cigarettes, and she turned to me and said, "Why, we can smoke, can't we?"

When it was time for her to go home, we told her that her mother could smell the smoke in her breath.

She said, "What am I going to do?"

We told her to get an onion from the store next door and eat some of it. Then her mother would not smell it.

She went to the store next door and brought back an onion. She ate some of it, and we had her blow in our face to see if we could still smell the smoke. We kept saying we could smell it so she would eat some more. She ate so much, she had to go out into our backyard and throw up.

I feel rotten about this because I know we shouldn't have made her sick. The next Sunday, my Sunday-school teacher taught a lesson on doing to others as you would have them do unto you. I just hung my head because I felt so ashamed.

(Wonder why her mother would not let her play with us.)

GAMES ON THE SQUARE

Martha Herbert, Evelyn Crawford, and Ione Herbert

My friends and I love the afternoons in beautiful weather when the ladies come to the Square in their beautiful dresses to play crocket. We follow them around to watch, and hope that we will someday be as pretty and as fashionable as they are. When we play dress-up, we sometimes play like we are some of those ladies: Charlotte Wakefield, Ann Wakefield, Virginia Bryan, Mary Jo Chambers, Opal Anderson, Christine Prater, Katie Anderson, Ione Herbert, Martha Herbert Campbell, Neva White, Catherine Crawford, Christine Bell Booth, Geneva Smith, Ada Ross Waters, Viola Gray, Jewell Ledford, Jessie Martin, and Catherine Eller.

After a while, a group started playing horseshoes on the courthouse square. Many of the people in town became upset because it was ruining the grass and making an eyesore on the square. Needless to say, horseshoes did not last very long.

One of the things we like to play in the courtyard is hopscotch. No one ever says anything to us about drawing hopscotch squares on the side walk. We also love to sit on the rock wall around the Square and play jackstone.

MOONSHINERS HAVE COMPETITION—
BEER IS LEGAL

Clay County voted in beer and wine in the late thirties. Boy, this has caused a big commotion in Hayesville. We didn't need a vote for liquor, because Moonshine had always been made all over our Tusquittee Mountains. Moonshiners make their liquor with sugar and corn in what they call moonshine stills. The ones who sell moonshine are called *Bootleggers*. They also have what they call *Moonshine Runners* who load their cars with the liquor and go as fast as they can to get to Asheville, North Carolina, or other big cities. Sometimes they have to go very fast to get away from the law.

The moonshiners who have stills usually live way back in the mountains, and they live in constant fear of the Federal Revenuers. They carry shotguns all the time around their homes, and up to their stills because they never know when the revenue agents might come. They keep someone on the lookout all the time.

I remember when the revenuers came in and broke up a bunch of stills up there. The agents brought all the liquor they found to the town square. Most of it was in glass fruit jars. They unloaded all the liquor into one big pile, busted them, and let them run all over the street. It was a hot summer day, and the fumes could be smelled all over town. Many men just stood around rubbing their chins, saying, "What a waste of good liquor." The revenue agents had brought in the moonshiners they had caught. They were put in jail to be tried at the next court session.

The county sheriff and his deputies were hopping mad because the federal agents got in their cars and drove off, leaving broken glass all over the street. The sheriff let the moonshiners out of jail to go back to their homes.

I heard my Dad say, "The mountain people have always built stills to make liquor; it's their way of life and all they have ever known. It will not take long for them to rebuild their stills and make their moonshine as they always have."

I think the men whom I hear talk know what they are talking about. They say the revenue agents waste their time and taxpayers' money. Moonshining goes on and on.

BEER JOINTS COME TO TOWN

Since the vote to legalize alcohol, beer joints are popping up overnight. We have Wily McGlamery's beer joint in an old tin building next to Everet Crawford's house. Across the Main Street on the other corner is Bass Duvall's beer joint. He sells Little Man Ale, and has a big neon sign up above his door, that of Little Man Ale holding a tray of ale bottles. His arms go back and forth holding the tray. This is one of the neatest things I have ever seen. His legs also move. I'll bet this sign cost Bass Duvall a lot of money. If the ladies in town have their way, they will vote out the beer and ale and Mr. Duvall will have to take his sign down.

McGlamery Red Top Beer

I don't go into either of these places. Up beside the Methodist Church on the Square is Violet Passmore's beer joint and sandwich shop. I did go into Violet's one time, because Mary Jo Chambers and Neva White took Mary Janice in there to get tomato sandwiches. I went in there to get Mary Janice to come out and play with me.

All of the beer joints seem to have a contest to see who can play their jukebox the loudest. The music is all over the Square, and it all runs together because they are playing different songs at each place. We don't play our restaurant jukebox really loud. People living in town are as mad as hornets because the music is so loud.

Ms. Juliette Crawford and Mr. Everet Crawford are next door to the McGlamerys, and they say they can't hear each other talk in their own house. The nights are booming here in Hayesville; there are always lot of things going on around the square.

(Hayesville did not keep beer legal for very long).

WINDOW VIEW OF NIGHTS ON THE SQUARE

Mother works late in the restaurant every night, so she always has a girl take me over to bed and stay with me. Long before we go, Dad builds a fire in my bedroom and the sitting room. Mother has someone at the restaurant fill up our hot water bottles to warm our beds. Some of the girls who stay with me have boyfriends who come to see them without Mother knowing. After putting me to bed, the girl meets her boyfriend out back in the gazebo. I don't mind this, because when they go outside, I get up and go to the front-room window. I raise it up just far enough so I can see and hear everything on the Square. Our front-room windows go from the ceiling to the floor and have weights in them. Although I am small, I can put my hands in the two handles at the bottom and raise the window.

In the winter, I wrap up in a quilt and put my hot water bottle against my stomach at the window. Many nights, there are fights outside the beer joints. The police come to lock people up, and one of the deputies loves to use his blackjack. Dr. May has an office on the Square across from our house. Some nights, Dr. May comes to his office to treat people hurt in fights or car wrecks. Many times, they have to take them up the stairs to his office on a stretcher.

The other night, it was very late when Cardine Moore was in a wreck, and he had to be brought to Dr. May's office. Dr. May took very good care of him, and now Cardine is all right. I am sure Dr. May regrets they ever started selling beer on the Square. Although we always had people drinking Tusquittee Moonshine, the town was never as wild as it is now.

When I sit in my window, I stay on the lookout to see when the lights go out at Mom's restaurant. The girl out in the gazebo watches, too. She comes in the backdoor and jumps in her bed. I am already in mine and pretend to be asleep. Mother always checks on me before she goes to bed. I never forget to let the window down. Mother told Dad that he wastes his time building fires. She says this is the coldest house she has ever seen. We have lots of quilts on our beds, and our water bottles keep us warm.

I wear flannel pajamas and a bath robe that looks like an Indian blanket. It has a twisted cord that looks like a rope with tassels on the end for a belt. I sometimes wear my Brother Ray's leather jacket over my robe.

My wine-colored house shoes are made out of felt. These house shoes only come in wine or navy blue. Men can get them in wine, blue, or brown. Almost everyone has these house shoes and Indian blanket bath robes. Dad used to have them in the store where I got mine; now you can buy them anywhere. The only things I take off when I jump in bed are the house shoes. Sometimes, after I get in bed, I'll find I still have one house shoe on.

My bed is wonderful. It has a big, fluffy feather bed mattress on it that my Grannie Cearley gave to me. I snuggle down, and the feather bed comes up around me, and it feels good and warm. Mother has Mentory take it off when spring comes. If I had my way, I would leave it on all year round.

ILLEGAL SLOT MACHINES IN HAYESVILLE

Vaughn Cannon, out of Asheville, North Carolina, brought slot machines to Hayesville after beer became legal. All of the beer joints and Mother's restaurant had them. The beer was legal, but the slot machines were not. Everyone knew it was against the law to have slot machines in North Carolina. It was also against the law to make moonshine whisky, but people did.

When the Feds found out that Hayesville had slot machines, they came into town to pull them out of the businesses. Dad heard they were in town when they were on the other side of the Square. He and some of the men who were in the restaurant threw his slot machines on the back of a truck and covered them up. They took them up Tusquittee to Boss Cothern's house before the Feds got to our restaurant. When they got to the Cotherns, they were not at home. Dad and the men went ahead and put the slot machines through a small opening into the attic. Boss and his wife came home later, and they never knew the slot machines were there.

Meanwhile, the Feds took the slot machines out on the corner of the square, and busted them up with sledgehammers. Money was all over the street. Before they left town, they swept up the money and put it in cloth bags and left with it. They didn't get my Dad's.

Dad later had Vaughn Cannon come over from Asheville, North Carolina, to get his slot machines. The first time Boss Cothern knew the slot machines were in his attic was when Dad and Vaughn

Cannon came to his house to get them. Vaughn Cannon was very pleased to get his slot machines back.

(Vaughn later served time for illegal activities in North Carolina.)

DREAM OR NOT?

Did you know that in Thompson's store, just past the barbershop, a man was hypnotized? He peddled a stationary bike in the window which did not go anywhere. Seeing him gives me the creeps, and I don't have them often. I don't know how many days he was in there. I watched for his eyes to blink, but they never did. I can't believe that he doesn't know everything that is going on. I knock on the window, but he never moves, except to pedal his bicycle. They say he goes from town to town doing this.

I guess Mr. Thompson has to pay him. One night, I slipped out of the house after Mom and Dad had gone to bed to see if he was still there at night. He was still sitting in the window, pedaling away. I got back to our house, and no one knew I had been out there.

(Years later, no one I mention this to ever remembers this event—the rider in the window. It is so vivid in my mind that I cannot believe it was a dream. If anyone remembers this, I would like to know. Does anyone else remember this?)

STEALING A BALLOON

Mr. Leonard "Shorty" Crawford owns the dime store right next to our restaurant. We all love to go in and look around. He has some candy we like that only cost a penny. I save my money and often buy something that cost more than a penny and sometimes more than a dime. When I have a quarter or fifty cents, I can buy something very nice.

All my friends must be at home today, and I am bored. I am trying to find something to do, so I go over to the store by myself. I look around the store a good while, and I don't see anything I want. I know I should not do this, but I pick up a penny balloon, look around to see if anyone is watching, put it in my pocket, and leave the store. It only costs a penny, and I can afford to buy as many balloons as I want. I go over to the restaurant to our sitting room and blow up the balloon.

Mother comes in and I quickly let the air out to try to hide it.

I said, "It isn't anything."

She said, "Get up and let me see. Where did you get the balloon?"

I said, "Over at the dime store."

She said, "Why are you hiding it? Did you pay for it?"

I said, "No," and started crying.

She said, "You know you shouldn't have taken the balloon. You know it is stealing. Bring the balloon and come with me, and we are going over to Mr. Crawford's to tell him what you did."

I said, "Do we have to do this? I will never be able to go into that store again if you make me do this."

Mother said, "Betty, you should have thought about that before you took something that didn't belong to you."

I took a penny and the balloon; we went over to tell Mr. Crawford that I came in his store and stole a balloon. I told him I was very sorry, and I would never steal anything from him again. We went back to the restaurant, and I lie down on the wicker sofa and cry and cry because I knew Mr. Crawford would never trust me again.

I do go back in the store, but only when my friends are with me. I always put my hands behind my back and clasp them together. I never touch anything. I just look at things because I don't want Mr. Crawford to think I am about to steal something. I sure wish I had never stolen that balloon. I still don't know why I had the urge to do it.

Christmas is coming. It has been a while since I stole the balloon. One day, Mr. Crawford came over to eat lunch at the restaurant.

He asked me to come over to his table and said, "Betty, would you like to have a job?"

I replied, "What kind of job?"

He said, "If it is all right with your Mother and Dad, I would like for you to be a floor walker during the Christmas season."

I said, "What does a floor walker do?"

He said, "All you have to do is walk around the store and act like you are shopping, but keep an eye on all the people in the store, and make sure that no one is taking anything. This is to be a secret between us, because it wouldn't do good for people to know they were being watched."

This made me feel wonderful. I know now that Mr. Crawford believed me when I told him I would never take anything again. I go to work every day, get a lunch break, and go back to work in the afternoon. I can't tell my friends that I have this job.

CURTIS HOUSE—WELFARE

The Curtis house is on the corner, up the sidewalk from my house, past the barbershop and Thompson's store. This is at the corner of the square and Tusquittee Street. It is a big two-storey house similar to ours, with porches upstairs and down. I always think of it being bigger than ours, because you have to go up more steps to get on the downstairs front porch. Our front porch is low to the ground. Mr. Ed Curtis was raised in this house.

Due to the Depression, President Roosevelt has set up places all over the country to give food, clothing, and other items to help the needy. There are a number of women who come to the Curtis House every day to make clothes and mattresses for people on welfare. This house is known as the sewing room. They get in yards and yards of blue and wine corduroy cloth. The kids who wear these clothes are known as the corduroy kids. I feel sad when I see them; I try to be nice and friendly to them.

The ladies who work at the sewing room also make mattresses for people who have none. Some of the people out in the country sew feed sacks or burlap sacks together, and stuff them with wheat straw to make their mattresses. Some of them stuff their mattresses with corn shucks. The mattresses made in the sewing room are stuffed with cotton batting with a cover of mattress ticking over it. I am sure these mattresses are better to sleep on than the ones stuffed with straw or corn shucks.

The Curtis house is also used as the welfare place where the government gives out food to the needy. Many of the people on welfare live in the Tusquittee Mountains, and a lot of them don't have cars. They get together and come to town with people who own cars. They go to the welfare office and pick up their food. After getting the food, they wait on the side of the road, across from Dad's stable, to catch their rides back home. They are given grits, meal, rice, and flour in great, big bags like those holding my dad's livestock feed. They can't just take what food they want; they have to take everything they are given.

While they wait for their rides, they cut holes in the bags of the things they don't want, and pour it out on the side of the road.

Sometimes, the ditches are full of rice and grits. I think most of them take the meal and flour home. We sometimes have fun sliding around in the grits and rice they have thrown out.

They get big cans of all kinds of food—pork and beans, prunes, raisins, oatmeals, peaches, and apricots. If there is any food they don't want, they just leave the cans on the side of the road. They leave a lot of canned apricots, carrots, and prunes.

Sometimes, my friends and I carry the cans up to our play house in the gazebo. Once, we ate so many prunes that I don't have to tell you what happened. They also get canned ham, turkey, roast beef, and chicken. They are given big rolls of bologna, just like you see over at Tiger's Store before it gets sliced.

Big rounds of hoop cheese in round wooden boxes are given, and sometimes they have more of this than they want. Dad told them not to throw the cheese away, so they sometimes give him some. They are given big boxes of pudding mix, peanut butter, oatmeal, big boxes of powdered milk, and lots of fresh fruit, along with bags of oranges, grapefruits, and apples.

One time, they came down in front of our stables with big hundred-pound bags of grapefruits. They were so excited, but thought these were big oranges. Since they had to wait for their ride, they decided to sample some of their big oranges. Several of them bit into the grapefruit and were shocked with the taste and started cursing, saying, "These are the worst oranges I've ever tasted." They had a great time reaching in their big bags and throwing the big grapefruits against the bank and bursting them. Those grapefruits just flew all over.

The Curtis house has become overcrowded with sewing, making mattresses, and giving out food. The government rented Dad's vacated store building to house and give out food to the needy. Everyone had known where Dad's store was located.

When people came into town to get their government food, they went to the sewing room at the Curtis House where they were getting food before. They were told the food had been moved to the Old Benedict Store. Many people did not understand and thought that Dad was in charge of the food given out at his new location, Mother's Restaurant. Dad had to explain that the food was where his old store had been. People keep coming in and saying they were told the food had been moved to the, *Jews' Place*. We did not know until then that many people thought we were Jews. Dad says it is a compliment, that Jews are very hardworking people and great businessmen.

WPA

The WPA is another government program making jobs for people who need them. They did a lot of work just to be working. They built out door toilets all over town and out in the country. They would build you a toilet whether you needed one or not. The first thing we knew, we had an outdoor toilet between our house and Dad's stable. It was made out of nice creosote-treated wood. It had a concrete floor and a poured concrete thing like a commode that had a wooden seat that you could raise and close. We didn't need one because we had a toilet in our house.

This was just up my friends and my alley. We got some old satin cloth and some silver tinsel that you put on Christmas trees. We put the satin over the seat with the lid closed and draped it all down on the floor. We draped the tinsel all over the inside walls. We had a crown to play with, and we took turns being the queen. We dressed up in all our finery, and sat on our throne in the WPA toilet. We spent many hours playing there. Dad would bring his buddies from the stable to see our throne.

The WPA workers came to the square and built wonderful circular wooden benches around some of our trees. Everyone loved this. It was not only wonderful to sit on the benches, but it made our courtyard look beautiful. My friends and I play paper dolls upstairs on the benches in the courtroom when it is rainy or or when the weather is bad. We love our outdoor benches, because we play paper dolls under the trees in beautiful weather. It didn't seem to me like our benches lasted very long. People started carving initials or writing on them with their knives. The benches became such an eyesore that the city decided to take them out. Everyone said that all of the drunks from the beer joints were the ones who ruined them. They also made use of them at night. They would bring their beer outside, sit on the benches, and argue and curse very late. After the benches were gone, they did not come over into the Square as much.

GYPSIES IN TOWN

There are always strange things and strange people coming to our town. The gypsies come almost every spring in a gypsy caravan, and park down at the knoll behind the restaurant. I don't know if they ask anyone if they can camp there or not. They are a bad lot. My friends and I would never go over to the knoll to see the gypsies, because we are afraid of them. Everyone in town gets upset with their presence here.

They walk around in droves all over town. They visit our restaurant and the stores, and steal anything they can get their hands on. People sometimes see them take things, but they are afraid of them, so they just let them steal and go. This makes me very nervous. I dread them coming every year, and the whole town rejoices when they leave.

My friends and I sometimes dress up like the gypsies. We pull our soda box table right up to the edge of the sidewalk in front of our house. We offer to tell fortunes for the people passing by. We have a cup on our table for people to leave us money, if they want to, after we have told their fortune. We don't ask them for money. If Mother finds out we are telling fortunes for money, she will make us stop. I usually read palms, and Amelia uses her mother's playing cards to tell their fortune. I would like to have a crystal ball. They say you can see futures in those.

The interesting thing is that it seems no women want their fortunes told. Our customers are always men. Sometimes we get a quarter, dime, or penny. Amelia and I go over to Tiger's store with our money and buy stuffed green olives in a jar. We pull out the red stuff, and eat it first, and then we eat the rest of the olive.

Sometimes, we take our money to Mr. Frank Herbert's pool room, and buy those big dill pickles for a nickel that he has in a large jar on the counter. Mother has plenty of dill pickles, but we think Mr. Herbert's are better because they are bigger.

RIVER OF MEMORIES

Allen Bell has a favorite song—"Did You Ever Go Sailing." It is on our jukebox in the restaurant, and he plays it everytime he comes into the restaurant. It costs five cents to play a record.

I learned the song from start to finish by listening to the jukebox. I told him that I knew his song, and I could sing it. He asked me to sing it for him. I did, and he gave me a large fifty-cent piece. He told me that he would rather hear me sing, than to listen to the record with someone singing who he does not know.

Allen Bell

Fifty cents is a lot of money. I went to the dime store next door, and bought me a set of tools. It had a large handsaw, hammer, chisel, square, pliers, screw driver, level, and a measuring tape. I got all of this with my fifty cents.

Mr. Bell is a wonderful man and a great entertainer. He can stand straight up, and throw his leg across his shoulders behind his head. He dances around on one leg and makes everyone laugh. When we have cake walks and entertainment at our school, he loves to do this to get people in a good party mood.

Now, whenever I meet him, he wants me to sing his song. I sing it at the Square, or on the sidewalk; each time, he gives me a fifty-cent piece. Other people often gather around and listen. He asked me not to spend my money on anyone but myself. He said that he had heard about the nice things I did by spending my money on other children. I think Allen Bell is one of the best friends I have.

(Allen Bell later became superintendent of Clay County Schools.)

PAINTING

One morning, I got up and looked out my window at the square. There was an old, run-down paneled truck pulled up against the rock wall. There was a man pulling out all kinds of boards. He pulled out an artist easel, and set one of the boards on it. He had a big case of paints and started painting on the board.

I couldn't wait to get over there to see what he was doing. I pulled on my clothes with Mentory screaming at me to comb my

River of Memories

hair. I combed my hair, and went over to the Square. I told the man I was Betty Benedict, and asked him his name. He said it was John. I asked him what he did with his paintings.

He said, "I will sell them to anyone who will buy them."

I couldn't wait to tell my friends. We all gather around him and watch him paint. People are buying his paintings, and I think he is making lots of money. One day, when I was watching him paint on a little narrow board, I was amazed when it was almost finished because there it was, right before my eyes, Allen Bell's *River of Memories*. I asked John not to sell the picture because I wanted it. I told him I would go get my Dad.

I brought Dad across the Square, and he gave John a dollar for the painting. My oil painting was still wet when we took it home. John said to be very careful with it for a couple of days and to bring it back and he would frame it. He frames all of his oil paintings with scrap pieces of moldings. I set my oil painting on my chest of drawers at the foot of my bed. I make believe that I am there in the painting, in the boat, sailing down my *River of Memories*.

(I still have this painting in my upstairs parlor. I often look at it and imagine that Allen Bell and I are in that boat sailing around our *River of Memories*.)

THE EARLY ANDERSON HOUSE

Across the street from the sewing room is Early Anderson's big two-storey house. My brother Ray's friend, Hoover Anderson, known as *Brother*, lives there. Mrs. Mamie Anderson and Mr. Early have a large family. The ones I know are Omar Lee, who is a lawyer, and married to the prettiest woman in town, Katie Anderson. They now live in Mr. Bud Anderson and Mrs. Edna Anderson's old house. Omar Lee and Katy eat dinner at our restaurant every evening.

The other children whom I know are Charles, Kermit, and Hugh (Hugie), Sally Jo, and Betty Jean. Betty Jean is several years older than me, but she still takes time to play with me. Her dad, Early, has a store and workshop right below their house down the sidewalk on Tusquittee Street. Betty Jean helps me dye my eggs at Easter time in one of their egg-candling buildings. Her dad buys eggs, chickens, wild animals, and animal hides that people have tanned on boards. Sometimes, it does not smell very good there.

They have a staircase that goes to an upstairs window that is octagon-shaped. I would love to have a window like that in my house. It would be a wonderful place to play in, like you were on a ship.

Hugie has always been very nice to me; he has a tricycle that is very old. He was pushing me one day on the tricycle when I got my big toe hung in the pedal, and it tore my toenail off. Blood was flying everywhere. Hugie grabbed me and ran with me to Dr. May's office. He fixed me right up, and my toe healed good as new. I got a brand new tricycle out of the deal, courtesy of Dad.

(Hugie became a lawyer, like his brother Omar Lee. Mrs. Mamie taught school for many years at Hayesville High School. She taught me in Home Economics for two years.)

FRED PASS DRUGSTORE AND SODA SHOP

Across the street from the Anderson house and down the street on the Square is a soda shop owned by Fred Pass. He has little Coca-Cola tables in there that have seats that swing out from under the table. I can't get on one of these seats unless someone holds it out, because it will swing back in before I get on.

I like to sit at the soda fountain, anyway. The stools are tall, but I can get on them. There is a bright, shiny black top on the counter that looks like marble. The reason I like to sit at the counter is that I can talk to my friend Wallace Crawford, who works there after school. I check with people to find out when school is out every day, because I cannot tell time.

Not too long ago, Mother's brother, Paul Cearley, came to see us. Uncle Paul and I walked across the Square to the Fred Pass drugstore to have a treat. I had seen people ordering Alka-Seltzer, and it looked like a fun drink to me.

Wallace Crawford asked, "What would you like?"

I said, "I'll have an Alka-Seltzer."

Uncle Paul and Wallace said at the same time, "You don't want an Alka-Seltzer."

I said, "I want one."

Wallace gave me a glass of water and a tiny package that had the Alka-Seltzer tablet wrapped in it. I opened the pack, and dropped it into my glass of water. I was so excited to see it fizzle. I brought it up to take a sip; the bubbles tickled my nose, and I still thought I had done something great. Then I took a sip while they were both watching me. I swallowed it, smiled, and acted just like I was in Heaven. I drank the rest of it, and thought I was going to throw up. Needless to say, I will never want another Alka-Seltzer.

Soda fountains all have these white paper cups that are twisted around and glued and have a very sharp point at the bottom. They have a black cup holder to put them in so they will set up. If you want to take your drink with you, you can take it out of the holder and hold it around the point. These cups do not hold very much. I would much rather get a coke in a bottle, because you get more for your money. They are both five cents.

MASONIC TEMPLE

The steps on the right side of Fred Pass's soda shop go up to the Masonic Temple. They have secrets I would like to know. I've heard they ride Billy Goats, but I don't think they do it up there. They wear silly little aprons and strange hats. They dress up like Arabs. Mother sometimes takes food upstairs when they have dinner.

The Eastern Star ladies also meet up there. They install their officers and swear in a woman they call a *Worthy Matron*. One time, they asked me to sing at their program, and I did. I got confused up there as they walked around little tables, lighting candles. I know it must be something good, because the ladies who belong to it would not join if it wasn't. The one thing I liked is that they wear fancy, long evening gowns. I don't know anywhere else in town where you would wear a long evening gown.

TELEPHONE CENTRAL OFFICE

The steps on the left side of the soda shop go up to the Telephone Central Office. Mr. Jim Penland, who is blind, owns our phone company. Christine Prater works at the switchboard. She sits all day long at a desk-like thing that has a tall board behind it with lots of little holes. She has electrical cords that have a plug on the end. They plug into one of the many holes in the big board. Everyone who has a phone in Hayesville has one of the holes assigned to them in Christine's switchboard. Every one with a phone has a cord with a plug on it. Your cord stays in your hole, unless someone is calling you. When someone calls you, she takes your cord and drops it down and places your callers' plug in your hole, and that connects your phone to theirs. Each person is assigned a ring.

When our phone rings, it rings a long-short-long; we have no private lines in Hayesville. I think the most private line you can have is a three-party line. You can hear the rings of each party on your line. If you hear their rings, you are not supposed to pick up the phone, but many people do. This is called eavesdropping. One lady on our three-party line listens to every call on her line. She knows all the gossip in town.

Glen and Christine Prater and their daughter Glenda Prater live in the back of the central office. They have a living room, two bedrooms, a kitchen, and a long room that runs across the back of the building. They have a commode and lavatory in a small room in the back. They have a long folding canvas bath tub. I can't figure out how they empty the water. I always wanted to take a bath in it. Glenda is one of my good friends, and she plays with me every day on the Square.

POST OFFICE

Down from the phone office is an old bank building, but we don't have a bank now. The bank went broke when the stock market crashed, and lots of people did not get their money out. It is now the post office where Uncle Ed Mease works.

Hayesville Bank

The first time Mother let me go to the post office to get our mail, I was so excited my tongue got twisted.

I said, "Any Mease, Mr. Mail?"

I will never live that down with Uncle Ed. He always reminds me of this every time I enter the post office.

He says, "Any Mease, Mr. Mail?"

Uncle Ed says that I am the smartest, friendliest girl in town. He always greets me anytime I meet him. Dad told me he knows just about everyone in the county. He was a county land surveyor for many years. I think he is one of the nicest men I know.

DIDLEY BRYAN

Didley Bryan

Fred Pass's Pure Oil Service Station is on the opposite side of the Square from my house. W. T. Hunt and Didley Bryan work there. Fred wears his glasses

Fred Pass Pure Oil and Crawford Sinclair at the Red light Pass Hotel at the back of Sinclair

on top of his head. I don't know what good they do, unless he has a set of eyes that I don't know about.

Didley Bryan is one of my bestfriends. The station gets in little books that they

WT Hunt

give out when people buy gas. These books are for little children, and Didley always saves one of each for me.

Some of them are coloring books, others are paper-doll books, and some are hard cardboard punch-outs. You can put them together to make different things like cars, trucks, boats, and airplanes. These are very hard for me to put together. Didley helps me put them together when he has time. Didley can fix anything and does repair work for people. He is a plumber, and he put our bathroom in under the stairs. If I break something, I always know that Didley will fix it.

I have a small ironing board that is made of wood, and it folds up when I am not using it. I had it set up one day over at our restaurant, and a drunken man came in and sat down on it. He went to the floor, and the legs of my ironing board were broken to pieces. I grabbed the pieces and ran crying across the Square calling for Didley. He came to meet me and wanted to know what was wrong. I showed him my broken ironing board.

He said, "Stop crying and don't worry, I will take it home and fix it tonight."

He brought it back the next day, and it worked fine. It is good to have a friend like Didley Bryan who can fix anything.

TIGER'S DEPARTMENT STORE

TIGER'S CASH STORE: Formerly WALKER STORE - Located on Site of CHINQUAPINS

Mr. Tiger's Department Store is up from the Pure Oil Station and is a big green wooden building with display windows on each side. It has nice steps for running up and down. My friend Star Bristol works here.

I come here to try on ladies' beautiful, fancy hats. I especially like the ones that have veils to pull down over your face. I make sure my hands are clean before I touch the hats. They have a beautiful hand mirror with a long handle. It is green and has flowers painted on the back. The hats are on little hat racks for display on each side of a dressing table. The table has a big mirror on the back and adjustable mirrors on each side. Sitting in a chair, you can see the hat on your head from all angles.

A man named Mr. Booth built a Rexall Drug Store between Mr. Tiger's store and the Pure Oil Station. Star left Mr. Tiger and went to work for Mr. Booth next door. Neva White, my friend Mary Janice's mother, came to work for Mr. Tiger. I was making my regular rounds one day, and I went in to try on hats. I sat down at the little table and put one of the hats on my head and picked up the mirror.

About that time, Neva White said, "No, no, Betty, don't touch those hats."

Mr. Tiger heard her, and said to her, "Always let Betty try on the hats; that's why she comes in here."

I have always liked Mr. Bob Tiger, and after this, he is a special person to me. I don't think Mother would like it if she knew about me trying on hats. I don't tell her.

(The lot for this location was purchased in 1910 by Bob Tiger and Frank Herbert for $50.00.)

COMMERCIAL HOTEL AND MRS. LAURA SCROGGS

Mrs. Laura Scroggs owns and lives in the Commercial Hotel on the corner just across the street from Mr. Tiger's store. She is my friend Frances Beal's grandmother. I visit her almost every day. She is a grand lady to me. She is very old, and is always sitting in the same room even when there are many rooms in the hotel not in use. Miss Fronnie Bramlett stays with her. Mrs. Scroggs has Miss Fronnie bring in a pretty tea set with a cup and saucer on a pretty tray. Mrs. Scroggs pours hot water into her cup. She never has any tea or anything in the hot water. She drinks hot water every afternoon.

I asked Mother to give me some tea bags and sugar cubes to take to Mrs. Scroggs. I figured she was down on her luck, and could not afford to buy tea. I was happy the day I could take her some tea and sugar. When I gave it to her, she thanked me for it, and told Miss Fronnie to bring me a cup and saucer. She put a tea bag and a cube of sugar in my cup and poured hot water on it. She then put hot water in her cup and started drinking it. I explained to her that I had brought the tea for her. She told me that she drank hot water every afternoon for her constitution.

I didn't ask her what her constitution was, but I wanted to remember that word so I could ask Mother what it meant. I could hardly listen to Mrs. Scroggs talk because I was repeating over and over in my mind "constitution," "constitution." I didn't go down to see Mrs. Lizzy Scroggs and her daughter Becky Scroggs that day. I went straight to the restaurant. All the way, I kept repeating "constitution" in my mind. I went straight to Mother and asked her what "constitution" meant. She started telling me about our country's constitution and Bill of Rights. I still cannot figure why Mrs. Scroggs drinks hot water for our country's constitution. I am confused.

Commercial Hotel—Mrs. Laura Scroggs

Each time I go to see Mrs. Scroggs, I love to look at her pretty white bisque figurines. They set in shelves on each side of her mantle. The figurines are cherubs and angels. I told her one day that I could paint them with my crayons if she wanted me to. I told her I thought they would look better. I had planned to ask her this for some time. She said that would be great. I took my crayons the next time I went to see her, and she had Miss Fronnie Bramlett get one down for me to paint. I finished, and Mrs. Scroggs said it was very pretty. She liked it very much. She had Miss Fronnie set it back up on the shelf. Each time I go to visit, she has Miss Fronnie get a figurine down for me to paint. Mrs. Scroggs likes for me to come visit, and especially color the figurines.

Miss Fronnie just shakes her head and makes grunting noises. I can tell she thinks I am a pest. She would rather that I not come at all. What she thinks doesn't bother me.

MISS LIZZIE AND MR. PEARL SCROGGS

After I visit Mrs. Laura Scroggs, I go down the little street between the Commercial Hotel and Mr. Bob Tiger's Store. There is a pretty little yellow two-storey house with white ginger bread trim where Mr. Pearl Scroggs and his wife Miss Lizzie live. Before Miss Lizzie was married, she was a Haigler. Their house is the old G. H. Haigler House where she grew up, and she and her daughter, Rebecca Scroggs, are usually at home. I love their house; it has many interesting things.

The thing I like most is a pair of wooden shoes from Holland. They set on a table in the front parlor. I went there many times before I got the nerve to ask Rebecca if I could try them on. She and Miss. Lizzy seemed glad for me to wear them. The wonderful thing is that they fit my small feet. I clump around their house, and sometimes while I am wearing the shoes, Rebecca takes me upstairs to see the things in her room.

Lizzy Scroggs

Pearl Scroggs

Miss Lizzy and Mr. Pearl Scroggs's Home

The stairs curve with tiny, little steps, and they end right at Rebecca's room. You must step high at the last step to get up to her room. It is difficult for me since I am wearing the wooden shoes. I don't think an old person would be able to get up there. I think it must be neat sleeping there. The wooden shoes clonk-clonk up the stairs and back down again. We come down stairs, and I take off the wooden shoes. I thank them for letting me wear them. They usually give me a hug and tell me to come back any time and wear them.

I can tell when people want me to visit by the way they act. Mother is afraid that I worry people by visiting them. I would not go if I thought I wasn't welcome.

HERBERT HOUSE

Pearl & Frank Herbert

The next stop I make *Winding Round the Square* is up the little street and just across from the Commercial Hotel to Mrs. Pearl Herbert's house. It is a two-storey house with a large porch on the front, facing the square. Mr. Frank and Mrs. Herbert have a large family. All of their children are grown-ups. They have a big side porch on the street facing the Commercial Hotel, and it is very private. They eat out there in the summer, and every afternoon they serve tea.

Martha is the oldest daughter and is married to Percy Campbell. She is always so glad to see me that she grabs me and hugs me no matter where we meet in town. I love Martha, but sometimes I dodge her. Every time she hugs me, she bends way down, and my face gets buried between her big boobs. I am almost smothered.

Their children, Frank Junior Herbert, Ione Herbert, Clara Herbert, and Robert Herbert are always glad to see me. They offer me a glass of ice tea. I don't care about the tea, but the ice tea spoons they have are wonderful. The spoons are made of something called celluloid. You can put your mouth on it, and draw the tea up just like a straw. On the other end is a spoon for stirring your tea. They have them in many colors. I wish Mother would get some of these. I think they are wonderful. I drink my tea, thank them, get hugs all the way around, and tell them goodbye.

One day, when I was making my rounds, I stopped by Mrs. Pearl's; she was all excited. She seemed to be what you call agitated. Frank Junior is in the service; he is very handsome in his uniform. He is stationed away from home, and has met a girl named Carmella. He called the family to tell them that he was bringing her home to meet them. Mrs. Pearl was wringing her hands, and saying over and over that Frank Junior was bringing *that Italian* home. She probably was worried that Carmella would look down her nose at our little mountain town. I didn't know what an Italian was.

They told me when he was coming home. I didn't go back for a couple of days after he came home. I knew they would want time to get acquainted with Carmella. It was hard on me to stay away because I wanted to see what *that Italian* looked like. When I got there, I found Carmella and Mrs. Pearl sitting on the front porch, and I could tell Mrs. Pearl was very pleased with her. Carmella Herbert is a cute little lady with a great personality. I am sure Mrs. Pearl never referred to her as *that Italian* again.

OMAR LEE AND KATIE ANDERSON HOUSE

The little street between the Commercial Hotel and Mr. Herbert's house leads down to the old Bud Anderson house. The lawyer Omar Lee Anderson and his wife Katie live there. Katie is not from

Hayesville. I am not sure where she is from, maybe Asheville, North Carolina. She is the most beautiful woman that has ever lived in Clay County. As a matter of fact, if there is any prettier lady in the world, I have never seen her.

When my friends and I want to play like we are grown-ups, we want to look just like Katie. Sometimes when I visit Katie, she takes me in her bedroom and lets me hold the pretty doll on her bed. She does not know how to cook anything, so they eat something like donuts or cereal for breakfast. They eat something for breakfast and lunch at their house. After they eat, Katie rakes the plates out and drops them down in a big wooden barrel of water on the back porch. Mentory goes every afternoon and washes the dishes at Katie's house. Katie and Omar Lee eat at Mother's restaurant every night.

FRANK HERBERT'S POOL ROOM

Ed Mease and Frank Herbert

Mr. Frank Herbert's Pool Room is next-door to his house facing the square. Mr. Herbert has a card that stands up on the counter with toy watches on it. The watches have colored elastic bands. I get up on a stool and look at these watches every time I go there. Although the men are there playing pool, Mother doesn't mind me going in the pool room because Mr. Herbert is a nice man and runs a good pool hall. There is a great big jar of dill pickles on the counter. If you buy a dill pickle, he reaches in, gets one, and hands it to you. These are the best dill pickles you can buy anywhere for a nickel.

One day, while I was visiting Mr. Herbert, he told me to pick me out a watch.

I said, "Mr. Herbert, I don't have any money."

He said, "It is a gift from me."

He took the watches off the card, and I tried on every one of them, trying to decide which one I wanted. Mr. Herbert said he thought the pink one matched my dress, so I took it. I hugged his neck and ran home to show Mom and Dad my new pink watch.

Mother said, "Betty, I have told you not to ask for things."

I told her that I did not ask Mr. Herbert for it; he just gave me one. I don't know why Mr. Herbert has those children's watches in his pool room, but I love my gift.

Facing the Square next door to the pool room is Mr. Angel's shoe shop. Everyone wears their shoes until they get holes in the bottom. Mr. Angel can put a half sole on them and make them almost like new. I don't stop at the shoe shop because nothing really interests me there.

DOCTOR MAY

I'm now at the stairsteps that lead up to Dr. May's office. I think you could say my friends and I are *crazy* about Dr. May. If Dr. May is not busy when I go upstairs to see him, he will ask me if I am not feeling well. I say I am not, and he gives me several little pink candy pills. All of my friends and I love these candy pills.

Dr. May tells me the reason I am so smart is because he gave me smart pills when I was born. He says they were special pills, and he chose me to give them to. He says I am the smartest child for my age of any child he knows.

Dr. JM May

Dr. May will come to your house any time you call him if you are sick. Dr. May is very busy these days. The beer joints keep him busy at night. I don't see how he makes it with no more sleep that he gets. Our little town is very fortunate to have a good doctor like Dr. May.

DOCTOR MAY

Betty Benedict

Dr. May brought me into the world
He's one of my best friends.
He calls me Cooter Bug,
And pats me on the chin
He knows if I am really sick
When I stay out of school
He scolds me just a little bit,
But doesn't tell my mother
He gives me pink candy pills
I run to meet him on the Square
He loves all the children here
Because he brought them all
He doctors us when we are sick
And comes running when we call
He says I'm his special Buddy
Because I like him so
He says I know more for my age
Than any child he knows
He gave me smart pills when I was born
And slapped me on the butt
To set me into motion
Since then, I haven't stopped.

OLD HAYESVILLE METHODIST CHURCH

When I come down the stairs from Dr. May's office, next to the stairs is Violet Passmore's beer joint. Next to that is the Hayesville Methodist Church, an old, white, wooden building, with a steeple and belfry on top. The church is across the street from Mother's restaurant.

On Sunday morning, I get up across the street at our house, go across to our restaurant, eat my breakfast, and Mother checks me to make sure I am dressed all right for church. I then walk to

Joy Padgett

Frances Beal

the Methodist Church by myself and go into Sunday school class. I always sit with Joy Padgett and Frances Beal. After Sunday school, we listen to the preacher preach the sermon, and I often go home with Joy to eat lunch.

Her mother, Mrs. Lucille Padgett, makes the best meat loaf I have ever eaten. Sometimes, Joy and I play there at her house on Riverside. We play paper dolls and games like Tiddley Winks and others.

Some Sundays we go back to my house and play with paper dolls or dress-up at the Square. When we go back to town on Sunday, some of our other friends like Amelia Standridge, Mary Janice White, and Glenda Prater might come to play with us. We may walk down to see Frances Beal, because her mother does not let her play on the square. Her mother is glad for us to come play with Frances at her house.

The Beals's place is a fun place to play because there is a big meadow with a persimmon tree out back. In the fall of the year, these persimmons are so good to eat. Also, Town Creek runs through the meadow beside their house. There is a tall thing, called a culvert, that goes from their meadow under the road to the other side. Town Creek runs through it, and we love to walk through the culvert while playing in the creek. I am so glad there are things called culverts.

FIRST CAMPING TRIP

Glenda and I have been bored. This has been a day when none of our other friends have come to play. We have large mud holes in our street that goes around the Square; they fill with water when it rains. We pretend to fish in them, but we don't have any hooks that the big people use when they go fishing. We get a stick, tie a string on it, and fish in the mud holes. We have been fishing for a good while, and we are trying to figure out what we can do for the rest of the day.

Glenda Prater

We decide we would like to go camping. We first go over to the phone office to ask Glenda's mother, Christine Prater, if it will be all right with her if we go camping.

She said, "Yes, go ahead, and have a good time."

We go over to the restaurant, but Mother is busy. I asked her if we could go camping, and she said yes. I told her we needed some food to take with us. She told me to go in the supply room and get two cans of Dad's Vienna sausage and some crackers. I got them, put them in a small brown paper bag, and we set out on our camping adventure.

We go across town behind the jail and down the hill to Town Creek. We are having such a good time fishing. We go up and down the creek with our fishing poles, trying every fishing hole. We sit down and talk, pretending we have a campfire. It starts getting dark; we walk up and down the creek bank. We lie down every once in a while in a spot that looks comfortable. We think we are supposed to sleep on the edge of the creek bank. We talk about how we can listen to the water, and it will put us to sleep.

We are still trying to find a place to sleep, when all of a sudden, we see all of these flashlights up near the jail shining all around. We decide a convict from the jail must have broken out. Glenda said we probably are safe where we are. The lights start coming down the hill. Bright lights start shining on us.

They started yelling, "Here they are, here they are. We've found them."

Glenda and I are puzzled. We know we had permission to go camping. It seems like all the men in town are swarming around us. They are telling us how worried they have been about us, and said our parents were just worried sick.

Dad and Glen Prater are with the group looking for us. I keep telling Dad over and over that we had permission to go.

I said, "Mother also gave us food to have in camp."

Dad said, "She thought you were going to camp in the Square or in our yard."

We would have never gone camping without asking. We thought we were doing the right thing, and we still got in trouble. I don't understand grown people.

(We had no idea that you took quilts and blankets when you went camping. We thought you slept out on the ground in the open.)

MOVIE THEATER IN OLD METHODIST CHURCH

I have heard some news that has upset me. The Methodist Church that I go to every Sunday has been sold. As soon as they get a new one built, we will no longer have services in our old, wooden church. A new church is going to be built all the way across town near the Baptist Church.

Many people say that this will be wonderful because we will have moving picture shows in the old church building. I have never been to a movie. The nearest movie theater is in Murphy, North Carolina, about twenty miles from Hayesville. Many people go to Murphy to the movies, but my family is too busy to go.

Mother belongs to the Baptist Church, and Dad's family belongs to the Christian Church. My friends and I always go to the Bible schools at all the churches in town, which are Methodist, Baptist, and Presbyterian. I don't think that the Church of God has Bible school. If they do, we have never heard of it.

Later on after the church moved, they built a little room that stuck out on the front of our old church building. It looks like it will only hold one chair or stool. They call this a box office for the new movie theatre. I walk up there, and watch the people pay to go into the movie. The lady that sits in the box office has a big roll of

**Betty at two with Mother
at the old Methodist
Church on the Square**

tickets. People give her money, and she gives them a ticket. They have someone standing outside the door of the theater. He takes their ticket, tears it in half, and keeps one half. He gives them one half, and lets them go into the movie house.

I want to go see a movie so badly. Every night, I follow Mother around in the restaurant, begging her to let me go to the movie. If they had them in the daytime, I could use some of my dancing money and go. At night, I can't go where I please. The theater has been there a long time now, and it seems they will never let me go.

I started pitching a fit. Which means I was crying and stomping around in the restaurant. Mother said she was going to whip me good when she finished work. She told me to go back in the sitting room in the back of the restaurant. I just kept on until finally, she told me that if I would hush, she would get my Christmas doll out for me to play with. I don't believe in Santa Claus, anyway.

Sisty and Betty Benedict

Regina Johnston and Sisty

She gave me my doll, I opened the box, and there was the sweetest, prettiest doll I have ever seen. President Roosevelt has a new granddaughter who is named Sisty. My doll has a tag around her arm with Sisty Roosevelt written on it. She is the size of a six-month-old baby. She wears six-month-old-baby clothes.

Sisty has a cotton-stuffed body, composition head, arms, and legs. She has eyes with eyelashes that open and close. She has a red velvet tongue with four white upper teeth that show because she is smiling.

I feel ashamed that I have acted so ugly. I know Mother loves me very much to get me the prettiest doll in the world. Mother kept her word and whipped me good when we got over to the house that night. I went to sleep crying with my new doll Sisty by my side. I often take money that Allen Bell gives me for singing to buy Sisty six-month-old baby clothes at the dime store.

MY FIRST MOVIE

Mom and Dad finally let me go see my first movie in the old church building that was made into a movie theater. It was after dark when Dad took me by the hand, and we walked across the street to the movie. He bought my ticket, and told me he would come back to get me when the movie was over. He told me to wait for him at the front of the movie theater, and he would come when he saw everyone was leaving.

This was a very big deal for me. I sat down near the back of the theatre; no one was on the seats beside me. When the movie came on, it was really something to see. The people seemed much bigger than in real life. The movie was something about the law chasing gangsters. I was doing all right even though I was a little nervous, when all of a sudden, a car came off the screen right toward me. I could see the bottom of it!

I jumped up and ran out of there as fast as I could go. I did not stop until I was in our restaurant next door.

Dad said, "Betty, what's wrong? Why didn't you stay for the movie?"

I told him I didn't like it, but I didn't admit I was scared. I don't ask to go to the movie anymore. That's one thing they won't have to worry about.

GIFTS FOR BETTY

When traveling salesmen come through Hayesville, they stay at one of the hotels at night, and eat their meals at Mother's restaurant. One of the salesmen, Mr. McClain, sells shoes which he carries in a sample case. He used to take his case to my Dad's store to sell shoes. On one trip, he brought me a pair of red shoes. I don't ever remember being so proud of anything. I put them on; they could not get them off of me that night. I slept in them.

Mr. Charles Higdon lives in Andrews, North Carolina, and services our jukeboxes in the restaurant. He takes the money out of the jukebox, counts it, and gives some to Mother. He changes the records with all the latest hits, and takes off the records that have been there a while. He lets me tell him which of the old records I want, and he gives them to me. He puts them in paper envelopes that have holes in the middle. This lets you read the title of the record without taking it out.

I have stacks and stacks of records over at my house that Mr. Charles Higdon has given me, but I don't have a record player to play them on. Mr. Higdon has told me that someday he may find a record player for me. Mother told him not to do that; also he didn't need to be giving me all those records.

One morning after eating my breakfast, I was sitting at a table in our restaurant playing with my catalog paper dolls. All of my friends and I have bought all of the paper dolls we want. They are only a dime a book at the ten-cent store. We had much rather play with the paper dolls we cut from a catalog, or better still, a pattern book. If any of us can get our hands on a pattern book, we love it because they are our favorites. This particular morning, a lady and her husband were having breakfast, and they watched me cutting paper dolls from a catalog. They finished their meal and left.

About two weeks later, a big box came in the mail addressed to *The Little Girl at the Hayesville Café, Hayesville, North Carolina.*

Dad brought the package from the post office, and I was very excited when I opened it. Inside the box were heavy cardboard paper dolls with metal stands. The paper dolls were Princess Elizabeth and Princess Margaret Rose of England.

A note in the box said, "This is for the little girl who sat so patiently playing with her catalog paper dolls while her mother prepared our delicious breakfast."

The nice people were from New Jersey, and probably thought I never had bought any paper dolls.

Another traveling salesman that comes to our town, Mr. Bennett, has only one arm. He brings me a present every time he comes to town. He brings dolls, and one time, he gave me a little birdcage that you wind up to make the bird sing. He brings all kinds of special toys. I look forward to Mr. Bennett's visits, but Mother told Mr. Bennett not to bring me any more presents.

She said, "Enough is enough."

She hurt my feelings; I hope she didn't hurt his, because I think he enjoys bringing me things.

JOHN BRISTOL

I usually go over to our restaurant every afternoon when our housekeepers—Mentory, Tish and Teddy—leave our house to go home. I stay there until my bedtime, which is eight o'clock. The girl who stays with me at night comes to the restaurant in time for us to go to the house at bedtime. I enjoy being in the restaurant in the evenings because it is always busy with lots of people that I know who come in and talk to me.

John Bristol is another one of my favorite friends. We play a little game of make-believe each time he comes in. A waitress will go over to his table, and ask John what he would like to eat.

He says to them, "I am waiting for Betty, my favorite waitress."

I walk over and say, "Mr. Bristol, what would you like to eat?"

He says, "I would like a Heath Bar and a Coca-Cola. Could you take time to eat with me?"

I say, "Yes, I can."

He says, "Get a Heath Bar and a Coca-Cola for you."

Betty at Two Years Old

I can reach the candy case with no problem, so I get our candy and the cokes, and take them to the table. I sit down with John, and we have a nice talk.

Each time I see him, John says, "Betty, how old are you?"
I say, "I will be three the sixth of May."
(My friend John Benedict Bristol sent me a birthday card every year, until he died in 1975.)

FIRST DATE

**Victor Bell 1926 Mail Carrier
Brasstown, NC**

One day, one of the neatest things happened. Mr. Victor Bell came into the restaurant very excited because he had bought a brand new 1937 Buick. Everyone was coming from all over town to see his new car. Not many people can afford to buy a brand-new car; most people don't even have a car.

I think a Buick must be the finest car there is. It was big and so shiny; I could see myself in it. Mr. Bell knew I was excited over his new car, and that I wanted to ride in it. He asked me if I would like to take a ride.

He said, "We can have a date. I will pick you up at the restaurant tomorrow afternoon."

He went in with me to ask Mother if this was all right. I was so excited I could hardly sleep that night. The next day, I got dressed in my Sunday dress and went over to the restaurant to wait for Mr. Bell. He came for me, and we drove twenty miles to Murphy, North Carolina, where we had ice cream and a coke. I am the first one among my girlfriends to have a date and to ride in a brand-new car.

Mr. Vic Bell married one of Mother's best friends whom she had worked with in Murphy, North Carolina. Her name is Annie Mae Cagle. Vic Bell is Allen Bell's brother.

MOUNTAIN DIALECT

In our little town and the surrounding areas, most of the settlers came from Scotland and Ireland. Many of the people have a dialect they brought from the old countries many years before and handed down to their children. People who have not always lived in Hayesville have a hard time understanding our mountain people. I still get confused about the language. I grew up listening to Mother and Dad, and they have a different way of speaking than the local people. Sometimes, I have trouble understanding people who come into the restaurant.

One of my friends asked me if I wanted to go to the *far*. I had heard of people building a far in their far places. I thought she had invited me to a big bonfire where you roast marshmallows and hotdogs. I asked Mother if I could go, and she told me to get some money from Dad. I did get the money, and we went to Murphy. I was very happy when I saw we were at a real Fair. We rode all the rides and had a great time.

One time, an airplane got in trouble and had to land in a field below town. All the men kept talking about going down to see the plane. Most people had never even seen an airplane. This has caused a lot of excitement for the town. Everyone coming into the restaurant would say, "Have you been over to the garage to see the engine?"

I got very excited, and I went over there expecting to see an Indian. Most local people called Indians by the name Injun. I was very disappointed because it was just an airplane engine.

TENT REVIVAL

One afternoon, I was in the restaurant when some nice-looking people came in. They said they were having a revival in a tent on the knoll behind our restaurant. They wanted the children in town to come the next afternoon to practice singing songs for the revival. There were many children there. We practiced and learned many songs. Some were new to me, and some I had already known. My two favorites that we sang were "Running over, my cup is full and running over." We learned hand and body movements that went with these songs. The other one I really liked was "B-I-B-L-E. Yes, that's the book for me."

That night, we all went to the revival and sang our songs. After we sang, I sat down on the seat at the end of the aisle. We children got scattered from each other because seats were not available for us to sit together. Someone led the audience in singing several songs.

The preacher started preaching, and all of a sudden, a woman up front started shouting. Two or three more people got up and joined in the shouting. Some came running down the middle aisle. I was scared, jumped up, and ran to our restaurant. I didn't go back to the revival again.

I had heard of shouting, but we did not do this in any of our churches. I had been to revivals at the Baptist, Methodist, and Presbyterian churches, but I had never seen shouting before.

SAINTS

Betty Benedict

When the saints go marching in
Lord, I hope there's not a stampede
Wouldn't it be awful to get there
And have to turn and flee

When they open up them pearly gates
There's going to be a rush—
A pushing and a shoving
To get in before they close up.

Saint Peter's supposed to have
The key and he best watch out
Because the Saints can be a real rough bunch
When they begin to shout

I may just stay the way I am
And let time take its toll
I'd rather not be bored to death
Sitting around while these ages roll.

ELECTION NIGHTS IN HAYESVILLE

When we have national elections at Hayesville to elect our country's president, people take it very seriously. We have many Democrats in our county, but only a few Republicans. Dad says you never argue about politics or religion. Very few people out of town have radios, and when they do, they have to buy big batteries, almost as big as their radios, and heavier. They do not have electricity in the country. The batteries last only a short time and are very expensive. People sometimes heat the batteries in their oven to try to recharge them when they go dead.

We have electricity in town and have an electric radio sitting high on a shelf in the restaurant. We also have one in Mom and Dad's bedroom at the house. When election night comes, people from all over the countryside come to the public places in Hayesville that have radios. Mother's restaurant stays open on election until all the things—they call returns—are in. That is when you know who is going to be your new president, or if the old president will be the president again. Ever since I was born, no one wins except President Roosevelt. That man Dewey must be tired of running and not winning. I think he is ugly anyway; everyone else must think so, too. People drink a lot of moonshine on election night. People that you would not dream of come in our restaurant as high as a Georgia pine. Mother lets me stay up very late on election night. A lot of the men buck dance, and some of them who are drunk think they can dance, but they can't. It's funny to watch them try. Andrew Moore is always there to dance, and he is the best buck dancer in Hayesville.

POLITICS

Betty Benedict

The people who run for office
Get so very nice
Just before election time
to try to get your vote.
I've figured it out we should live our lives
As if we're in a campaign
Then anytime we need a boost
A favor or a vote
We won't have to run about like fools
We'll have it all sewed up

MY DOLL BED

I kept asking Dad for a doll bed, and he said you just cannot go anywhere around Hayesville and get a doll bed. He said they do not have any at the dime store. Not too long after that, I came in from playing one afternoon, and there set a doll bed in the middle of my bedroom with a mattress made from feathers. It had sheets on it, little pillows, and a tiny quilt. Dad had Didley Bryan put legs on a wooden tomato crate and build up one end with little pieces of wood to make the headboard. Sisty was too big for it, but Homer Gene fit in it perfectly. Grannie White made the mattress, small pillow, sheets, pillow case, and a little quilt. I just love my doll bed, and it's the best doll bed that anyone could have.

(My daughter Alisa Lyon and my granddaughter Shelby Sullins played with it when they were little. They still have it; they never wanted any other doll bed.)

THE GREAT DREAD

**Charles Thompson
First Grade**

It is getting time for me to start first grade. Many of my friends have already started. Amelia, Mary Janice, Gay Nell Mingus, and Frances all started school last year. We all know what happens before we start school in the first grade. They send a doctor from the Health Department in Asheville, North Carolina to take the children's tonsils out before they enter the first grade. They take all the seats out of the auditorium in the high school building and set up cots all over the place. They have big, galvanized wash tubs full of ice where they put cokes and ice cream in small dixie cups. They have small wooden paddles to eat the ice cream. They set up an operating room for Dr. Wichard, who comes from Asheville, upstairs in the home economics classroom. One by one, we are taken up to the doctor, and he gives you ether to put you to sleep. He takes your tonsils out right there in the classroom. Boy, we really dreaded this. The nurse told me his name right before they put the ether on my nose to put me to sleep. I hated that awful feeling as I went to sleep. While I was having my tonsils out, I dreamed that I was in an airplane flying around with Dr. Wichard.

The next thing I knew, I was on a cot right down in the auditorium, and the nurse was asking, "Betty, do you want some ice cream?"

Charles and Archie Thompson

I said I wanted some coke, but my throat was so sore I could not swallow it. Many of the children from the country had probably never had ice cream. I thought it was so cruel that the nurses all told the little kids they could have all the ice cream they wanted to eat after their tonsils were out. When they got their tonsils out, their throats were so sore they could hardly swallow, and the ice cream all melted in the ice, anyway. I know the kids were very disappointed.

I guess they were overcrowded at the school house because my friend Joy Padgett wound up at the Commercial Hotel in town to get her tonsils out. She woke up in a hotel room in bed with a little girl she had never seen before. My friend Bobbie Penland also had her tonsils removed at the Commercial Hotel. They said the ice cream they got was frozen. I guess they have freezers to keep things frozen at the hotel.

Two years ago, a little boy named Archie Thompson was getting ready to start in the first grade. He and his younger brother Charles Thompson were supposed to go to the high school to get their tonsils out. The morning they were supposed to go, Archie was missing. His worried family and his brother looked for him for several hours. The operating time was over at the school, and by the time they found Archie hiding under the bed, it was too late. Charles Thompson and Archie Thompson never had their tonsils out, and they did just fine. If I had heard this before I got mine out, I would have hidden somewhere.

FIRST GRADE

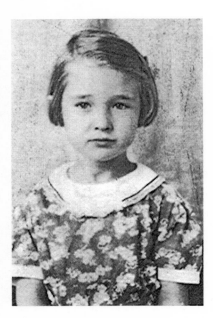

Betty at first grade

I enjoy first grade very much. My teacher is Miss Lenore Johnston, and we learn many things in her class. On my first day at school, the dress I wore was navy blue with bright red apples printed all over it. It has a white pique collar with a beautiful lace around it. My shoes are black patent leather Mary Jane shoes. I shine them with one of Mom's biscuits.

My friends and I all wear heavy wool snow suits under our dresses during the winter. Joy has a green one, I have a navy blue one, and Amelia has a brown one that is very neat. It is really a boy's suit with an aviator cap. I sure would like to have that aviator cap. The first day I wore my snow suit to school, it rubbed my legs so raw that I was miserable. After I came home from school, Mother sent someone with me over to Pauline Bryan's, who is a very good seamstress. She lined my pants with tan flannel, and I haven't had any trouble since.

Each day when we go to school, the bell rings and we must go into our classroom. Miss Johnston lines up all of us girls who have snow suits. She takes them off. We study until recess time. She lines us up again, puts our snow suits back on so we can go out to play. When we come back fifteen minutes later from recess, she takes them off again. We study until lunch, and she puts them back on before we go out for lunch. After lunch, they are off again and after noon recess, the same routine. I told my Dad how many times she has to change our clothes.

He said, "If I was her, I would just throw those things in the burning barrel."

GOLDILOCKS AND THE THREE BEARS

Bill Standridge

Bill Standridge and Miss Sue Haigler help with putting on operettas at our school. They are planning a big one, "Goldilocks and the Three Bears." The first, second, and third grades are to take part. We have to try out for parts, and they have leading parts and they have chorus children that dress up as if they are flowers. Patterns come with the operetta, and they make flower costumes from crepe paper. They told us that the older children in the higher grades would get the leading parts.

We all tried out. They decided that I should have the part of Goldilocks even though I was in first grade. I have lots and lots of lines to memorize. I sing and dance on my way through the forest before I come upon the three bears' house. Patsy Alexander is Mama Bear, Howard Alexander is Papa Bear, and Jerry Padgett is Baby Bear. I get very tired on the way, and I lie down on a log in the forest, and go to sleep. All of the little flowers dance around me, and I have a dream of a little elf dancing around my log.

(I later married this elf. His name is Quenton Lyon.)

People came from miles around to the high school auditorium to see this operetta. I was a great hit, and everyone told me I was a great Goldilocks. My teacher Lenore Johnston gave me a paper doll book of "Goldilocks and the Three Bears." She enclosed a note telling me what a good job I did.

(I took part in many operettas in my grammar school years, but I enjoyed this one the most.)

I dance and sing sometimes for people in the restaurant, and they give me money. Most of the men give me quarters. At school during recess, I take any of the kids who want to follow me down

Sue Haigler

to Mr. West's Store, across the road from the school. I can buy twenty five pieces of candy with a quarter. Most of the time, I have several quarters to spend. The kid's favorite candy is called Guess Whats, and it has a prize inside. We get little wax bottles of juice that are orange—or cherry-flavored. We like candy cigarettes, big red wax lips, wax teeth, marshmallow peanuts, waxed orange slices, peppermint sticks, and more. Each day, I give out as much candy as I have money. On the days I do not have any money, we just play and don't go to the store. I have all the candy I want to eat at the restaurant, anyway. It makes me feel good to give the Corduroy Kids candy treats.

THE BULLIES

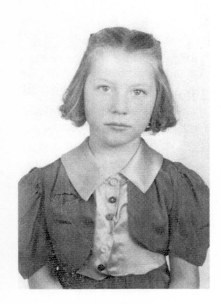

Joy Padgett

Many days after school, I go with Joy Padgett to her house down on Riverside, or we stay at my house at the Square and play. All of us kids have to walk to and from school because we live in town. The school buses pick up the children outside the city limits, but we must walk, rain, snow, or shine.

As Joy and I go down to her house, we have to pass the old state garage. The McTaggart family lives above the garage. One day, all of the McTaggart kids came out with knives. The largest had big butcher knives, and the tiny children had table knives. They chased us a great distance; we were scared to death.

When we got to Joy's house, we told her dad, Mr. Guy Padgett, about what happened. We figured he would do something about it. From that time on Joy and I would walk on the other side of the street to stay away from them.

At another day as we passed their place, they were waiting for us to come by, and they poured bags of gravel on our heads from their upstairs window. Our snow suits were heavy with the gravel lodged in them. Mother emptied my clothes of all the gravel, and put it in a brown paper bag to show to the sheriff, hoping he might do something about it. The McTaggart family moved, and we are very happy that we don't have to worry about them anymore.

TENNESSEE VALLEY AUTHORITY

Talk about excitement, the TVA has come to town. They are building a dam with a spillway located in our county. The dam will dam up the Hiawassee River and make a big lake. The name of the lake is an Indian name—Chatuge. This will change our community forever by creating this large lake.

Many families of the TVA workers move with them from place to place where they are building dams. The hotels in town are filled to overflowing. Many workers need places to stay. Almost every home in Hayesville, regardless of how small, has at least one room rented out to the workers. Dad has turned one of the large rooms upstairs in our house into a small apartment, and we have it rented out to a family named Aaron. Mrs. Aaron was married before, and her son is named Tommy Lawson. She is a wonderful cook and homemaker. They settled in the upstairs of our house, and I play with Tommy. He walks to and from school with my friends and me.

Our school is full and bursting at the seams with the children of the families moving in to build the dam. We needed about three more dining rooms in our restaurant. Mother

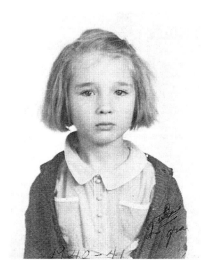

Betty at second grade

brought in more tables and chairs, and did whatever she could to make room for all the TVA workers. Most of the men who live in the hotels and room in homes come to eat at our restaurant.

Mother gets up earlier each morning to go to the restaurant, and pack lunches in brown bags for the workers to take with them to the job. These lunches are put up near the front door where the workers can come in, pick up their bag, and go on to work. They pay for these lunches by the month.

Betty at third grade with curls

CURLS, CURLS, CURLS

I find that I can make money easily by singing and dancing for customers at the restaurant. There is a man with the TVA who eats at our restaurant. His name is Mr. Purvis, and it bothers him that I have straight hair. He wants me to have curls like Shirley Temple, so he asked Mother if he could take me across the square to the beauty salon to get me a permanent wave. Mother said I couldn't have a permanent wave because I am too young. I am not too young; I am already in second grade. I like Mr. Purvis because he is interested in me looking like Shirley Temple. We kept begging Mother until finally, to make us shut up, she agreed that I could get one.

Mr. Purvis and I walked across the Square to the beauty salon where Mary Jo Chambers, Jessie Swanson, and Geneva Smith work. I did not know what I was in for; I just knew I wanted curls. They rolled my hair on

**Betty at fourth grade.
The curls are gone.**

some strange-looking metal rods with felt pads down on my scalp. I have a long skinny neck, and they had so much stuff in my hair, I could hardly hold my head up. They put some kind of silver pad over each curl that was wrapped on these rods. Then they took me over to this big machine that has cords hanging down with metal clips on each end. They clipped a cord to each metal rod. One of the ladies held my neck to keep my head from falling over with all the weight.

Then, as if I was not already scared, they turn on the machine, and it sent electricity to each curl. It sizzled and made frying sounds, and I could feel the heat. They had bellows to fan air on my head so it would not burn my scalp. I thought it would never end. I know now I will never want another permanent wave.

When they decided the curls were cooked enough, they unplugged me and took me over to a chair to remove all of the things from my hair. It took a long time to get it all out, but lo and behold, I had curls. Not quite like Shirley Temple, but I have curls, and I am glad that it is over. I have curls, and it was worth it all. Mr. Purvis paid them, and we went back across to the restaurant.

All I've heard for days is, "Oh Betty, how did you get all of those curls?"

HEAVY SLEDGEHAMMER HANDLES

Dad loves to play practical jokes on his friends. All of the men in town have a big time trying to get the best of each other.

Mother says, "This is all they have to do. If they had more work, they would not have time to dream up all this foolishness."

The principal of our school, Mr. J. Walter Moore, owns a hardware store on the Square, and Mr. Weaver Anderson works for him. Dad was visiting the store one day when one of the TVA workers came into the store, and asked if they had heavy sledgehammer handles.

After the man left, Mr. Anderson told J. Walter that he imagined they needed to order this type handle. Mr. Moore said to put down an order for one dozen. They continued to talk about how they might find out about other small equipment the workers might need to build the dam. They talked about making a lot of money by supplying these needs; of course, that was all Dad needed to hear.

Dad went out and asked another TVA worker to go into the hardware and ask to buy a heavy sledgehammer handle. He continued to ask other workers to do the same thing. Dad would go back into the store with the workers, and listen to Mr. Moore and Mr. Anderson talking about how many handles they should order.

Mr. Anderson said, "J. Walter, do you realize how much economic boost this is going to be for us and possibly the whole town?"

All of the men in town were getting a kick out of listening to the conversation about how many handles they should order. Everything was going well until Mr. Booth, dressed in a suit, who everyone knew had never struck a lick at a snake, went into the hardware. He asked Mr. Anderson if he had a heavy duty sledgehammer handle.

Mr. Anderson said, "J. Walter, that Red Benedict has set this whole thing up."

J. Walter said, "We should have known better. Have you noticed that every man in Hayesville has been hanging around here all day just watching us making a fool of ourselves?"

They took it all in stride and joined in the laughter. I am sure they were very disappointed that all those big dreams of all those sales went down the drain.

TRADING FOR A ROLLTOP DESK

I sometimes walk up the street to the furniture store. I keep looking at a pretty little rolltop desk. I mention it to Dad several times, thinking he might buy it for me, but he never seems interested. I even think I might walk into my room one day and see it there.

I make many trips, hoping each time I go into the furniture store, that it will still be there, since it isn't at my house. One day, I told the man at the furniture store that I had a beautiful little baby bed that I slept in when I was a baby. It is white iron with little fancy roses, and I keep my dolls setting on it in my room. I tell him I will trade my baby bed for the desk. He says that is fine with him, but he will have to talk to Dad.

I immediately run to find Dad. He is in the restaurant, and I know he probably will agree to the deal. I am not sure what Mother will say. To make a long story short, I now have the rolltop desk in my room. I love my desk. I get my lessons there when I have home work and my friends, and I like to play office with it.

The next thing I want to work on getting is a record player. I have all my records that Mr. Charles Higdon gave me, but I still don't have a way to play them.

CHARLIE McCARTHY

Betty, Charlie, and Ginger, and Sandra Gray

Silvey Penland came into the restaurant the other day with a big smile on his face.

He asked, "Where is Betty?" I went running to meet him.

He had a large box that he handed to me saying, "I brought you a present."

When I finally got the box opened, to my surprise, it was a Charlie McCarthy dummy. I was so pleased, and I think it shocked Mr. Penland when I threw my arms around him and gave him a big hug.

Dad is a good ventriloquist. He can throw his voice without moving his lips. He is trying to teach me. We are having fun, and Dad gets a big kick out of trying to teach me. I also have to practice making Charlie's mouth move when I talk. I try to practice some every day, but this is very hard.

I figure I can make some money by putting on shows with Charlie. Tomorrow, I will take him to show all my friends around the Square. I would like to have a tuxedo to wear when I put on my shows, but I don't know where to get one.

POLLY PARROT

We have a bird that is a small green Amazon Parrot. Dad's Aunt Belle Mitcham bought our bird at a pet shop up in Kentucky and named her Polly. She was six weeks old when she bought her. The man at the shop told Aunt Belle that if Polly didn't speak by the time she was six months old, he would refund her money and take Polly back.

Polly has a wide vocabulary and talks very much when alone with our family. Mother and Dad carry her back and forth from the house to the restaurant. She stays at the restaurant from opening in the morning until closing time at night.

Betty at six with Polly

Sometimes, Mother keeps Polly under the counter up at the cash register. Polly often calls out, "Come back to see us."

If a customer is not ready to leave, they turn to Mother and say, "I am not leaving yet." They think Polly's voice is Mother talking.

Sometimes, Mother moves Polly from behind the counter to a stool. People come in just to see Polly. I think she is the only parrot to ever be in Hayesville. They try to talk to her; she just sits and sulks like she cannot talk. After people leave, she laughs and says everything they have said to her.

She says, "Pretty Polly, talk to me Polly. Can you talk Polly? Does Polly want a Cracker? Come on, say something, Polly, What a bird. What a bird. Bye, Polly."

Then she laughs some more. Polly sounds like a witch when she laughs. She mainly eats sunflower seeds.

Aunt Belle set up a trust for Polly to be in effect when she died. Christine Bowles Jones, my cousin, was left in charge of the trust. Christine decides which family Polly is to live with. The trust states that Polly is to be left in a family where children live. Polly came to live with us when I was four. She loves my dad more than anyone. I don't know why Aunt Belle wanted her to go where there were children. Polly doesn't like them. She is very jealous of me and Sisty, my doll. If Dad shows me any affection while Polly is around, she gets upset.

Sometimes, Mother turns Polly loose outside in front of the restaurant. She will sit on the bench outside and up on the gas pumps. When Polly is out, I cannot go barefoot or wear open-toe shoes because she will peck my toes, and her beak is very strong.

Every evening about dusk, Polly starts calling "Miss Belle, Miss Belle" over and over.

She says "Miss Belle, come cover me up," over and over until Mother puts the cloth cover over her cage.

This is eerie since Miss Belle has been dead for years. Every Sunday morning, Mother turns the radio on in the restaurant to a station that plays hymns. Polly will start singing. She drowns the radio out as she starts singing "When the Roll is called up Yonder." She sounds just like a drunk. Sometimes, Mother has to turn the radio off to get Polly to hush.

(Polly died in 1952 at the age of eighty-two.}

POLLY—POLLY

Betty Benedict

Polly—Polly why did Aunt Belle name you such
A common name because you're such a special bird
Polly wants a cracker—Where
There she is sitting on the back of Dad's chair

Waiting and waiting for Red to come home
She loves him so
There she is sitting on Dad's shoulder
Rubbing her head against his cheek
There she is in the old maple tree
Aiming to glide down and get my feet
She's even jealous of Sisty my doll.
She wants all the attention we have
Every night in the twilight she still calls Great Aunt Belle
Oh she's a very special bird and she is loved so well

MERINGUE MISHAP

I like to visit Mrs. Aaron in the apartment upstairs at our house. She makes wonderful pies. Mother told me if she offered me pie, I could take it, but I must eat all of it including the meringue. I love the pie, but I hate meringue. The Aarons's apartment upstairs has a door to a front porch over the street facing the courthouse. We have a tiny yard below the porch near the sidewalk beside the street. When Mrs. Aaron gives me a piece of pie with meringue on it, I go to the edge of the porch, take my fork, and flip the meringue off down to the grass. I am good at this. After I eat my pie, I run downstairs and stomp the meringue until it disappears into the grass.

One time, I had a wonderful piece of chocolate pie with meringue. I always look both ways to make sure no one will see me flip the meringue. I looked both ways; I don't know what happened, but the minute I flipped that meringue, I heard a splat. I looked down; it had hit a bald-headed man on the top of his head. I ran and fell down on my stomach and flattened myself out on the upstairs porch floor. I was too late; he knew who did it. Needless to say, after letting out a string of curse words, he went across to the restaurant and told on me.

I was in trouble again.

MY NIGHTS IN JAIL

Hayesville Jail

Mary Janice's father, Ruel White, Grannie White's son, has been appointed Deputy Sherriff for the county. He and his wife, Neva White, and their daughter, Mary Janice, have moved into the jail.

When I spend the night in the jail with Mary Janice, I think it is great fun to be able to tell people that I spent the night in jail last night.

They have a nice little apartment, and Neva feeds the prisoners. Mary Janice recently had a birthday party there in the jail. She had a Mexican piñata hanging from the ceiling. We were all blindfolded and had sticks to break the piñata open. Loads of candy and little toys fell from it, and we could keep the things we picked up. I had never seen one of these before. I don't know where they got it, but it was great fun.

ITCH AND LICE

Our school at Hayesville has many children who come from out in the county. Their homes don't have conveniences, and they often are not as clean as they should be. We have outbreaks of lice and itch in school. Leave it to me to catch both of them at the same time.

Mother saw some little white things in my hair, and she sent me over to the house. Mentory looked through my hair and said that I had the lice.

Then she saw me scratching my hand and said, "Lord, have Mercy, you have the itch and the lice."

She sent someone over to the restaurant to tell Mother that I had a case of the itch and the lice. Mother would not let me get into our bathtub under the stairs. They brought a big round galvanized wash tub in to give me a bath. They filled it with water, and put something with a terrible smell called citicide for the itch. Many families use a combination of sulfur and lard to cure the itch. They had me get into the stinking tub and lathered up my head with something they called larkspur to get rid of the lice.

They took my clothes out and burned them. Dr. May said they were being overly cautious. They wore rubber gloves to touch me. I felt like I was ruined forever. They took all the sheets off my bed, and didn't let me sleep in it. I slept on a pallet on some old worn-out quilts that they later threw away. I finally was cured, and they treated me like a human again. Every night before I go to bed, they put a white piece of cloth over my lap, make me bend my head over it, and comb through my hair with a fine-toothed comb. They inspect the cloth to see if any lice fall out. You can get these combs at the dime store. Oh Lord, don't let me ever go through this again.

DAD AND THE RED RIBBON

We have a lounge in the back of the restaurant, near the ladies' restroom. Mom and Dad can go to rest when we have no business up front. I play there sometimes. When my girlfriends come, we play paper dolls back there. Grannie Cearley's old wicker sofa and two matching chairs are there for us to sit on.

I went back there the other day, and Dad was in one of the chairs, snoozing. I slipped in and very carefully braided a small braid in the top of his hair. I tied it with a little red ribbon to make a bow. We have a bell on the front door, so we can hear when someone comes into the restaurant. The bell rang and Dad jumped out of his chair, and went up front to wait on some people who were from out of town. I guess they thought Dad was a freak.

They stared at him as he told them to be seated; a waitress would be right with them. I guess he saw them staring at him because he put his hand on his head to smooth his hair. The ribbon came out of his hair into his hand. He tried to explain to them that he was taking a nap in the back, and he had a very mischievous daughter. They had a good laugh. Dad said he was glad it was not any of his local cronies there to see the ribbon, or he would never live this one down. Dad is a good sport when it comes to pranks because he is usually the one pulling the pranks on others.

PLAYING SICK

I like school, but I miss staying at home and at the restaurant. I am afraid I will miss something. I don't see any of the interesting salesmen I used to see on their routine visits. They come during the day while I am at school. I miss getting records from the jukebox. Charles Higdon usually comes around lunchtime. I decided to stay out of school when some of them were coming.

I knew I would have to be sick to stay home. I would say my stomach hurt. I don't think Mother believed me because she called Dr. May. He told her to give me a dose of castor oil. She put the castor oil in a glass and poured Nehi Grape on it. She handed me the glass along with the rest of the grape drink. I sat and looked at it for a long time. The smell was terrible. I really wanted to stay home. I finally managed to drink it down with the grape drink behind it.

I tried going back to the restroom to pour it in the commode. This didn't work because Mother went with me. This ruined my day off from school because my stomach started rolling, and I had to run to the bathroom all day.

One day, I really wanted to stay home again so I put on a good show. I bent over holding my stomach, acting like I was in a lot of pain. Mother called Dr. May. He soon came over to the restaurant where I was in the lounge, lying on the wicker sofa.

Dr. May said to Mother, "I don't know what is wrong with her, but I can tell she is very sick."

He asked Mother to get me a glass of water. I was lying there thinking I had finally fooled them.

As soon as Mother left the room, Dr. May said, "Betty, you lie here for a little while, then tell your Mother you feel better. You get up and go to school. I don't want to come back here again when you have one of your spells."

Boy, this sure put cold water on my being sick. Needless to say, I shortly got up and went to school. I met Dr. May on the Square a few days later. He took my hand, gave it a pat, and told me that our secret is between us. We are still friends. I love Dr. May, and I am glad he isn't mad at me.

BATHROOM AT OUR HOUSE

We have a bathroom in our house on the Square. Didley Bryan put it under the stairs. He put the bathtub under the upstairs steps. I am the only one in my family who can sit up at that end of the bathtub. Big people have to put their feet down at that end.

When I need to go to the bathroom, I always knock to be sure no one is in there. Sometimes, someone I do not know comes out of our bathroom. One day I had been playing outside, and I really needed to go. I waited and waited. Finally, a man came out, and I got to go in. Later that day, I told Mother I had almost gone in my pants because I had to wait so long to get into our bathroom.

Mother got very upset and said, "Fred, what in the world is Betty talking about? She said she had to wait to get in our bathroom, and some man came out."

Dad said, "Oh, I think people sometimes go in to use our bathroom."

I could tell Mother was hopping mad.

She said, "Fred that is our home. It's a terrible thing to have people from the street going into our house to use the bathroom."

She told Dad she wanted our house locked. He locked it, and I hate it. In the daytime, I have to knock on the door and wait for someone to let me in.

The surprising thing is that many people in town are angry at Dad because he locked our door. Mother said it is ridiculous for them to feel that way. Anyone can use our public restrooms at the restaurant.

BEGINNING OF WORLD WAR II

People come into the restaurant more than usual to listen to the news on the radio. War is raging in Europe, and I don't understand it, but I feel the unrest and anxiety that the grown-ups are feeling. I got up one morning, December 7, 1941, and went over to the restaurant for breakfast. The minute I opened the door and walked in, I knew something was terribly wrong.

People were talking about Pearl Harbor; I didn't know what they were talking about. I had never heard of Pearl Harbor. I soon found out that it is a place that had been bombed by the Japanese. At first, I thought they were talking about a place in our country. I know that the Japanese made most of the toys I have.

The war brought with it so much heartache and worry. We, along with many other families in Clay County, were under tremendous stress. We didn't know if we would ever see our loved ones again. I know this is something very bad. I have never seen people so upset and afraid. People gather in the churches to pray.

I am praying very hard and asking God to take care of my brother, Ray Benedict, who is in the U.S. Navy. Mother told me to not only pray for Ray, but for all the boys in our armed forces.

This was the beginning of the nightmare of World War II. Almost overnight, all kinds of little pins were in the stores. They have the word *Remember,* and instead of the word *Pearl,* there is a little pearl and then the word *Harbor.*

Everytime you turn on the radio, you hear "Remember Pearl Harbor" over and over again. President Roosevelt comes on the radio and tries to make people feel calmer. He tells us that our country must declare war on Japan.

Edwin and Ray in San Francisco, 1942

He said, "We have nothing to fear, but fear itself."

A new hit song soon came out entitled "Let's Remember Pearl Harbor as we did the Alamo."

Families who have a member in service display a banner in their door or window. The banner has a blue star for each member serving their country. A gold star represents a member killed in action. During this time of war, our entire country is joining together to support the war effort. People go to the Red Cross headquarters and make bandages. Women work in plants making war materials. For the first time, women have to assume responsibilities that they have never experienced before.

Every eligible man was drafted into military service, and very few were left at home. My brother, Edwin, was drafted into the army. By chance, Edwin and Ray accidentally met in San Francisco during the war. This picture was made of them during this time. (There was no television, so we didn't get to see the things that were happening to our service men on a daily basis.)

News correspondents are on the fighting lines, making movies and sending them home to be shown in the theaters. These are shown before the main attraction. The movies are very patriotic. The hit songs are written about patriotism and support for our service men. Some of the songs are "Praise the Lord and Pass the Ammunition, and We'll all Stay Free," "God Bless America," and "White Cliffs of Dover."

Ray was trained and is serving as an Aviation Ordinance man. His job is to service all the munitions, guns, bombs, and other ordinance equipment for the U.S. Naval Aircraft. Ray's first aircraft carrier assignment was on September 30, 1937. It was a new carrier named the *Yorktown*. He was on the shakedown cruise which was the first operation after christening. He sent me many souvenirs from the *Yorktown* during this time while on the Atlantic east coast and in the Caribbean Sea.

After the war began in 1941, we knew that Ray was on the *Yorktown*. We heard that the *Yorktown* was damaged while fighting in the battle of the Coral Sea. We soon had a letter from Ray telling us that he was well and not injured.

A short time later, we heard about the Battle of Midway taking place in the Pacific. They reported the aircraft carriers that were being attacked by the Japanese. The news reported that the *Yorktown* had gone down on June 7, 1942.

The agony that we are going through during this time is so intense that I can't do anything but sit at my desk at school and worry. Mother tells me to pray and ask for Ray's safety. Of course, we have done this since he went into service. I don't believe there is a minute of the day that I don't pray to God to bring Ray home safely. I don't hear what people are saying when people are talking to me. I don't hear my teachers; I just pray constantly. It seems like this worry will never end.

I am in third grade, and time passes by so slowly. We have an old crank telephone on the wall at our home in West Hayesville, but we don't always have dependable long-distance service. One day, Ray just showed up on our doorstep, and our rejoicing was unbelievable. The Navy lets you come home for one month when a ship is shot out from under you. My brother is only twenty-four, and he looks as if he has aged ten years. Since he has been home, he talks very little about his ordeals.

(Many years later, he talked a little about being on a life raft with several others. They had drifted in the ocean for several weeks. Planes would be flying over, and they could not signal for rescue because their flares on the raft were all wet. After several weeks, they came upon an island. Fortunately for them, U.S. Army soldiers were on the island, and they contacted the Navy and a plane was sent for them.)

After Ray's stay at home, he was assigned to the *USS Wasp* aircraft carrier. The carrier was hit by six Japanese torpedoes and sank a day later on September 16, 1942, in the Pacific Ocean near the San Cristobal Island. Many sailors lost their lives; all surviving sailors abandoned ship to life rafts. We did not know he was on this carrier at the time. Ray came home again for thirty days after surviving the second ship shot out from under him.

Ray was later assigned to serve on the *USS Saratoga* carrier, and it survived the war in the Pacific for several years before a major battle.

On February 21, 1945, the carrier was launching fighters in support of Iwo Jima raids. Six Japanese aircraft dropped bombs on the ship, doing major damage and causing the death of over 123 sailors. This was the last battle of the war for the *USS Saratoga*. Ray came home again for thirty days; a few months before the end of the war.

When Ray played football for Hayesville High School, he carried a silver dollar for good luck. He had this silver dollar in his pocket when he survived the carriers sinking during the war. After the third ship was shot from under him, he brought the silver dollar home and gave it to me. He said after three ships being blown out from under him, he couldn't think of it as being good luck.

I told him, "Maybe it was good luck, because you did survive all three."

(I still have the silver dollar.)

WAR ON THE HOME FRONT

Life goes on in Hayesville, but the atmosphere is so different. I wonder if it will ever be the same again. The TVA is still with us, and they work day and night to finish the Chatuge Dam. Hayesville people worry that after the dam is built, it could break and flood our entire community. Now, they also have the war to worry about. People who never wanted to be in military service are being called into the armed forces. In no time at all, it seems like everything we took for granted is now rationed. We have little ration coupon books with stamps in them to buy things that are necessary for us to live.

There is a shortage of almost everything. Anything that has metal in it is being used to build airplanes and bombs. People are talking about going to work in the Bell Bomber plant that has been started in Marietta, Georgia.

We must have been unprepared for this war because they are using whatever it takes to make our shoes. Ration stamps are given to buy a pair of shoes. Sears Roebuck has some neat shoes in their catalog. There are big-girl shoes that are sandals. They have really high wedge heels and platform soles. They make the soles out of old worn-out tire treads. They have cloth straps, and you can adjust the width of them by tying a bow across the top. You do not need a ration stamp to buy these. I wanted a pair of them, but I never got any. This is why they call the Sears Roebuck catalog the *Wish Book*.

The service stations are having a rough time, and so are we because we have gas pumps at the restaurant. Gas is rationed. After you use your monthly ration, you do not get any more until the next month.

A new product is out to take the place of dairy butter; it is called margarine. It comes in a clear bag, and it is white like lard. It has a little yellow pill in the bag, and you squeeze and squeeze the bag, until you get it warmed up with your hands. The little pill dissolves; you keep squeezing and squeezing until every bit of the white stuff is yellow through and through. You then put it in your butter mold, and hope that people will like it in the restaurant and think it is butter. I don't eat butter; I couldn't care less.

One of the neat things happening is the wonderful songs that have been written in praise of our country during this time of war. I love to hear Kate Smith sing "God Bless America." There is one thing about this war; it has brought Americans a feeling of pride and a love for their country.

THE WAR

Betty Benedict

They're all gone the town is quiet
Everyone left is sad
The distant cry of battle
Can be heard within my head
The stars hang in the windows to show the pride our
    people feel
A star is such an empty thing to take the place of life
I do not want to understand
I wouldn't want to know
This ugly thing that possesses men
Down the shaft of time
The thing that looms forever
A threat to all we love
If I had God's power, I'd make it stop
I'd crush the bad beneath my heel
And let the good remain
I'd have no more war and no more suffering and pain

WASHING CLOTHES AND LINENS

Between our house and the gazebo in our backyard is a large area set up for washing clothes. We have four big galvanized wash tubs setting on a bench in the shade of the trees. Five large black cast iron wash pots stand up on their feet and have a fire built under them. Octagon or homemade lye soap is used in the first tub. A scrub board is in the first tub to get out the heavy stains. The clothes are then put in one of the black wash pots to boil and loosen all the dirt. All of the white clothes are washed and put in separate pots. Wooden sticks are used to keep the wash punched down into the boiling water. These sticks are also used to lift the hot clothes out of the pots. They are taken over to go through three tubs of rinsing water. The fourth rinse water tub has bluing in it. Only the white clothes are put into this tub to keep them snow-white. The clothes are then wrung out by hand.

They are hung on rows of clotheslines to dry. The items needing starch are placed into a tub containing starch before hanging them to dry. Even in the winter, the wash has to go on. If it is very cold, the clothes freeze on the line. When the sun comes out, they thaw and dry no matter how cold the day.

Mother uses white tablecloths and white covers for the chairbacks in her restaurant. They are made of Huck toweling. It requires constant washing and ironing to keep all of these things clean for the restaurant. Mother has three or four ladies at the house to keep up with these jobs. My friends and I enjoy playing in the yard when the washing is going on. There is always singing, laughing, and cutting-up as the ladies do the wash. I learned many of the old spiritual songs while playing in the yard during wash time.

THE DISSAPEARING PLAYHOUSE

One time, someone parked a large tractor trailer between our restaurant and the Methodist Church. The tractor was gone, but the trailer was parked there for a few days. My friends and I got the backdoor open and decided we could play house in this big trailer. We worked hard to get our playhouse fixed up so we could start playing. We carried things like blankets and quilts to make beds. We carried a footstool and used it as a table. We took Mother's clock from the house and put it on the footstool. We also brought some of our dress-up clothes and shoes. Each one of us brought books and magazines to read. It was a wonderful place to play; we had so much fun. We decided it was the best playhouse we ever had.

I got up one morning to go over to the restaurant for breakfast. Lo and behold, our trailer was gone. The owner had apparently taken it away during the night. I ran over where the trailer had been parked to see if our things had been thrown out. There was nothing there; all of our things were gone.

I wonder what the truck driver thought when he opened the trailer and found our nice playhouse there. I thought he might bring our things back, but he never did. Mother missed her clock and wondered what had happened to it; I sure didn't tell. I am so thankful that Homer Gene wasn't in there. Amelia said we could also have been in there. Wouldn't that have been something?

(Many years later, I told Mother what happened to her clock. After all those years, she still did not take it too well.)

THE DOLLHOUSE

I love late fall because we get the Christmas catalog from Sears Roebuck. I love to look at this catalog, and usually by Christmastime, it is worn-out. My friends and I lie across the bed in my room and pick out the things we would like to have for Christmas.

Every year, I talk to my parents about a beautiful dollhouse that is in the catalog. It has two stories and is filled with furniture. It has a nice kitchen with the latest stoves and refrigerators. You have everything you need to keep house. I told Mom and Dad for the last two years that I want it. Dad told me that Santa Claus tried to get it, but he ran out before he got to my house.

I know that just means that Sears had run out of them before Mom ordered it. I think that all little girls must want a dollhouse, and they are not making enough to go around. I feel sure that Mom will order it earlier this year. I am looking forward to Christmas morning. I just know I will have the dollhouse for my own. I am not asking for a lot of things this year because I know that pretty little house will be the nicest present I will ever get. My friends and I will be able to play with our dolls and pretend we are grown-ups. I am going to bed early Christmas eve so they will be able to get it all fixed for me by the time I get up on Christmas morning. I bet it will take half the night or more.

I know it can be done because there are some people who live in big houses they order from Sears. They call those houses Craftsman Bungalows. People live in these all over the country. I don't know how long it takes them to build the bigger houses, but I know they can do mine in one night.

Christmas morning has finally come. I jump out of my bed and run to the back of the house to look in the yard. I don't see my house there. I was almost in tears because I know Sears Roebuck was out of them again. It will be a long time to have to wait another year.

I come back to the living room to see what other things I had under our tree. There sat a little house just about the size of a milk crate. It looked like the house I wanted, but it was very small.

Dad said, "Look Betty, Santa has brought the dollhouse you wanted."

I said, "Do you mean this is it?"

He said, "Isn't this the one you wanted?"

I just lay down on the floor and started crying.

I said, "This is not what I wanted. I thought it would be in the backyard, and I could get in it and play. "

Mother said, "Betty, it is a dollhouse."

I said, "I don't have a doll you can get in that house. I don't have a paper doll you could stand up in it. That is good for nothing."

Mother said, "Well, Santa Claus can just take it back and all of your other things. If you ever needed a good spanking, it is right now. I don't know what to do with you."

The whole time Dad tried to calm Mother down.

I said, "It's okay. It's okay."

I knew they were getting into an argument. I said, "I will put it on a shelf in my room."

Mother said, "If you are not going to play with it, I am going to give it to some little girl who will love it."

I had been mixed up about the size of the dollhouse. I thought it would be built in the backyard and we could play in it. Dad talked to me, and told me that I was wrong to pitch a fit when Santa was trying his best to make me happy.

He said, "Santa has feelings, too."

I know this means Mother and Dad have feelings, and I have hurt them. I told Mother that I was sorry that I acted so badly. I told her I loved the baby carriage, the doll, and the blankets I got.

Amelia came over to see what I got for Christmas. She had gotten a Scarlet O'Hara doll and a small baby doll bed. She carried it to my house to show me. When I told her about my dollhouse, she said she knew all the time it would be too little to get in. I asked her why she didn't tell me that. Amelia told me she didn't know I had any idea I could get into it. I think that whatever I get for Christmas from now on, I will pretend I like it even if I don't.

INDIANS CAPTURE WHITE LADY

A group of my friends and I were playing out in the backyard. We saw the little girl who could not play with us, walking down the street wearing a straw hat. Her mother insisted she wear this hat to keep her from getting freckles and keep the sun out of her eyes.

Betty at Mom's restaurant

We were playing Indians, and we decided to capture her. We started doing our Indian war dance, whooping and hollering as we captured the white lady. We took her to the Indian chief (Amelia), and he commanded us to tie her up in the gazebo. We then built a fire right in the middle of the backyard, took her straw hat, threw it in the fire and did our war dance around the hat as it burned. We didn't have a very good fire; her hat only got scorched.

Of course we were told on, and again, I was the one to get the spanking. Worst of all was the talk Dad gave us about thinking of other people's feelings and not ever destroying anything that belongs to someone else. We felt like two cents. Dad had us tell the little girl how sorry we were. We promised her we would never do this again. We also told her that it was not us that did this; we were Indians at the time.

CHRISTMASTIME

We have punch boards in the restaurant for our customers. You pay a fee for the number of punches you want to make to try to win the big prize. Many of the boards have names on each punch. The men punch the name of their girlfriend or wife and hope to win the big prize. Everyone wins a tiny prize like a candy bar. If the punch board is for candy, the big prize is a big box of chocolates. At Christmas, we always have chocolate-covered cherries on the punch board. The board with peppermint stick candy has one big peppermint stick, the size of a fireplace log, for the grand prize.

Christmas at the restaurant has always been a great time for me. We have a large live tree that goes almost to the ceiling. We put tinsel and green and red roping on it. We have little bells that fold up flat when not in use, and when you open them, they are tissue paper that magically unfolds into a bell. We have a star to put on the top of our tree. We have many different colored balls that are made of thin glass. The lights are all colors; they are big and in the shape of candle flames. We have tin foil ice cycles on the tree that reflect the colors of the lights.

I love this time of year. Santa Claus comes to see me over at our house, and when I get up on Christmas morning, there is a big fire in the parlor fireplace. All of my presents are over near the tree. Santa is usually good to me, although I don't believe in him. I know it is just a made-up thing to make kids be good. I haven't told Dad that I don't believe because he gets a kick out of telling me Santa Claus stories.

Someone always helps me take all my toys over to the restaurant. I put them around the tree, and show them to people who want to look at them. One year, I actually found one of my Santa Claus gifts, a big paint set, that had been hidden under Mother and Dad's bed. After that, I started hunting for my gifts. I usually find quite a few of them before Christmas.

One year, I went to the storeroom at the back of the restaurant to look for my gifts. I climbed the rolling ladder they use to get the supplies from the tall shelves that go up to the ceiling. I found a large box behind the cans on the top shelf. I could tell there was a doll in it because there was a picture on the side of the box. I had to work to get the box open and found a large rubber doll with a bottle. I would have thrown the box down to the floor, but the bottle was glass, and I knew it would break. I thought someone would hear the box fall and come to see what happened. My doll was tied inside the box, and it took me some time to get it loose.

I managed to carry the doll down the ladder. I laid the doll down on the floor at the bottom of the ladder and went back up to get the bottle. I closed the box and hid it back behind the cans. Needless to say, Mother saw me coming out of the storeroom, holding my doll with a big grin on my face.

Mother said, "You are going to keep on until you will get nothing for Christmas."

I loved that doll.

(This doll is the one that Grannie White named Homer Gene.)

This became a game for me. I would find my presents, and let Mom and Dad know I found them. Mother got angry about this. She told me that if I found my toys and gifts that year, the only thing I would have on Christmas morning would be what I had not found. I went ahead with the search for my toys. I thought surely she was only teasing. They would always get me other things for Christmas.

I got up Christmas morning, and all I had was a tin bugle. I acted like I was thrilled, and I carried it over to the restaurant and put it under the tree.

Everyone who came in would say, "Betty, what did you get for Christmas?"

I would go over to the tree, get my bugle, and show it to them.

They would say, "What else did you get?"

I would say, "Just the tin bugle." Mother would have to explain the whole thing. This went on and on all day long.

MY LIFE IS CHANGING

Mother's restaurant is called the Hayesville Café. The highway in front of our restaurant brings salesmen and travelers passing through Hayesville on their way to Murphy and western North Carolina. Our little restaurant has been fairly prosperous during these difficult times. We have Gulf Oil Company gas pumps out front. Being the first gas station on the main highway entering town gives us a lot of gasoline sales.

The TVA has almost finished building the Chatuge Dam and rerouting the roads and highways. The main highway through town to Murphy will no longer come past our restaurant.

Mr. Jeter Coffee and his family have moved into the right side of our house. Mr. Coffee is a watch repairer. This spot on the square is ideal for him. He has his work bench in front of the window facing the street. People can come on the porch and talk to him through the window. His customers never need to come into the house.

Dad felt that it was time to sell the restaurant and establish more of a home life for me. He bought a house and acreage out in West Hayesville. Since he sold the restaurant, Mother had to cook in our home on the square until we moved to our new place. It was just like playing house. Mother cooked with old time pots on the open fireplace just like they did in olden times. Dad bought a table and chairs at the furniture store owned by Andy Padgett.

Mother bakes corn bread and biscuits in a cast iron oven on the hearth of the fireplace. Red hot coals are underneath the oven and in the cast iron lid on top. She cooks pinto beans in a pot that swings from the arm over the fire in the fireplace. In the evenings, Dad plays his guitar and we sing old songs, like "When the works all done this fall, Old Shep" and many old hymns.

No matter what we are singing, Polly tries to drown us out with her song "When the Roll is called up Yonder." Often Dad takes Polly out of the cage, she sits on his shoulder, and rubs her head against his cheek. I have tried hard to make Polly like me. I am fighting a losing battle.

We have a Hastings catalog that we enjoy looking at each night. We discuss what we would like to grow in our garden and what flowers to plant at our new home in West Hayesville. Our family will have a real kitchen, and be able to sit down at a table and have our meals together. This is something I have never had. I usually ate my meals at the restaurant by myself unless some of my friends were with me.

My friends are looking forward to the great time we can have in Town Creek which flows through our new property down below the stables. We will have a big bank of Kaolin, snow white rocks, and big sheets of isinglass. Kaolin is snow-white clay. There are big veins of this white dirt on the bank of our creek. The creek keeps it moist. We can play with this like modeling clay. Kaolin has been used for years by families to whitewash their chimneys and fire places. This is done in the spring of the year to cover the smoke and soot produced during the winters. All the fireplaces are beautifully white all summer. Kaolin is also used to make fine china. I will miss my old house on the Square, but I look forward to a new kind of life.

MOVE TO WEST HAYESVILLE

Moving day is finally here. We bought our place from George Thompson. The house was originally built and owned by Mr. Will Winchester so it is known as *Winchester Place*. We can only move into half of our house because Dad made an agreement with Mr. Thompson. They can live in one side of our house for six months while they build their new one. Mother is not happy with the situation. She wanted the new Harley Hampton house across from the water tank on US 64.

We moved into one side of the house with no water. We have a sink in the kitchen with no faucet. It is used to pour water out, and the water just runs out under the house. We have a well on the back porch, and city water outside in the front yard and on all sides of the house. There are four faucets outdoors, but none in the house. A kitchen was made for the Thompsons in the back bedroom that opens onto the porch, and they moved their wood cook stove in there. I guess they didn't miss much; they just didn't have a sink to pour out their water.

We have an outdoor toilet that is shared by both families. The walls and ceilings of our house are all bead board planks that has never been painted. The front door opens to a large hallway about ten feet wide. It runs the full length of the house and the walls are so dark you feel like you are in a dungeon.

My bed is in the front room where the parlor is supposed to be; it is a large room and easily holds my bed and our sitting room furniture. The second room down the hall is supposed to be the dining room, but Mother and Dad have their bed there. The next room is our kitchen; there are no cabinets. Mother put a counter, a Hoosier cabinet, an enamel metal top table and four chairs in the kitchen. She has a new cook stove called Allen's Princess. It has white enamel with a shiny black top.

Dad bought a large table top Motorola Radio with push buttons for our new house. We are very pleased with it because we can get radio stations we could never hear before. Stations are strong, loud, and clear. The cabinet is mahogany, and it sets on top of our wash stand that we have owned forever. Of course, Dad bought our new furniture from Andy Padgett's furniture store.

We have a small Philco refrigerator that holds only four ice trays. We have a screen porch off the kitchen with a nice table and chairs. We have an ice box out there, and in the summertime, the ice truck comes from Murphy to deliver ice. In winter, our screen porch is used as a refrigerator. Mother often puts Jello out there to cool.

The first time it rained, water came in from the roof, and we had to put buckets in several places to catch it. I have never seen Mother in such bad humor. The war is raging, and with everything rationed, we cannot buy nails for a new roof.

Dad has hired Glen Byers and his twin boys, Harold and Carol, to come and roof the house. He hired every teenager and many younger children to come and pick the nails out of the old roofing to install the new shingles. We all sat close to the house to dodge the old shingles being thrown off the roof. Dad furnished all of us with little brown cotton gloves, a pair of pliers, and a quart mason jar to collect the nails from the old shingles. There must have been twenty of us working. Dad called us the *assembly line*. The nails were used to put on the new shingles. We have no more leaks because the old nails worked just fine. Mr. Byers did a great job.

Benedict Home West Hayesville

Mr. and Mrs. Thompson have a teenage son named Addison. He gave me his red Radio Flyer wagon and a bookcase especially made to hold Big Little Books. He also gave me his complete collection of books for the case. He gave me many comic books to go with my collection. I like to take my wagon around to my friends' houses and trade comic books.

(Wish I had saved all the old comic books.)

LAZY

Betty Benedict

Whoop-se-Daisy, I sure feel lazy
Today is a beautiful day
If I slip on the grass and bust my ass
I won't get up from the fall
I'll just lie here and enjoy myself
and look at the beautiful sky
The clouds float about and form different things
They make me glad that I'm living

I can smell the grass and corn and horses
All this is part of my world
So Whoop-se-Daisy if I want to be lazy
I will till I hear Mother call

Our West Hayesville house is in a very good location for me because I get to see some of my friends more than when I lived on the square. Tommy Gray lives right down from me. Gay Nell Mingus lives just up the street, and Frances Beal lives across the highway and up the meadow from the water tank. I can walk down through the woods across from my house to the water tank, cross the highway, and through the meadow to Frances Beal's house. She waits for me, and we walk up the hill to school from her house. I don't think this is much further to school than from my house on the Square.

WEST HAYESVILLE WORLD

Betty Benedict

I run my world from West Hayesville and I like it pretty good
If I didn't I'd change it to something else, I would
I like to ride old Bess and really make her fly
I love to shoot my rifle, or climb a tree so high
I really like the summers while playing in Town Creek
I dam it up, but every time, it always springs a leak
I like to play cowboy and sometimes paper dolls
It's fun to make believe and be anything I want
I sometimes go to the stockyard and that is lots of fun
I brought home a Palomino and he could really run
We sold him to the Wimpey's that made me very sad
I just don't think of sad things much. I'm too busy having fun
After all I have my great big world to run

We don't have a lunchroom at our school so Mother packs me a lunch. There is a rumor that we may soon get a place to eat at school that is called the *soup room*. They will serve nothing but soup and milk. They are trying to get the state to help them provide a lunch room.

HOME WHEN THE WHISTLE BLOWS

When school is out each day, I usually take the long way around and go through town. I do this to see my friends on the square. If I tell Mother I am going through town, she tells me to start going home at five o'clock when the whistle blows at the Ritter's Lumber Company.

On the weekends, our house is a gathering place for my friends. We have a larger group than we ever had on the square. Now, Mary Catherine Bradshaw, Frances Beal, Tommy Gray, Regina Johnston, Amelia Standridge, Glenda Prater, and Joy Padgett come to play in our barn, in the creek, and on the kaolin bank.

**Ritter Lumber Company
Saw Mill—our clock**

We work very hard at digging up what we think are Indian graves. This project came to an end when we dug up half of an arrow head. We thought we would soon find Indian bones so we stopped digging. Later we found out that these were just mounds of earth thrown up on the bank when a bridge was built across the creek.

HAND-ME-DOWNS

All of my girlfriends except Mary Janice get clothes from some of their relatives who are older, and most of these clothes are very pretty. When anyone tells them they have on pretty clothes, they say it is just an old hand-me-down. They usually say it is from one of their cousins or an older sister. Mary Janice and I have no older

Gypsy, Brother Ed, and Dad

sisters and no older cousins to give us their clothes. I would like to have hand-me-downs.

All of my clothes that I outgrow are given to my cousin Pat Nash in Athens. Amelia has a cousin in South Georgia that sometimes sends her clothes. I was telling Amelia's mother, Bill Standridge, that I would like some hand-me-downs so she saved some of Amelia's things that had been given to them by Amelia's cousin. Amelia had worn them until they were too small for her, and I got them because I am smaller. I think I was prouder of these clothes than any new clothes I ever had.

Now if anyone says, "Betty you have on a pretty dress," I can say, "It's just an old hand-me-down."

A RECORD PLAYER AT LAST!

My family goes to Athens, Georgia, to visit my Grandmother Cearley more often than we could when Mother had the restaurant. There is a wonderful place to play at my Aunt Bob's house. We all gather there. My Nash cousins—Bill, Bob, and Pat—are there. Down the street from my grandmother's and Aunt Bob's house is a little girl named Freddie Orr, and she comes to play with us. She mentioned to me that she had a new record player. She said that she could carry it from place to place because it was in a little suitcase. I asked her if she would bring it to my grandmothers so we could listen to it. When I saw it, I wanted it badly. I told Freddie that I would give her fifty cents for it. She couldn't believe I had a whole fifty-cent piece. I went in and got my fifty-cent piece from my suitcase at Grannie's to show her. She said she had never had that much money. We made the deal. I gave her my fifty cents, and she gave me her record player. I was so happy because this was a dream I have had for so long. I can now play all the records that Charles Higdon has given me.

Docia Low Cearley

We were eating dinner that night at Grannie's house when the telephone rang. Someone answered the phone and said that Fred Orr, Freddie's dad, was on the phone, very upset. He said he wanted to talk to one of Betty's parents. Dad went to the phone. He didn't know at that time that I had the record player. Mr. Orr told him that his daughter had taken Freddie's record player from her.

I heard Dad say, "Mr. Orr, let me call you right back."

Dad went into the living room and called me in there. I knew I was in trouble. Here came Mother before I had a chance to tell Dad that I had made an honest deal. Mother wouldn't give me a chance to talk; she was so excited and aggravated.

Dad said, "Carrie, lets listen to what Betty has to say."

I said, "Freddie Orr went home very happy. I gave her fifty cents for that record player."

Mother was carrying on, and I said, "Mother, Charles Higdon would have given me a record player if you had let him."

She said, "If you say one more thing, I will wear you out."

She said, "You knew better than to give that child fifty cents and take her record player."

Dad said, "Just let me go down and talk to Mr. Orr."

He had me go in our bedroom and get the record player. I had put it under the bed, waiting for the right time to tell them what I had done. Dad came back much later with the record player. He had paid Mr. Orr enough to buy Freddie another one.

Mother was not mad at me anymore; she was hopping mad at Dad.

She said, "There is no chance of me ever teaching her anything. All you ever do is get her out of trouble."

Mom said, "You knew good and well that fifty cents for the record player was not right."

Dad told me, as he so often did when mother was upset with us, "Betty, you know the Good Woman is right about this. Just remember, she wrote the book!"

Dad tells me to listen to Mother. I have looked everywhere for the book, but I can't find it. It must have all of her rules that she made for me to live by. If I could read it, I might do a better job of staying out of trouble.

I had told my friends in Hayesville that I was going to have a record player to play my records on. I couldn't wait to get back home to tell them that our dream had come true. We will be able to dance to the music we have, and I can take the player from house to house which will be wonderful for us. This record player is electric, but it is not automatic. You have to lift up the arm and put the needle down on the beginning grove of the record. When the record finishes, you have to lift the arm off the record. I have to buy little packs of needles that have about one hundred in a pack. One needle plays about ten records before changing them. We save our old needles and put them in a little jar. We reuse these when we are out of money.

Mother has never fussed again about my record player. She never complains no matter how much we play music or shake the house dancing. She enjoys knowing we are safe at home and having fun.

I never have to ask Mother if I can bring my friends home. They are always welcome. My friends often spend the night, but I do have to ask her if I spend the night at my friend's house. At our house, we always feel comfortable to play anything we want.

THE SECRET CLUB

Dad brought home a box of new cereal that we had never seen before. The name of it is Corn Kix. It is good cereal, but the thing that interests me most is the advertisement on the back of the box. You can send a box top with a coupon to the company to get a secret compartment ring. It is adjustable to fit any finger. I told my friends about it, and they are all buying the cereal, and sending for the ring. We decided to form a secret club, and the rings will be part of our club to show that we are members. We were very pleased when our rings came. They have small secret compartments that slide out of the top of the ring. We write our club rules in small writing, and fold it up to put in the top of our rings. We decided we must take our rings off each time we wash our hands to keep water from going into the secret compartment.

We decided to find a tile under the sidewalk to use for our secret mailbox. There are several tiles under the sidewalk from my house to town. We set up our mailbox in the round tile that runs under the sidewalk between Amelia's and Mary Catherine Bradshaw's house. We write secret messages to each other and put them in the mailbox. We go by every afternoon after school and get the mail that is addressed to us. I usually have five or six notes. I answer them, and put them back in the mailbox the next morning on the way to school.

This club is a lot of fun. We have meetings on Saturday at one of our houses. It seems that no one else has bought the Kix cereal because we are asked everyday at school by someone where we got our rings. We tell them we can't tell because they are secret club rings. Everything was going great until a big rain came. We went by our mailbox on the way to school and found all the notes washed out into the street. They were all sopping wet and the ink had run all over them. We did not know our mailbox was a drain tile that was put there to carry rain water under the sidewalk.

We talked about getting Dad to put up a mailbox for us somewhere along the sidewalk. When we asked him about it, he said he didn't think we would be allowed to put a mailbox up in town. We still have our rings, and we still play and have secret club meetings even without a mailbox.

COURTHOUSE REVIVAL

Not very long after our move to West Hayesville, a traveling evangelist came to town. He set up a revival in the courtroom of the courthouse, and someone told him I could sing. I told him I would sing if I could get Peggy Crawford to play the piano for me. Many people go up front when he has altar call, and a lot of them are children. After every revival that we have in town, people talk about the children going up to the altar.

They say, "Oh, nothing but a bunch of kids went up, and they don't know what they are doing."

One night at the revival, I sang "Jesus Paid it All," and went down and took my seat. I felt very guilty that night, and felt like I needed to try to be a better person. The preacher had preached about accepting Jesus as a personal savior. In my mind, a personal savior is someone who is yours. I thought it was very neat to be able to have Jesus with you all the time. I am only nine years old, but I feel that I have done lots of things to be forgiven. I am not sure how long it will take for God to work through all these things.

I knew I couldn't go up like other people did. I didn't want people thinking that I was one of those kids who didn't know what they were doing. I just prayed, and asked Jesus to come into my heart and be my personal savior. I felt sure he did. I did not tell anyone that this had happened to me. I talk to Jesus all the time, and He is my personal savior and my personal friend.

When I jump rope, and they are raising the rope higher and higher, I ask Jesus to help me jump, no matter how high they lift the rope. Sometimes I miss, and I begin to wonder if Jesus can hear me if I don't talk out loud to him. I can't ask anyone so I decide I will talk out loud. I decide that if I talked very low, He will hear me. I didn't want Him to think I was talking to someone else, so I told Him that I will just give Him another name. I gave Jesus the name *Coggie*. Whenever I call this name, Jesus will know I am talking to Him.

This did not work out too well. Mother overheard me talking to *Coggie*, and she thinks I have gone loony. She thinks they needed to get me some help. I told Jesus that He was going to have to be patient with me. I will talk to Him in my mind whenever someone is around, and I hope He can hear me. I try very hard to be a good girl; sometimes it isn't easy.

THIRD GRADE

Mabel Thompson

When I go to the third grade classroom, I have Miss Mabel Thompson for my teacher. A little girl named Clara Jane Taylor and I can't seem to get along. We both get a whipping almost every day. I have started wearing my boots and jodhpurs to school. Miss Mabel always says she has to switch me harder because Clara Jane has on a dress.

As I walk to school each day, I make up my mind not to do anything to cause me to get a whipping. Somehow without fail, I manage to get one. Clara Jane Taylor and I have a fuss. We pull hair or shove each other over nothing. We both get a whipping. Mother has not found out that I was getting into so much trouble at school. This was a bad year.

BREAKING HORSES—RODEO DREAMS

I have a wonderful place to ride my horses in West Hayesville. While we were in town, Dad had to rent pasture land for his livestock, and we often had horses scattered about the pastures around town. We now have enough pasture land behind our house below the barn to keep all our horses. Sometimes we have large numbers of horses; other times only one or two.

Dad often gets a large truckload of horses that are wild western stock. These horses are taken off the open ranges out west. They are usually very beautiful horses. They are mustangs, paint, and palomino horses. Dad breaks and trains these horses himself. I am always excited when a new load of horses come.

On horse-breaking day, John S. Jones and Otis Williams are usually there to help hold the horses for him. I always enjoy watching, but Mother never does. Dad is often thrown, and Otis and John S. help get him back on the horse. Most of the horses throw him more than once. Dad will get back on the horse and keep riding until the horse is worn-out. The falls never seem to hurt him; he says he knows how to fall.

It is so much fun watching Dad break horses. Amelia and I decided to call this a rodeo and sell tickets for the horse breakings. Dad is usually such a good sport; it shocked us that he would not let us do this. Another fortune down the drain!

One fall day, Dad met his match. He was bucked off, and forgot how to fall. He landed on his face and busted up his teeth really badly. He got back on that horse and broke the horse that day. He never gives up! He also never went to the dentist. He went through the rest of his life snaggletooth. Mother says Dad was very good-looking before he got his teeth knocked out. Dad said at least he never lost his hair.

Dad and I were walking down to the barn one day.

I said, "Dad, you just know everything there is to know about a horse, don't you?"

He said, "Lord, yes, I could make one if I had the stuff."

The horse we took from the town stable is named Charming Charlie. I ride this horse, and it is nice to have a place to ride without having to worry about cars making Charlie shy. We have thirty eight acres in which to ride and play. At this time, we have another horse that Dad rides when I ride Charlie. This horse is named Royal Bess, and she is really a fast saddle horse with five gates. Dad takes me for rides on her, and I sit in front of him in the saddle. When we take a curve, it is like we are leaning sideways. I kept on at Dad until he finally let me ride Bess by myself. We ride Bess with an English saddle. I wanted a western saddle for Charlie, and Dad finally got me one. I love this saddle because one of our favorite games is to play cowboy.

POOR LITTLE FROG

I have something bothering me very much, but I haven't had time to tell Dad. I did something very bad the other day. I was going down to the barn to sit in the loft and do my lessons. I was about half way between our house and the barn when I saw a cute little frog. I don't know what came over me, but I picked up a good-sized rock and killed the little frog.

As soon as I did this, I had this horrible feeling come over me. I just felt terrible, and so very sad that I had killed that poor little frog. I wish I could give that frog back its life. I feel so guilty, and I just wish there was something I could do. The little frog was not hurting anyone, and it was terrible for me to take its life.

When I finally got up the nerve to tell Dad about this, he said, "Many times people do things that can never be fixed. We must be very careful, and always try not to do things that we can never make right again."

He said, "The little frog is dead, and you can never make that different. You can go on from here and try to always do what is right and never bring harm to something innocent that is not hurting you. Betty, don't worry about the feelings of the little frog because he is dead and doesn't know about the way you feel. You are the one suffering. You have to go on from here. You know you were not right, but I am glad you could talk to me about it."

Dad said he had done things that he would give anything in the world to take back. "These are life's lessons, and we must learn from them."

I always feel better when I talk to Dad. I think he is very wise. I just hope I will never do anything like that again. I will never understand why I did it.

Dad said, "Betty, it hurt you worse than it hurt the frog."

MOVIES IN THE COURTHOUSE

The theater at the old Methodist Church building went out of business. We now have western movies each Saturday night at the courthouse. Dad takes me to town and stays at Bob Tiger's store where a bunch of the fathers gather to wait on their children to get out of the movies. I sometimes get out of the movie and walk over to Bob Tiger's store. The men are laughing and cutting up and having a great time. I think they have more fun than we do at the movie.

Although we go to the movies and the men are having a good time, we still have a dark cloud over us. We all have our loved ones in the war to worry about. Everything is still rationed, but life goes on as much as possible under these conditions. I pray in my heart every minute of the day for my brothers to be safe. I try to be happy.

PLAYING IN THE BARN LOFT

Our barn is a great place to play in. In the loft, we have a bar set up to play cowboy like in the saloons we see in the western movies. We sometimes bring our soda tables and use them as card tables in the saloon. Amelia brings her mother's playing cards, and we pretend to be gamblers. We pretend to smoke our Bull Durham roll-your-own cigarettes.

We have holsters with cap pistols, and most of us have cowboy outfits. I let someone else wear my cowboy outfit, and I wear my boots and jodhpurs. I wear a flannel shirt and a vest over it. We got some brown oilcloth and cut-out chaps. These are things the cowboys wear over their pants. Ours didn't work too well because we could not keep them on.

Grandmother Cearley came to visit and she sewed ribbons on the chaps so we could tie them on. We took the scissors and cut into the oilcloth to make fringe. I guess the cowboys wore these to protect their pants.

I had a hard time getting a cowboy suit because everyone thought I should have a cowgirl suit with one of those tacky little skirts. We don't play cowgirl; we play cowboy. If we have girls in our plots, we play like we are saloon girls. Some of us dress up in all our western

Betty Playing Cowboy

finery to play this part. We wear a long off-the-shoulder dress as the saloon girls do. The saloon girls deal the cards at the gaming tables. They go to the bar for fresh drinks for the cowboys. We plan the plot we are going to play, and everyone is assigned a special part. Some of our cowboys are good guys, and some are bad. We usually use names of the cowboys we see in movies, like Tim Holt, Lone Ranger, Roy Rogers, Gene Autry, The Three Musketeers, and others. Sometimes we play like we are chewing tobacco when we are the bad cowboys. We use tootsie rolls for this. We usually have one of the saloon girls sing. If there are enough of us to dress up, we have a chorus line.

We play our record player in the loft. Didley rigged me up a power cord to plug in the player. Mother keeps worrying about this because she says we are apt to cause a fire. For a guitar, we cut off a broom handle to use. I want a real one, but I haven't managed that yet. I want a gun more than a guitar.

Right now, I am planning on how to get a real rifle. I have found one in the Sears Roebuck catalog that costs nine dollars and ninety-eight cents. To buy one, it would take twenty times for me to sing "Did you ever go sailing" for Allen Bell. I don't think I can ever manage to get money for the gun. It would take a long time.

GROVE ACROSS THE STREET

We have so many good places to play in. Dad owns the land across the street from our house. There is a shady grove that looks like a place where a wagon train might rest and camp out. We play like we are camping there, and I told Dad that we needed a tent. He nailed a two-by-four between two trees, and put a brand new tarpaulin over the plank. He drove stakes in the ground and tied the tarp down. This tent is so tall we can all stand up in it. It makes us a big room so we can put our soda tables in it. We brought our nail kegs and planks from the barn to use for a table or bar.

We sometimes play like we are in Africa on a Safari. Someone gave Amelia a jungle hat that we would all like to have. We don't know where to get them.

UNCLES AND PALM LEAVES

Mr. Ed Crawford and Mr. Henley Crawford own and operate a Sinclair Service Station on the Square in town. I visit them every afternoon on my way home from school. When I go by the station they pay me to sweep the floors. I don't mind doing this. It is not dusty because there is a lot of oil mixed in with the dirt. I use the money to buy cokes for Amelia and me at Star's drugstore.

One time, someone they know went to Florida, and brought back these big palm leaves that look like big fans with fringe hanging from them. They must have twelve of them. They put them in the window of the station, and they have been there a long time. I want these palm leaves to put in my tent to make it look more like a jungle. I don't know how to get them, and I know Mother would be mad if I asked for them. I am sure Uncle Ed and Uncle Henley would let me have them, if they knew I wanted them.

About once a week, I stack up all the palm leaves and wipe out the window with a cloth. I dust the palm leaves and put them back in the window. Many months seem to go by.

One afternoon, Uncle Ed said, "Betty, would you like to have those palm leaves?"

I was so happy. I took them and Dad stuck them on each side of the two-by-four up in the top of our tent. This makes our tent look like a jungle. I know why Uncle Ed gave them to me. I told him if I ever got to Florida that I was going to bring me some home. That did it. If Mother knew this she would say that I was not supposed to hint for things.

Uncle Ed and Uncle Henley tease me and try to get me to say which one of them I like better. They give me presents on my birthday and Christmas and try to get me to say which gift I like better. There is no way I would pick one over the other. I love both of them. Uncle Ed Crawford is my friend Wallace's Dad. Wallace is in the war, I pray for him too.

STAR AND SARAH BRISTOL

I sometimes go to Star's during school lunch period. She and Sarah have food cooked, and I eat my lunch there. I always get permission to leave the school grounds. I can go home for lunch if I want to. It is more fun to visit with my friends Star and Sarah at the drugstore.

Star and Sarah always have something interesting and funny happening in their lives. They love to entertain their customers with these funny stories. Two of their neatest stories were in Hugh Park's article in the Atlanta Journal Newspaper.

Twice a year, they go to the Merchandise Mart in Atlanta, Georgia to shop for replenishing their store. They enjoy these buying trips very much. They go to Canton, Georgia where their niece lives, and she drives them to the mart. Their niece's husband has a woodyard in Canton. They spent the night in Canton, went out the next morning, and got into their niece's car, and it would not start. Their niece called her husband and he told them to take his car, and he would get the car fixed while they were gone. He was getting ready to leave for the woodyard and didn't think they would be driving off in his car immediately. They got to the Merchandise Mart, parked the car in the parking garage and went shopping till noon. One of the highlights of their day is to go to a fine restaurant to have a leisurely lunch before continuing with their shopping. They shop until five o'clock.

At the end of their shopping, they went back to the garage, got into the car, and started for home. Sarah was sitting in the back seat, and she kept telling them there was something loud bumping around in the trunk. They kept on their way, and when they got almost to Canton, they stopped to get gas. Sarah said she thought they should check the trunk.

When they opened the trunk out jumped three big bird dogs, and they ran down to the curb to relieve themselves. They said you would have thought a fire hydrant had broken, there was so much water running down the street. After the poor dogs finished, they jumped back into the trunk and just sat there and waited for them to close the lid. The niece's husband had worried about his dogs all day, but had no way to contact them. The dogs ride with him every day to the woodyard. They had no idea they were driving off with the dogs in the car.

The next story also made the Atlanta Journal some time later. The same niece in Canton, Georgia decided to remodel her den and give it a very rustic country look. Her father-in-law in Shooting Creek, North Carolina had an old chicken house. She asked him if she could have the weathered boards off the outside of his chicken house to use on her den walls. He said she could if she replaced the old wood with new timbers.

The niece hired a crew of men to take a truck of new lumber from Canton, Georgia and go to Shooting Creek. They would remove and replace the siding on the chicken house. They arrived and knocked on the father-in-law's door. He came to the door half-asleep. They explained what they were there for, and he sleepily pointed in the general direction to the chicken house and went back inside.

The men took the old timbers off a chicken house and replaced them with new. That night, well after dark, the neighbors of the father-in-law came home from visiting their children. They went to bed and the next morning at early daylight the neighbor came out side to have his morning coffee. To his surprise, he saw a new chicken house in place of his old one.

He called to his wife, "Lord, have mercy, you are not going to believe this. Someone has built us a new chicken house."

His wife said, "What could have happened? What could it be?"

He said, "Your guess is good as mine. It must have been the Chicken House Fairy."

They were proud of their new chicken house. The father-in-law just lost out. If you snooze, you lose.

Sarah is dating Mr. Guy Wheeler who is in the Army. Sarah has a beautiful glow about her now. Star says she is in love. My friends and I love to watch them walking around the square. Sarah Bristol is in her beautiful winter coat and Mr. Wheeler in his uniform. They are a very

Guy Wheeler

handsome couple. My friends and I often pretend that our names are Sarah and Guy. I am sure they will marry soon.

BUGGY TO RIDE

My friends and I often play dress-up, pretending that we are opera stars. We think we can sing opera quite well. We play on a small platform we made from milk crates with plywood over them and pretend this is our stage. We pretend we are in a buggy with fringe and sing "Surry with the Fringe on Top." We carry our umbrellas and pretend they are beautiful parasols. Someone came up with the idea that we needed a real buggy.

I mentioned to Dad that I wanted a buggy. I can ask my own dad for anything I want. Mother has never made a rule against that. I don't know where Dad got the buggy. I came home from school one afternoon, and over across the street beside our tent set a buggy. It looked brand new. It had a pretty black leather seat and a convertible top.

We play on that buggy so much and use it for so many things. We play cowboy and pretend we are getting away from the bad guys in the buggy. We dress up like ladies and dress up like opera stars. We pretend that the buggy is on our stage while we are singing. We are always plotting to get Dad to hook a horse to our buggy so we can go on rides. He sometimes hooks Bess to the buggy. I can drive out to the end of our street and back.

Dad sometimes has Otis Williams take us for rides in the buggy. We get all dressed up like ladies and pretend Otis is our chauffeur. We put the buggy top down on sunny days and carry our umbrellas as parasols for our ride. We sometimes go up Town Mountain and then to down town Hayesville. Otis will have Bess in a beautiful trot-strutting around the square. We frequently drive down Tusquittee Road to Boice Supply at the head of the railroad. We turn around, come back up around the square, and then go home. Otis enjoys our outings as much as we do.

After returning home, we park over near the tent in our grove of trees. Otis unhitches Bess and takes her to the barn or pasture. We will get homemade cinnamon buns or cookies, grape juice, or lemonade. We carry these over to our soda tables, and pretend to have a ladies tea. We always invite Otis to have tea with us.

After tea, we often sit outside out tent, and Otis entertains us with stories of his life. He tells us many things. I sometimes wonder if he tells us these stories just for entertainment. He tells us that while living in Africa, an enemy tribe captured him and his friends, and sold them to a white slave merchant. He said they stacked them like sardines in the bottom of a boat. The trip to America was long, and they had to ride this way for weeks.

I asked Dad if he thought this was true. Dad said that it probably happened to Otis's family, and they had told him this story. Otis has the nickname of Bozo Williams, and most people call him this. Dad says to call him Otis, which shows our respect for him.

TWO HOUSES IN THE WOODS

Soon after we moved to West Hayesville, Dad built two small houses on our property across the creek from our house. This is a beautiful wooded area, and to me it is like a fairy land. There are all kinds of beautiful wild flowers in the woodland. There are two pretty springs of water that have beautiful moss and ferns growing around them.

Dad built a little frame house for Otis Williams and his wife Edna. Edna took white feed sacks and bleached them as white as snow. She made curtains for her windows, and embroidered them with beautiful flowers. She starched them and hung them in her little cottage. I love to go over and visit Edna in her little home.

Edna has a sister, Frankie, who married a man named Frank Lloyd. Edna and Frankie's maiden name was Murphy. Frankie is a talented artist, and she saves any kind of board that she can find for painting her pictures. Dad built her a little log cabin, and she has it decorated with her beautiful paintings. There is a white picket fence around her log cabin, and she has planted beautiful flowers and shrubs there. The cabin has a fireplace, and it has a room added on the back called a *lean to*. This is the kitchen.

Frankie and Edna carry water from the springs as there is no running water in the house. It is not unusual to not have running water in your house. My friend Regina Johnston's family use a spring for their water. Most of the people living outside town have a spring or a well for water.

Edna has large iron wash pots and tubs set up outside. People bring their washing to her. They call this *taking in washing*. Edna charges fifty cents a load. She washes, starches, and irons them. She uses irons she heats on the kitchen stove. Edna says she would rather use the flat irons than an electric iron. Some people call them smoothing irons.

WASHING AND IRONING

Edna comes to our house every Monday to help Mother do her wash. The only difference in washing at our house is that we have running water. All washing is done outside and is boiled in an iron wash pot heated by wood fire.

Mother expects me to iron my clothes which are mostly dresses. This is really the only chore I do. My dresses are starched and sprinkled, rolled up, and put in our refrigerator for a few hours. Being cold seems to make them iron better. We even iron our underclothes.

Everything we wear, like slips and panties, are made of rayon. Most of our slips have beautiful lace, and when you wash them, they wrinkle up and look almost like doll clothes. When they are sprinkled and ironed, all of the wrinkles come out, and they regain their size.

(There was no nylon, polyester, or perma-press.)

Mother lightly starches our sheets and pillowcases before they are ironed. My grandmother makes lace to go on all of her families sheets. Our beds are pretty, and it's nice to crawl into them on Monday night when we have fresh sheets.

WHITE FEED SACKS TO FINERY

Many people make sheets from four white feed sacks sewn together. Grandmother Cearley makes all of her families white pillow cases and napkins out of feed sacks. Only our Sunday napkins are linen. Grannie bleaches the feed sacks snow-white then hemstitches the pillow cases and the napkins. When they are starched and ironed, they look like beautiful linen. These have to be washed, starched, and ironed after each use.

We never have paper napkins at our house. Every Monday, Mother puts a fresh napkin at our place at the table. After we eat, we fold it and lay it in our chair. If we don't have anything messy, we use the napkin all week. I wish we could have paper napkins because most of my friends do. I guess Mother doesn't want to spend the money for them.

I ask Mother if we could buy some paper napkins, and she said, "Why on earth do you want paper napkins when you can have beautiful cloth napkins?"

Grandmother is a great believer in ladies learning how to do needlework. She told me my Mother would never sit still long enough to learn. Aunt Bob Parham learned to do all of the needlework. At night after dinner, Aunt Bob and Uncle Clyde Parham sit in their parlor and listen to the radio. Aunt Bob always has some needlework to do. When I go to Athens to stay with her in summer, we go to town, pick out some pretty material, and she makes me a beautiful dress.

ATHENS WITH BILL, BOB, AND PAT

I enjoy staying on the farm with my Uncle Andrew Nash and Aunt Fern Nash. I have a good time playing with my cousins Bill, Bob, and Pat. There are many interesting things on the farm. We climb up on the smoke house roof and have grapes all around us. We reach up and pick them and eat until we want no more. We go into the barn loft, and sit among peanuts that are all around us. They pull them from the ground, vines and all, then put them in the barn loft to dry. I love raw peanuts.

BORED

Betty Benedict

Bored, no I'll never be
I won't allow it to happen to me
I'll find something if its nothing
It's the way you approach it, you see
Boredom can fart at the wind and drift away
Or tie its tail to a kite
I don't care where it goes

Or how the wind blows
As long as it stays in flight
I'll laugh in the daytime and howl at the moon
I may burst at the seams any minute
It surely is an exciting world and I'm so glad I'm in it

Uncle Andrew told us that he would pay us if we would chop cotton, so they showed me how. We started chopping, and I thought I would never get to the end of that row. The sun was hot, and we were tired. There was a little bush at the end of the rows we were chopping. Bob Nash and I crawled up under the bush and just stayed there for the longest time. Uncle Andrew was trying to figure out where we were. I was never eager to chop cotton again.

That afternoon Bob told me that he would ask his mother, Aunt Fern, to make us some tea cakes. I had never had any tea cakes, but I imagined that they were going to be something great. I imagined they would be some fancy cakes with some sort of icing on them. Aunt Fern called us to come in the screen porch for tea cakes and grape juice. On the table sat a big platter of plain old sugar cookies. They were like the cookies everyone made in Hayesville when they didn't have time to make something better. I had never heard plain cookies called tea cakes. I didn't let on; I acted thrilled. They were very good especially with the cold grape juice.

My Athens cousins enjoyed coming to see us when we lived in our house on the Square. They grew up on a farm, and were amazed to be able to order anything they wanted to eat at our restaurant. Dad would get a kick out of letting them eat all the candy and drink all the cokes they wanted.

(My cousin Bob Nash became a missionary and was in charge of the Baptist Missions in Southeast Asia. Even after traveling the world, I think his Hayesville visits remain special to him.)

THE NIGHTMARE

In the summer after I completed third grade, Mother, Dad, and I went to Athens, Georgia to visit Grandmother. She and Aunt Bob live next door to each other. We had finished a big dinner at Aunt Bob's. My cousins were all there from the farm just north of Athens. We had played together all day and had such a good time.

Mother and Dad started packing up our things to go back home to Hayesville, but I wanted to stay. I started one of my spells bending over and pretending my stomach was hurting very badly. Everyone became alarmed so Grannie ran to the phone and called Dr. Harry Talmadge. He is a friend of the family and a surgeon. He soon came to the house and examined me. He poked around on my stomach, and asked me if it hurt. I would bend double and moan. Mother told him that I had complained of this hurting several times before.

He said, "I believe she has appendicitis. I think we need to get her to the hospital as soon as possible. We will be able to take a blood count there." This was turning into the worst mess I had ever been in. I started telling them that I was feeling better and Dr. Talmadge said this often happens with appendicitis.

He said, "I wouldn't risk taking her back to Hayesville."

I was beginning to panic. I thought that when they got me to the hospital, they would figure out that I didn't have appendicitis. It didn't happen that way; I was scared to death. I think I now know what a nervous breakdown feels like.

On top of it all, I found myself in St. Mary's Hospital. This hospital was swarming with Catholic nuns. I had never even seen a picture of one. I knew there was no way I could tell

Betty after surgery

Mother that I was putting on. Even as scared as I was, I thought about what Dr. May would say to me when I got home. I knew that Dr. May would know that I did not have appendicitis.

They put me in a room, and did what they called a blood count, which was just sticking my finger. By this time I was praying. I told God I had been bad pretending to be sick. I asked him just to get me out of this, and I would never pretend to be sick again. A man came into my room that had on a white jacket. I asked Him if I could go home now. I told him I really think that I am okay.

He said, "Young lady, we will have you well in no time. I am going to give you a shot. It will make you a little sleepy. In just a few minutes, we will roll you down to the operating room, and put you to sleep. When you wake up, you will not have that old bad appendix anymore."

My heart was pounding so that I was having trouble getting my breath. I told the man I really did not think I needed this operation. He seemed to be amused. The nuns came in rolling a big table; they lifted me up and put me on it. They rolled me down a hall way and into an elevator. I was asking them if I could just please do without this operation. They assured me that I would feel much better after it was over.

I had heard at church that *the wages of sin are death*; I truly felt I might not live through this. They took me into a room with all of these bright lights shining down on me. The sisters were all around me. The man who had talked to me in my room put a thing over my nose, and I tried to fight. I could hardly move because I was pinned down. They told me they were giving me gas; everything started whirling round and round and I was scared to death.

The last thing I knew I heard one of the sisters say, "Your Mother is with you. Your Mother is with you."

The next thing I knew I was awake in a room, and one of the sisters told me it was the recovery room.

She said, "It's all over, and you will not have the stomachache anymore." The Catholic nuns were very nice to me.

They took me to my room and Dr. Talmadge came in to see me; he had on some funny blue clothes. He told me that my incision was only an inch long with two stitches.

He said, "You must stay off your feet because we don't want you to get adhesions."

Mother and Dad came in; I could tell I had put them through a lot. I have never felt so guilty in all my life. Mother stayed for a while; Aunt Bob came to take her back to her house. Mother told me that I would be fine; the nurses would take good care of me.

In all of my life, I have never minded being left alone. I feel like I am a terrible person; I have been so bad to my family. I think they may leave me here and never come back for me. I am very frightened. I wish I could be home in Hayesville.

I dream that Dr. May will hate me and tell Mother and Dad I was never sick. I know this is costing Mom and Dad a lot of money. The day Dad left to go home, I heard him tell Mother he had to pay for the operation. This stay in the hospital has been awful. I am so scared I am going to be left here. Everyone in my Grannie's neighborhood has sent me comic books. I have flowers on the windowsill of my room. I don't know how I am ever going to get over this worried feeling.

After ten days in the hospital, Dad came back to get Mother and me to return to Hayesville. Being back home in Hayesville did not help my guilty feelings. I have always been very comfortable at night. I have never thought about anything bothering me. Now, I sometimes think something is under my bed, and I get out of the bed by jumping way out from it. I turn on the light to make sure that nothing is there.

LITTLE GREEN MAN DREAM

Before I went to Athens and had the operation, we often played up in Dot Matheson's barn loft. She had some old wicker furniture up there and a table with a fishbowl on it. We got some of the lacy stuff we call fish food that grows in Town Creek and put it into the fishbowl. We took green leaves and put them in the water for fish. I did not go back there to play after I came home from Athens because of this dream.

One night, I had a terrible dream about looking in that fishbowl and seeing a tiny, little green man in the water. My friends in the dream said that he was a little green man from Africa, and if he got out of the bowl and stung you, you would die. I thought he was gone when I turned around and looked in the bowl again. In my dream, all of us were scared and we looked everywhere, but couldn't find him in the barn. We had to be very careful everywhere we went to be sure he would not sting us. I thought someone saw him in Pansy Bradshaw's yard. They said he was in the big tiger lily bush right next to the sidewalk.

After having this dream, I am now afraid to go anywhere. I cannot get this dream out of my head. I think this little green man is going to jump out and get me for sure.

I know this is not real; I just can't get it out of my mind. I don't mention the crazy way I feel to anyone; I know I will get over it. It is just because I was so bad to pretend I was sick in Athens. From now on, I am going to try hard to be good and honest in everything I do. That's my promise.

I also continue to dream about dodging Dr. May in town. I dream I meet him on the Square; he gives me a hug and tells me he has been missing me. I think he must know that I am dodging him. He does not act mad at me and this makes me feel better.

(Interestingly, Dr. May died three years before this, but I never acknowledged his passing.)

RAGGEDY BETTY ELLEN

My friends and I are playing in the creek and on the old Kaolin mine. I am feeling much better. I go to the library to get some books to read. I think everyone in town has heard about my appendix operation. Miss Ellen Scroggs keeps the library in the courthouse, and I have never thought she liked me very much. When all of us go in the library, she seemed anxious to get us out. I am sure she remembers all the times we came through the hall of the courthouse on our roller skates. This time, Miss Scroggs was very friendly, and she asked me how I am feeling. She helps me pick out some very good books that I cannot find by myself.

When I start to leave the library, Miss Ellen asks, "Betty, have you ever made a rag doll?"

I tell her, "No, I have not."

She says that she has a pattern, and she thinks she has everything we will need to make one. She says she has always wanted to make one, but has no little girl to give it to. She said that we can make one at her house. I go over and hug her neck. She seems so stiff, but she tries to hug me back. I don't believe she has ever hugged anyone before. Now I think of Miss Ellen differently. She told me what time to come to her house. I went home and told Mother, and she thinks this is wonderful.

I go to Miss Ellen's house every evening after dinner. We sew on our rag doll until after dark. She has many interesting things that she lets me see. She has a clear liquid filled glass globe with skaters in it. You shake the globe and the snow in the liquid swirls around them.

Our rag doll is coming along great. We use white feed sacks to make her body, head, arms, and legs. Miss Ellen gets Rit dye and mixes it to make our feed sack cloth flesh color. She mixes pink and brown colors to get the flesh shade. We hang these on a line to dry. The pattern she has told me about is one cut out of newspapers. After the cloth is dry, we lay the pattern on it. Miss Ellen put table knives on top of the pattern to hold it down while we cut. She let me cut until the scissors hurt my finger. She then finished cutting out our doll.

She said, "Now, this is the face. We have to draw a mouth, nose, eyes, and eyebrows."

She told me to bring my crayons. We have a good time painting our doll's face. I make her big blue eyes with long eyelashes.

Miss Ellen said, "Don't you think we should make her rosy cheeks? We don't want her to look sick."

She laughs at some of the things I say. I bet that I am the only person in Hayesville that has ever heard her laugh. My rag doll has black shoes made from black material sewn on her feet. We decide we need some dimples in her legs to show where her knees bend. We do this with a pink crayon.

We sew her up with a needle and thread and start stuffing her with cotton.

Miss Ellen says, "We don't want her too stiff with cotton. A rag doll should be soft and floppy."

When we have her stuffed just right, Miss Ellen sews her head, arms, and legs to her body.

I tell her that I am going to draw the doll a belly button. I do this with brown and pink crayons. We giggle about this. Before we make her dress, Miss Ellen gets out a roll of yellow yarn. She uses a big needle, and we make our doll's hair by looping yarn all over her head. After this, she gets out some beautiful material. We have a little pattern to cut out a dress for our doll; Miss Ellen does the dress. It is too hard for me to do. Miss Ellen thinks she needs buttons on her shoes. She sews two black buttons on each shoe.

I tell Mother, "I want to name my rag doll Raggedy Ellen. Do you think this will make Miss Ellen mad?"

Mother said, "I think she will be pleased, but you will have to ask her if it will be all right." I told Miss Ellen that I am so happy to have a pretty rag doll, and I want to name our doll Raggedy Ellen.

She said, "We both made her; you did as much work making her as I did. Let's name her Raggedy Betty Ellen".

I thought this was a great idea, and said, "That's a nice name for her."

So that is how my rag doll got her name. She is the only doll I have except Homer Gene that has a double name.

TIGER'S STORE, UPSTAIRS

Upstairs in Mr. Tigers store is a place people never get to go. You go up a long set of stairs at the back of the store to get there. I have wanted to go up there for a long time. I asked Dad what he thought was up there. He explained to me that it was a place like our storeroom in back if our restaurant.

He said, "This is where Mr. Tiger stores stock to be brought down later. The Christmas stock that didn't sell is stored up there until next Christmas."

My imagination ran wild. I can just see all the toys up there. I picture it being like Toy Land in books I read. I am plotting on how to get up there. If Star hadn't left Mr. Tiger's and gone next door, she would take me up there.

Bob Tiger in his Store

I went over to Booth's drugstore, and asked Star if she could think of some way I could get up there.

Star said, "Ask Mr. Tiger to take you up there. You have never been bashful about asking before."

I told her it wasn't because I was bashful; it was because Mother would get upset if she found out. Star told me to save my money, and ask Mr. Tiger if I could please go upstairs and look at the toys. She also said to tell him I had money to buy something.

When I had saved the money, I went to Mr. Tiger's store. I told him I had looked over his whole store and can't find anything to spend it on.

I said, "Would there be anything upstairs left over from Christmas that I might want to buy?"

He said, "We can go see."

We went up the stairs, and I was a little disappointed. Most of the things were winter coats and bathrobes. There was a long table stacked up with toys. I found a rag doll with long arms and legs like Raggedy Betty Ellen. She didn't look like a Raggedy Ann doll at all. She had a sunbonnet on with brown hair around the front of her face. When you take off her bonnet, she is bald. I can keep her bonnet on, or I might get some yarn and put hair on her head. I asked Mr. Tiger what he would sell her for.

He said, "How much money do you have? "

I told him I had a dollar. He asked me if I thought seventy-five cents would be a fair price.

I said, "It's a deal."

I gave him my two fifty-cent pieces, and he gave me a quarter back. I bought her to be friends with Raggedy Betty Ellen; I think they will like each other.

I did not want to give my whole dollar for her. I remember that Grannie White thought it was terrible for her son Ruel and his wife Neva to pay a whole dollar for my friend Mary Janice's doll at Christmas. That was many years ago and things have gone up in price.

MILK COW EPISODE

Our school principal, Mr. J. Walter Moore, asked Dad to find him a cow that gave good milk. Something had gone wrong with the cow that Mr. Moore had owned for several years.

J. Walter Moore

Dad said, "Walter, I have the cow you need."

Walter told Dad that he did not believe he already had the cow he needed and said, "Red, I don't want any of your foolishness. I am very serious about needing a cow. My wife Gussie likes to have enough milk for the family with plenty left over to sell to the neighbors."

Dad answered, "Walter, you know I wouldn't joke about something like this. I happen to have the very cow that will suit your needs. I wouldn't try to pull anything over on you."

"Now, Red, you know I don't believe that. There is no way you can come up with the right cow just at the moment I need one. I have been around you long enough to know you will seize on any opportunity to pull something over on me. I don't trust you, and I don't know why I even try to deal with you."

This went on for about two weeks. Walter would ask his friends if Dad had mentioned pulling a trick on him. They told Walter that Dad was serious this time.

Walter finally purchased the cow from Dad. Walter and his family live on Riverside in the city limits. Dad had lined up his friends to go every morning before Walter got up to milk the cow at Walters's barn. Each man signed up for a morning. After they milked the cow, they waited down the street until Walter left home for school. They would then take the milk in to Gussie. Gussie was a good sport. She was in on the prank. Walter thought she was buying milk when she actually had plenty to sell the neighbors.

Walter would complain to Dad every day. He came out to the house mad, saying, "Red, you have done it to me again. This is not funny. I can't believe you would do this to Gussie. I know you like to pull your jokes on me, but Gussie is the one taking the blunt of this."

Dad said, "Walter, there is absolutely nothing wrong with that cow. You just do not know how to milk. If you would like, I can come down and give you lessons."

This made Walter so mad he was practically jumping up and down and said, "I have been milking since I was a young boy, Red, don't try pulling that stuff with me."

Dad looked at him and said, "I am afraid you are going to ruin that good cow. If you can't milk her properly, she will dry up."

Walter angrily said, "That cow is as dry as she can be, and you knew it when you sold her to me."

Mother told Dad that she was afraid Walter was going to have a stroke.

I could never see how Dad could take all that heat. Every man in town was leading Walter on; this went on for a week. Then all of Dad's friends decided to turn the tables on him. They decided they would tip Walter off the Sunday morning Dad was to milk the cow. They told Walter that Dad had been milking his cow every morning, and taking his milk. They told him that Dad was sick of selling the cow to Walter and had another buyer who offered more money for the cow. They said Dad was trying to get the cow back. Walter told them that he did not believe one word they were saying.

He said, "I know Red Benedict well enough to know he would not get up at the crack of dawn for a whole week, and come down to my house and milk a cow."

They told J. Walter if he didn't believe them, he could find out for himself. He could go to the barn on Sunday morning at five o'clock and catch him. The men all told Gussie about them setting Red up to be caught by Walter on Sunday morning.

Gussie called Dad and told him his buddies had set him up to be caught by Walter. She told Dad not to come out. So Dad stayed home on the Sunday and Walter got a big bucket of milk.

(This tale was told over and over for many years by the men participating in the prank. Here are a few of the names: Mr. Henley Crawford, Mr. Ed Crawford, Mr. Royal Hedden, Mr. Norman Alexander, and Mr. Red Benedict.)

FOURTH GRADE—MISS SUE HAIGLER

I will soon be going back to school and will be in fourth grade. Miss Sue Haigler will be my teacher. She is Miss Lizzy Scroggs's sister. I know her and like her very much. She and Mrs. Bill Standridge directed me in the "Goldilocks and the Three Bears" operetta when I was in the first grade.

Miss Sue Haigler is a very good teacher. She teaches class in an interesting way. She explains our lesson in an interesting way that is easy to remember. Every morning before she starts our lesson, we sing songs. We sing "Good Morning to you, good morning to you. We are all in our places with sunshiny faces. Oh this is the way to start a new day."

Singing makes me happy, and the lessons seem to go by quickly. We are soon out to recess, and I never do anything that gets me in trouble. This is a very happy school year. I believe that God has forgiven me for the terrible thing I did in Athens. I am glad He has, but I am sure Mother never will.

No one knows I didn't need that operation except God and me and possibly Dr. May. I went through this complete school year without a whipping. I don't remember Miss Haigler ever being angry with me.

I often get permission to go home with Regina Johnston from school. We walk across the road and through the Baptist-Presbyterian Cemetery. We have a good time making up stories about the people in the graves. Regina is lots of fun; she keeps me laughing all the time. The cemetery is very grown up with weeds and bushes which are all around and on the graves. Regina says there is no danger of the people coming out of those graves, they would get tangled up in briars and never catch us.

I met Regina Johnston in the first grade. Her dad's sister, Lenore Johnston, was our teacher. We have been friends ever since. After I moved to West Hayesville, Regina and I go back and forth from my house to hers. Her mother Cora Johnston is Mr. Luther Matheson's daughter. She has a twin sister Ora Matheson who is not married. She dates a TVA worker, Mr. Turner, and they plan to marry soon. My first grade teacher is going to marry Mr. Floyd Fender. Regina loves to tell about these courtships.

Regina's sister, Susan Johnston, is two years younger than us. Regina doesn't want Susan to play with us. They came to spend the night with me, but Regina didn't want Susan to come. This time her mother would not let Regina spend the night unless Susan came also. Regina treated Susan so badly at our home that Mother told her, "If you aren't nicer to your sister, you will have to go home."

I like Susan fine. Mother says that she was sometimes like that to my Aunt Bob when they were children. She said older children think they are wiser but they are really just jealous.

Regina's mother, Cora Johnston, is a wonderful cook. She has four girls. Cora continues to be pregnant and has children which are always girls. They live on a hill, and Regina's dad says he will cover the hill with children until he gets a boy. His children are Regina, Susan, Carolyn, Mary Ann, Abigail, and Roberta. Roberta was the Robert he never had.

Sunday dinners at the Johnstons are always special. I ask Regina how her mother knew how much food to cook.

She said, "Every time another youngin comes along, she just throws another tater in the pot."

(Robert and Cora had six girls and never had a boy.)

SINGING SOLOS IN CHURCH AND ALL-DAY SINGINGS

Regina's grandfather, Luther Matheson, owns and operates a small store a short walk from our house. If Mother needs something, she usually sends me there to buy it. Mr. Matheson is a musician and belongs to a wonderful quartet, "The Ritter Quartet." He sings the lead, Strubbie Galloway sings tenor, Doc Stanley sings alto, and Glen Byers sings bass. When people hear this quartet, they go wild. The quartet performs at all the singings. These singings are called convention singings. They are also referred to as *All day singings with dinner on the ground*. We often have singings in our courthouse on the Square.

Mr. Luther leads the singing at the Baptist Church. I was at his store one afternoon, when the quartet was practicing. I joined in on one of the songs and sang a line or two.

Mr. Luther stopped and said, "Come here Betty, you have a beautiful voice. I would like for you to sing at church. You can come to the store, and I will help you practice a song for church."

The first song I sang was "Love Lifted Me." This is how I started singing in churches.

Mr. Matheson asked me if I would like to travel with the quartet and sing at the convention singings. Mother and Dad knew all of these wonderful men in the quartet, and I was allowed to travel with them.

The Ritter Quartet seems to be the main attraction at these singings. They bring the house down when they perform. The crowd keeps on applauding until they do an encore. The ladies who bring picnic lunches all ask the quartet to eat with them. Many of these people are regulars at the singings. The quartet tries to take turns eating with different families. The food is delicious. Each group or individual who sings at the convention are on a list. The master of ceremonies calls out the name when it is your turn to sing.

(Many years after I left Hayesville, I was told that my name was still being called at the conventions.)

Betty and dogwood flowers by Tom Gray

Mr. Matheson writes songs, words, and the music. The most popular convention singing song books are printed by the "Stamps Baxter Company." Mr. Matheson has had several of his songs, words, and music, published by them. I often sing one of Mr. Matheson's songs, "Will He be Ashamed of Me." It pleases Mr. Matheson that I like to sing his song.

Helen Herbert

HELEN HERBERT, MY NEW FRIEND

We have a new neighbor, Tom Herbert, who has built a new house in West Hayesville not far from our house. He is married to Edna Evans, and they have a young daughter, Helen Herbert, who has become our friend. We play with her at her house and she visits us. Helen is older than us, but likes to play our games.

The Herberts have big, cured hams in their smokehouse. We take sharp knives and slice thin slivers of the cured ham, and we think this is better than jerky. We eat these small slivers and they are very tasty. We also like to eat the seeds out of the big sunflowers they grow in their yard. They also gave me some pumpkin seeds to eat from their garden. I had never eaten pumpkin seeds. They are good when they are dried.

When we play at each other's houses, we mix coco and sugar and pretend to be old ladies or cowboys dipping and spitting snuff. We also like to eat raw oatmeal. It has a good nutty flavor. When I was in the Hospital the catholic sisters taught me how to eat oatmeal with toast and eggs, just like grits. I had never liked oatmeal with sugar and milk.

MY SECOND FAMILY

Susan Gray

I spend a lot of time down at the Gray's house. They live in an old house that belonged to their family for years. It is nice and doesn't look like an old house. They are like my second family.

Tommy Gray and I have been friends since the first grade. He has two younger sisters, Ginger and Sandra Gray. Their dad, Tom Senior, is a lawyer, and their mother, Viola, is a teacher. We play the Green Hornet and other characters from our comic books.

Dr. Staton, one of the doctors now in Hayesville, gave Tommy some things to make a doctor's kit. Sometimes my doll gets sick, and Tommy makes it well. We are all gathered around Viola out in the yard most of the time and she supervises many of our games. Tommy has learned how to make neat little tents with a sheet and wooden stakes. We play under these tents a lot.

Viola feels like I have missed a lot since I don't have brothers or sisters at

Viola Gray

Sandra Gray

home. She tries to include me in all of their family activities. When they go to the movies at Murphy, I am invited to go. I especially love the musicals we see. Some of the stars that sing and dance are Ginger Rogers, Fred Astaire, Betty Grable, and Dick Haynes. Some of the popular songs from these movies are: "I'll Get By," "I'm Always Chasing Rainbows," "Elmer's Tune," "That's for Me," and many more. We often act out these movies, and pretend that we are the actors and actresses. One of the movies that I like most is the Jolson Story. Al Jolson was played by Larry Parks. I practice singing all of his songs, and I think I do a pretty good job sounding like him.

Ginger and Sandra are very pretty little girls with cute personalities. Sometimes Sandra comes to our house for a visit. Dad enjoys talking to her and hearing her tell jokes she has heard the grown people tell. She tells the joke and says she doesn't understand it, but everyone always laughs. She told about three little birds going south for the winter. Papa bird was in front, Mama Bird next, and Baby bird in the back.

PaPa bird said, "Mama, my instincts tell me we have turned around and flying back north."

Ginger Gray

Mama said. "No, Papa, my instincts tell me we are still headed south."

The baby bird said, "My end stinks too, but it doesn't tell me where to go."

Sandra said, "I know another one if you would like to hear it."

Tommy Gray

Dad always said, "Go ahead and tell it."

She said, "There were three little moles going through a mole hill—Papa, Mama and Baby mole."

Papa said, "Mama, I smell cabbage."

Mama said, "I smell carrots."

Baby mole said, "All I smell is molasses."

Viola Gray has a new baby named Susan. She is a cute little thing and gets a lot of our attention. The Grays and I spend a lot of time playing in our Town Creek and the Kaolin mine. Tommy does a good job of damming up the creek, but it still springs a leak. He has had a crush on Emogene Carringer ever since we were in the second grade. Most of us have boyfriends at school.

BLUE JEANS COME TO HAYESVILLE

Mattie Lou Penland's fifth and sixth grade

We are in the sixth grade in Mattie Lou Penland's room. She is teaching the fifth and sixth grade. Many of my friends who are a year below me are in this class. Mrs. Penland's daughter Bobbie Penland is my friend, and we have always been in the same class together. We are glad Bobbie is in this class because we were afraid she would be sent to another sixth-grade class since her mother will be our teacher.

We have worn dresses to school almost every year because they just don't make slacks to fit girls our age. I had one pair of slacks when I was in the second grade and I kept wearing them until they were too short. Dad called them my high water britches. I could wear them to play in after they became too short, but I do not wear them to school. We get the American Girl magazine, and we look at the Seventeen Magazine that Star sells at Booth's Drugstore. This is the way we keep up with the latest fashions.

It has now become the rage for girls to wear boys' blue jeans. A lot of the parents don't like this idea, but most of us have managed to get a pair of Tuff Nut jeans from Bob Tiger's store. The fashion is to roll the pants up to mid calf of our legs, and wear one of our dad's white shirts. The bigger the shirt, the better!

The older teenage girls are wearing blue jeans, and we always try to copy them. Some of my friends' fathers don't have white shirts except for the ones they wear on Sunday. Dad has furnished most of us with some of his old white shirts. We have no dress code at our school so we wear our blue jeans to school. Since this is the style, we now wear jeans more often than dresses.

We already had saddle oxford shoes, and we wear these or penny loafers with our jeans. I love to wear moccasins, and I have worn these for many years even with dresses. We go to Bob Tiger's store and buy tennis shoes that are made for boys because he doesn't carry girls' tennis shoes.

(At this time, there were no girls' tennis shoes except white tennis shoes made for playing basketball. There was no plastic to make buttons so regardless of how inexpensive the shirt, the buttons were made of real *mother of pearl*.)

REMODELING OUR HOUSE

Mother had Mr. Ed McConnell and his son Lyle come to the house to give her a price on putting sheet rock, a new kind of wall board, over all the walls in our house. She wants to make a room at the end of the long hallway for a bathroom. The Thompsons have moved out into their new house. Mother is now ready to make this old house more livable.

I now have my bedroom in the room that opens to the back porch. This is the room the Thompsons used for a kitchen. I have Ray's little bed in my room, and a pretty dressing table with a lace skirt around it. I have a nail keg with a pillow on the top and a lace skirt around it for a stool. I put my perfume and my hens that I got for my birthday on the dressing table. Dad bought me a chest of drawers from Andy Padgett's furniture store. I enjoy this bedroom.

My friends and I enjoy playing dress-up at the dressing table. We comb each other's hair and sometimes play beauty-shop. We put each other's hair in the latest grown-up styles like we see in magazines. They call one style a pompadour. We also have some nets that are called snoods. These come in different colors and the girls wear them in movies and magazines. Shoulder pads are the rage so we stuff cotton in the shoulders of our dresses.

All of the walls in the entire house are dark unpainted bead board. Mother told Dad she didn't think she could live in this dreary place unless she could brighten up the walls. Dad said the sheet rock was a good idea because it would insulate the house and make it warmer.

The McConnells started their work. Didley came and cut a double French door into the parlor from the big hall. Two French doors were hung with panes of glass in them. The doors open out into the hall. As soon as the McConnells finished all of their work, the house looked like a new and different home.

We have pine floors over the entire house. Mother had what they call inlaid linoleum put in the kitchen. She wants the bathroom put in right away. Didley said he had so much work for other people that he would have to let her know when he could get to it.

Mother had a good time painting the new walls and woodwork. She painted all the woodwork white. I wanted lavender for my bedroom, but you can't get lavender paint. Mother used a new water-based paint that was made for new sheetrock. This paint comes only in white. You get a tiny amount of the coloring you want, and mix it into the paint.

My room is pink, Mother's bedroom is ivory, and our guest bedroom is pale green. The dining room is a deeper shade of ivory. Our kitchen is all white, and we have red-and-white checked curtains with a red tablecloth on the table. All of this has made our house beautiful. Mother said she is beginning to love the old house, and this pleases Dad very much.

Pauline Bryan

Mother and I went to Blairsville, Georgia to visit her Aunt Dovie and Uncle Ira Butt. He prints the news paper for Blairsville, Towns and Union County Georgia. We went shopping and Mother bought some beautiful stripped fabric to cover our sofa and chair. When we returned home Mother had Pauline Bryan, Didley's wife, come out to the house to measure and make slip covers for the sofa and chair. We brought the piano from our house on the Square, and put it in our parlor. When Pauline finished the covers, they fit perfectly. The sofa and chair looked brand new. She is a talented lady.

We have lace curtains in our bedrooms and the dining room. When they are washed, they have to be put on curtain stretchers. These are wooden frames that you can adjust to any size. The stretchers have tiny sharp tacks about an inch apart on all four sides. While the curtains are wet, you carefully hook the edges over the little nails until you have the complete curtain stretched out. If you do not do this, your curtains draw up to nothing, and they would never fit your windows again. Even after the curtains have been stretched, they never look the same. There are scalloped pointed edges all the way around that were never there before.

Someone told Mother about the new draperies that had come out made of paper. Many people are buying these at Bob Tiger's store. Mother and I went over to the store, and picked out a beautiful pattern that looked good with our new sofa material. I think they are the prettiest window treatments I have ever seen. Mother said they are right tacky. We left them up for a while.

SORGHUM SYRUP FILLS THE BATHROOM

Mother finally had word from Didley. He gave her a date when he could be there to install the bathroom at the end of the hallway. She was very excited that we were going to have an indoor bathroom. The day before Didley was to come, a large truck pulled up at our house. Dad opened the door, and men started bringing in many gallon buckets. They stacked them to the ceiling in the room where Didley was supposed to put in the bathroom. These buckets were full of sorghum syrup.

Mother came running after Dad saying, "Fred, what on earth are you doing now?"

He told her he had traded a mule for the truckload of syrup.

She said, "This is the craziest thing you have ever done."

She told him that he knew Didley was to come tomorrow to put in the new bathroom.

He said, "I will have this syrup sold in no time."

She said, "By the time you get this stuff sold, Didley will be tied up again."

She threw her hands up, and went back to the kitchen.

Dad talked to Didley. In a few weeks, a truck drove up and loaded all the syrup. Didley came and at last we had our complete bathroom. Dad told Mother that he had cleared enough money on the syrup to pay for her bathroom.

Mother and Dad always have a cordial and loving relationship. Dad's nickname for Mother is *The Good Woman*. He refers to her in this manner in a loving and compassionate way. Dad often greets his friends in town when he meets them with "Hello, Good Man." Most men in town call him by the same name.

MRS. HYATT'S CAPE COD

Mrs. Girlie G. Hyatt lives in our community of West Hayesville. Her husband, Ute, works away from home. He comes in for a weekend about once a month. She has two grown daughters, Rita and Geneva, and they work away from home. Mother and Mrs. Hyatt are good friends, and they have tea almost every afternoon at our house or hers.

Betty's Hayesville Home—Hyatt House

Mrs. Hyatt built a new house before we moved to West Hayesville. Before she built her new house she gave her old house to my friend Regina Johnston's family. They moved the old house over behind Mrs. Carrie Johnston's house just past the water tank on old US 64.

Mrs. Hyatt built a new Cape Cod house on her property where the old house stood. She says, "My new house is a true Cape Cod.

She got her plans from up in New England and she says this is the only true Cape Cod house in the county. Didley Bryan soon built a similar house for him and his wife Pauline before the new Methodist Church was built across the street from them on May Street. The Bryan Cape Cod faces the back of the church.

Mr. Ute Hyatt is planning to retire so Mrs. Hyatt told Mother that the little Cape Cod house was not large enough for her and Ute. She built a new house about a block up the street. It is a spacious one-storey rock house. She and Mr. Ute moved into the new house, but Mrs. Hyatt lived for only a few months. Mr. Hyatt built a small brick house on another street near our home in West Hayesville. He sold his nice new home that Mrs. Hyatt had built to Joe and Roberta May.

BRIDAL PATH

Betty and Charlie

Betty and Gypsy

Ever since we moved to West Hayesville, Dad has talked about cutting a riding path through the woods up to the mountain top. The mountain is called Town Mountain. Dad usually gets things done quickly, but this seems to be something he just keeps talking about.

I would really like to have a bridal path because sometimes it gets boring just riding around on West Hayesville streets. The pavement is hot on my horse's feet, and Dad often doesn't want me to ride when it is hot on the gravel or pavement. One of our favorite things is playing in the woods across the creek from our house. There is always something interesting to see with the change of seasons. There are different kinds of flowers, mosses, and wild ferns that make a fairy land for us. I know it would be wonderful to have a bridal path there.

Dad came from town one day very excited. He told us that some loggers were coming in to clear a road on our property to the top of Town Mountain. He said he had made a deal to give them the timber in exchange for clearing a road for the bridal path. Dad, Otis Williams, and John S. Jones marked the trees he wanted taken out to make the path.

The loggers cleared all the stumps, and leveled the path that goes all the way from our barn across Town Creek and up through the woods to the top of Town Mountain. Dad had several loads of coal cinders delivered and put on the bridal path. These make a comfortable path for our horses, and it is very soft for their feet. Dad is protective of his horses and other animals. He put up several logs along the path for the horses to jump which makes riding more fun and the horses enjoy the jumps.

Amelia and Joy are the only friends who love riding with me. Most of my friends are uncomfortable around horses. Our path to the top of the mountain winds around with several switch back turns.

(Years later, I searched for the bridal path and could not find it. It was totally grown up. With tears in my eyes, I wrote the following poem.)

HORSES

Betty Benedict

Quick Silver, Royal Bess, Charming Charlie, Black Jack,
    Spot Light, Flash Light, Gypsy One, and Gypsy Two
What a grand parade of horses
What a show we used to make
How we used to blend together
With me upon their backs
Quick Silver, a Palomino, Royal Bess with chestnut lights
Charming Charlie was the deepest depths of darkest midnight
And Black Jack deeper still
Spot Light was the bay with mane and tail so dark
Flash Light was a miniature who glowed in pale moonlight
There was Gypsy One a sorrel
And Gypsy Two a bay with blaze and four white stocking feet
It still gives me a thrill to think of each in turn
Which one did I love most
I'll never, never know
I only know I remember, and happy thoughts abound
What a grand parade of horses
What a show we used to make
How we used to blend together
With me upon their backs

Along the cinder paths we trod
Most time in solitude,
Carefree swinging in the saddle
In tune with nature's abounding love
I don't ride now, they are gone
The path is found no more
Yet I sometime ride in dreams
Along the same old trails once more
And wind around the shadows of my mind
High in the saddle I travel back in time

Joy Padgett and Gypsy   **Betty Benedict and Gypsy**

AUNT OCTA AT TACKY PARTY

We often put on plays across the street in the grove. We invite the whole neighborhood, and we often have a good crowd. We decided to do something different and have a tacky party. Mother fixed refreshments for us to serve. Everyone dressed up as their favorite character, and we asked Dad and Uncle Ed Crawford to be our judges.

Uncle Ed took time off from his service station to do this. Everyone was gathering in the yard when Dad looked up the street.

He said to Uncle Ed, "Here comes Aunt Octa Herbert. I wonder if something has happened to her cow."

Dad told us that he had sold her a cow about three weeks before, and he couldn't imagine why she was coming to the house unless something was wrong.

Octa and John C. Herbert

Aunt Octa Herbert is a character. She came from down in Georgia and married Mr. John C. Herbert. He owns a large farm, and most of the mountain land in Fires Creek Mountains. In her younger days, they entertained the railroad executives when they came to Hayesville. Mr. John C. and Aunt Octa raised a large family of boys. Mr. John C. died several years ago. Aunt Octa is old and quite eccentric. She wears several layers of clothes, and is known to like a nip of moonshine occasionally. She carries a basket on her arm; people say she carries a nip in the basket. I don't know if this is true or not. She is a lovely lady and everyone loves her.

Dad greeted Aunt Octa as she came into our yard. Everyone started laughing. It was not Aunt Octa; it was her granddaughter, Helen Herbert. She dressed for the tacky party as Aunt Octa. Helen had the basket on her arm, and was wearing some of Aunt Octa's clothes. She had put some powder in her hair, and fixed it just like Aunt Octa fixes hers. Needless to say Helen won the Tacky Party Prize.

Years ago, Aunt Octa gave the railroad a right of way to cross her farm. The railroad also had a water tank on her farm to refill the train with water. One agreement she had negotiated was for the train to pick her up and give her a ride. They were to take her up to the head of the railroad at Boice's supply store near Hayesville. When the train returned, they were to bring her back to her home. This agreement went on very well for several years. Then apparently, a new boss came in over the railroad, and told Aunt Octa she could not ride the train any more. Aunt Octa immediately grabbed the water line filling the train. She told them they could not use her water.

Needless to say, Aunt Octa continued to ride the train.

GRANNIE CAT AND TRIXIE

When we bought the Winchester place in West Hayesville, the Thompsons had a cat they called Granny. When they moved to their new home, Granny would not go. We are very fond of Granny. One afternoon, Dad came home, and when he opened his coat, there was a tiny puppy inside. She was red like a fox, but we didn't know what kind of dog she was. Dad had bought her from Butter Hogsed who said that he had found the little dog wandering around in Asheville, North Carolina. He picked her up, and brought her to Hayesville.

I am so thrilled with my tiny sweet new puppy, Trixie. Granny, the cat, does not like her. When we feed Trixie out on the back porch, Granny runs and stands over the food to keep Trixie from eating.

After a few months, Trixie grew to be about the same size as Granny. We don't know how Trixie did it, but she turned the tables on Granny and will not let her eat. Now Dad has to feed Granny in the tack room at the barn.

MY POMERANIAN VALENTINE

Betty Benedict

I see her running around the house as fast as she can fly
She's red as a fox, and every bit as sly
She loves my mother dearly
Because she always there
She follows my dad into town
She's everybody's pet
She hears the rattle of candy jar
And jumps up in the air
She loves me most, because she is mine
My Pomeranian Valentine

Roger Curtis brings his mother's wash to Edna. He has a big bulldog named Hammer Head, that everyone in town is afraid of. Trixie evidently doesn't know she is so tiny. One day, she started barking at Hammer Head, and acted like she wanted to eat him up. Hammer Head jumped on Trixie and was slinging her around like a rag. We were so scared because we knew Trixie was going to die. Granny went running and jumped on Hammer Head's back. She started clawing his eyes and blood was flying everywhere. He let go of Trixie. Granny jumped off Hammer Head's back and ran to Trixie in a protective way. We couldn't believe this happened. Trixie and Granny are now the best of friends. Every time Roger and Hammer Head bring their wash, Hammer Head stays in the car and will not get out.

POLLY IN WEST HAYESVILLE

Mother lets Polly out of the cage to play in the front yard. Trixie and Granny, the cat, go about their business, and Polly never bothers them. Polly will climb up the tree in the front yard and glide down. She sits on the back of the front porch swing. I still don't dare go barefoot when she is out of her cage. If I do, she will make a dive for my toes.

If I can't see Polly, I am always afraid that she will swoop down out of the tree and try to peck my head. She just doesn't like me.

When J. Paul was small and Polly was living at Grannie Benedict's, he would chase her with a broom. She hates a broom and will dive on it and try to tear it up with her beak. If you have a broom, she will attack it no matter what she is doing. Mother catches her this way, and sweeps her off the broom into the cage. I found out that I could carry a broom with me and not have to wonder where she was. I would carry it out in front of me, and she would attack the broom.

Polly with Dad

When Polly is out in a tree and Dad comes home, she will glide down, land on his shoulder, and nuzzle her head against his cheek. When she is in her cage and no one else is around, she will start acting very nice to me.

She will say, "Come, rub Polly's head. Poor Polly, come shake hands with Polly."

Many times I have tried to do what she asks, and just as sure as I put my finger in her cage she tries to peck me with her beak. She puts her claw out to shake my hand and then tries to peck the dickens out of me.

Dad explained to me that she did not like Ray or J. Paul when they were children. When J. Paul was seven years old and living with Grannie Benedict, Polly was pulling her shake hands trick on him. She got hold of his finger, bit it and made a bad scar. He heated a poker in the fireplace, and asked her to shake hands with him. She grabbed the poker with her claw and burned it. Since then, she hates J. Paul with a passion.

When Polly first came to live with us, she had not seen J. Paul in fifteen years. When she saw him walk into the restaurant, she started to screech, saying, "J. Paul, J. Paul, J. Paul." She was going around and around in her cage with her feathers bristled out. Mother had to take her back to the sitting room to calm her down. Mother could never let Polly out if J. Paul was around. She now loves Ray and will sit on his shoulder.

Polly is jealous of children and wants all the attention herself. She does not like any of my friends. I soon learned her dislike of me is not personal.

SLEEPING IN THE BARN LOFT

My friends and I are having a wonderful time in West Hayesville. There are many more things to do that we could not do in town. We finally convinced Mom and Dad to let us sleep in the barn loft. Mother let us take quilts and pillows to make beds in the hay. Dad filled large galvanized wash tubs with water, and we hung lanterns from the ceiling over them. This was to prevent a fire if the lantern fell.

We play our country western records, and pretend we are cowboys around a campfire. Sometimes we take turns telling ghost stories, some of my friends get scared, but some never do. We like to have Dad come down and tell us stories of his adventures. I asked Dad if everything he tells us is true.

He replied, "No, some of it is purely entertainment."

The boys sometimes camp across from our house near the water tank. They come up after dark and ask Dad to come down to their campfire. If Mother answers the door, they ask her if Mr. Red can come down and tell some stories. Mother always gets a kick out of this.

Dad raises crops to feed his livestock, and often has large groups of teenage boys working for him. They seem to enjoy working and especially enjoy the meals Mother prepares for them at noon.

(Mr. Arthur Jones commented years later to me about how Dad could get so much work out of the teenagers. He said he was never this successful.)

PUPPET STAGE

One of the things we enjoy is my large puppet stage. It is made from very heavy cardboard and is assembled to make a stage for puppet shows. It is a yard wide, and the stage has a curtain. We have furniture for several different stage settings.

One of the stage settings includes a grand piano with a puppet called Professor Discord. He plays the piano for Madam Lotta Song. We play our record player to support the scene, and Amelia and I operate the puppets.

We also have comedians who are called Pete and Re-Pete. We wanted to do a puppet show for the community, so we planned to only charge five cents for the show. We made our billboards to put out all over town, but Mother found out and would not let us charge for the show. We marked out the five cents on all the posters, and put on a charge of ten buttons.

We had a large crowd of children in our yard to watch the show on our front porch. The show included a comedy with Pete and Re-Pete and Professor Discord with Madam Lotta Song. A cowboy show was included with the Lone Ranger and Tonto. We gave out lemonade with Ritz crackers and peanut butter. The children seemed to enjoy the show and wanted to know when we would have another one. We don't plan to have another one because we don't know what to do with all of the buttons. We got a quart jar full. I think Mother should have let us charge five cents.

We also play with our stage using our paper dolls. We play like they are actors and actresses. We enjoy this more than working the puppets; this is especially a great game to play on a rainy day.

BUILDING NAVY FLEET

I have a full fleet of all the Navy ships including every aircraft carrier, planes, battle ships, PT boats, and destroyers. My brother Ray sent them to me. They are made of heavy cardboard, and they came in a very large box. You punch them out and put them together. I was overwhelmed and thought I would never get this done.

I felt that I had outgrown my small rolltop desk, and I need a table to assemble my Navy fleet. I asked Andy Padgett if I could trade him my rolltop desk for a new card table and four chairs. He said he would talk to my dad about it. Dad approved the trade so I got the table and chairs.

We set the table and chairs in the dining room where we stay in the winter. This room is next to the kitchen, and we keep this room and the kitchen warm. Dad and I have worked on the ships and planes most of the winter.

I have two long tables in my bed room to display the Navy fleet. Amelia and I also spend many hours putting them together. Didley Bryan comes and gives us help when he has time. When we hear of a ship going down, we put it on the bottom shelf of the table. Mother says we should pray for all the people on these ships to be rescued and saved.

SUSAN GRAY

Little Susan Gray is now old enough to come to my house to visit. Dad gets a real kick out of having her sing for us. She sits down at a foot stool we have, and pretends it is a piano. She plays the piano and sings. A popular song now is "Sioux City Sue." Susan sings it this way,

"Sioux City Sue, Sioux City Sue, your eyes are red, your eyes are blue,

I'll wash my hair and die for you, Sioux City Sue, Sioux City Sue, there ain't no gal as true as my sweet Sioux City Sue."

The real words are:

"Sioux City Sue, Sioux City Sue, your hair is red, your eyes are blue,
I'll swap my horse and dog for you."
Naturally, Dad asks her to sing this song every time she visits.
(Susan has become an entertainer and travels with a band. She
has recorded several albums of her singing.)

THE MULE CHASE

Mother recently went to Athens and brought back a beautiful
Quaker lace tablecloth. She has wanted one for some time. We had
the pastor and his wife from our church to dinner on Sunday, and
Mother proudly used her tablecloth. She washed it on Monday, and
carefully spread it on our fence in the backyard to dry.

Dad had recently bought an old mule, or traded for it. He had
turned the mule out of the barn, and it came up to our backyard.
He grabbed the tablecloth, gave it a yank, and tore it.

Mother got a stick of wood, and chased the mule down the hill
toward the barn. When he got almost to the barn at the foot of the
hill, the mule keeled over and died. Dad had heard Mother yelling
at the mule, so he came out of the house to see what was going on.
He got to the foot of the hill, and Mother was standing there with a
surprised look on her face looking down at his dead mule.

All Dad said was "Carrie, you have killed my mule."

After that, whenever Dad does something Mother dislikes, he
reminds her, "Now Carrie, that's not as bad as killing my mule."

Dad bought her a new Quaker lace table cloth; she did not buy
him a mule.

HOG-KILLING TIME

When the weather gets cold we have hog-killing time. This is a
very exciting time for me and my friends. Neighbors come to help
Dad kill the hogs and cut up the meat. There are many people hired
to help, and we have a big fire going. Our hog pen is near the creek,
and there is a nice open space down the hill from our house for the
hog-killing.

The men build a big fire to heat a barrel of water. The hog is killed and immediately put into the barrel of hot water to remove all the hair. The hog is pulled from the water, and placed on a table made of boards on saw horses. The men scrape the hog's skin to remove all the hair.

The hog is then cut up into hams, shoulders, and tenderloin. Tenderloin is like pork chop without the bone, and we will have it for breakfast. Sausage is made, sacked, and canned. We like almost any part of the hog except the lites, which are the hog's lungs. Many people like them, and there is always someone there to take them home. The things we do not like someone else will. Dad says we save everything about the hog except the squeal!

On hog-killing day, Mother always cooks a big pot of many different scraps of meat. Some of the pieces are backbones, neck bones, liver, and kidney. Mother cooks this down and it makes brown gravy. We choose what we want from the pot, and eat it on rice. We call it *dirty rice*. My girlfriends and I look forward to having this special treat.

Fat is trimmed from the different parts of meat and put into a large black pot with a fire under it. This meat cooks until it is liquid. This is called rendering lard. Large strainers are pulled through the hot fat in the pot to get bits of crispy meat with all the fat removed by cooking. These pieces are put into a large metal can. When all the fat has cooled enough, several people lift the pot and strain the liquid through a cheese cloth into a large metal can. Any of the pieces left in the cheese cloth are placed in another can. When the liquid fat cools and hardens in the metal can, it is called lard. The lard is used for any cooking where shorting is needed.

The strained meat pieces are called "Cracklings." Cracklings are used for crackling corn bread, and we think of this as a special treat. Mom and Dad both love crackling corn bread and milk for supper. It is quite common here in the mountains for people to take a cold glass of milk, crumble corn bread into it, and eat it with a spoon.

One part of the hog that many people don't like is chitlings, so these are sometimes given to the workers that like them. The chitlings are made from the pig's intestine and stomach. The stomach is called the *hog maul*. Dad and I love chitlings and *hog maul*. Mother cleans them, and puts them in a large churn jar of salty water to soak. She changes the water, and washes them for several days and always puts them back into fresh, salty water.

Edna and Frankie usually share the chitlings with us; they like theirs boiled. Mother puts some garlic, pepper, and vinegar on them and marinates them over night. She washes them again, cuts them into small squares, dips them into beaten eggs and cracker meal. Then she deep-fries them, stacks them up on a large platter, and serves them with red seafood sauce. She makes the hog maul the same way, but cuts it sandwich-size to deep-fry. We eat this on light bread slices for sandwiches. Mother grinds horseradish for horseradish mustard to put on our sandwich. She does not eat any of this; Dad and I have a feast.

Mother gives the neighbors some of the best cuts of meat. When they kill hogs, they give us meat in return. This provides fresh meat for several weeks during the winter for us and our friends. I wanted to keep all the tenderloin, but Mother said we must share.

(When I was a child, you could buy lard in the stores made by Swift Meat Packing Company, and also a brand called Jewel. I had never seen Crisco or bottled oil at this time. Lard was used for all cooking purposes. It may not be good for you, but it makes the best biscuits and pie pastries in the world.)

MOTHER CAPTURES KILLER TURTLE

We have ducks and chickens. We have small ponds that are filled with water for the baby ducks to swim in. These ponds are on the other side of our backyard fence. The mother ducks found the creek below the barn, and they take the baby ducks down to swim in the creek. Every time they come back, two or three of the baby ducks are missing.

One day, Mother followed the ducks down the hill to the creek, and watched while they swam. It wasn't long until she saw one of the babies pulled under the water, and then another was pulled under. She had a big stick and dug down into the bank of the creek and up came a turtle. She grabbed the turtle by the tail.

We saw her coming up the hill with the turtle sticking his head out trying to bite her.

Dad said, "I want you to look at Good Woman coming up the hill; she has a turtle."

She took the turtle over to the chopping block and kept trying to get the turtles head out to chop it off. She finally got it. Can you believe we had turtle for dinner? She fried it, and it was delicious. Dad said Mom never fails to amaze him.

PRESERVING FOOD

Mother tries to have many different things to eat that we could not have when she had the restaurant. She tells us that when she was a young girl, no one knew how to can food. The only way to preserve food for the winter then was to dry or pickle it.

Hardly anyone in our town has much money. We may be poor, but we have the best food in the whole wide world and plenty of it. People here feed themselves by raising their own food. The only things they need to buy are salt, pepper, baking powder, soda, and sugar. People who do not mill their own flour buy large twenty-five-pound bags of it. Many of them never buy light bread at the store; they eat biscuits and corn bread.

All of the meat, hams, shoulder, and streak of lean are cured with salt in the smokehouse. Potatoes would keep well through the winter in the cellar where they would not freeze. Mother not only cans vegetables from our garden; she cans all of the meat that cannot be cured. This includes sausage, back bones, ribs, tenderloin, and chicken. Chicken is used for dumplings, salads, and casseroles.

Mother was born in 1899, and she remembers when canning was first introduced for preserving food. People today don't realize there was a time when people didn't know how to can. Mother says this was one of the greatest inventions for farm families. It forever changed the way we eat during the winter months. Preserving food from the garden provides healthy meals all year.

We have a large apple orchard and a grape vineyard, and we sell grapes from the vineyard. We have bins in the cellar under the house to sort and store our apples. My friends and I enjoy going to the cellar to choose the apple we want. Mother also dries apples to make delicious fried apple pies.

We also go down to the cellar to fill cups with pickled beans and corn. Mother has large churn jars of kraut down there, and we enjoy eating cups of it. The cellar is a favorite place to go to after school each day.

We have a large chicken brooder house where baby chicks are raised for wonderful meals of fried chicken. Laying hens provide eggs for our meals and cooking. We also eat duck eggs. I can't tell the difference in these and chicken eggs except they are bigger.

Many of my friends take eggs to the store, and trade them for candy and cokes. Frances Beal takes three eggs to the store and trades them for two candy bars. One is for her mother, and one is for herself. Her mother loves candy.

We often have duck for Sunday dinner, especially when Aunt Bob comes from Athens to visit. She enjoys the duck and orange sauce that Mother makes. We have had Peking duck, but Mother says it is too hard to make so she doesn't do it often.

Mother makes cottage cheese for Dad. I try very hard to eat cheese. I can eat almost everything and enjoy it, but I do not like milk, cheese, butter, or mayonnaise. I will try things and enjoy some that Mother will not eat. She didn't eat the turtle she fried. We sometimes have rabbit and squirrel, but she doesn't eat any of these.

Every Sunday morning, Mother gets up early to bake yeast bread to last us for the week. She makes dinner rolls, cinnamon rolls, and several loaves of light bread. Sometimes, she makes loaves with rye flour, and it is a special treat. We like it with caraway seed; my friends don't like it. Amelia said the seeds looked like rat poop. I told her she could not turn my stomach, no matter how hard she tried. I love rye bread.

(When I was a young teenager, home freezers were not available.)

MONSTER FISH—TOWN CREEK

We fish almost every day in Town Creek below the house. We have small poles with tiny hooks to catch minnows. We have been told that minnows are the only fish in our creek. There is a small hole that is deeper than any of the other parts of the creek. It is located below the jail house hill near Frances Beal's house.

We heard that the big boys who have nothing to do with us are trying to catch a monster fish in this hole. They say the monster fish straightens out their hooks when he gets hold of them. They have all changed to larger hooks but still can't catch him.

I got some larger hooks, and went down across the highway from my house to the monster hole. The boys were all around the hole. They were shoving each other trying to get up to the hole, but were being very quiet. I went down and tried to elbow my way in, but I couldn't get near the hole.

It didn't surprise me when they told me to go home.

I told them, "None of you own this creek."

One of the boys who lived across the creek said it was his. I told him it was not even on his side of the creek.

I finally went home, and decided I would go back later that afternoon. I went back after supper, and there were still boys there but not as many. Some of them were nice to me, and let me get near the hole.

I fished there every afternoon. I am not sure how many weeks it had been, but one afternoon, I caught the monster. It was about the size of Mother's hand, and the boys tried to take the fish away from me. I ran home as fast as I could go. I didn't even have time to take it off the line. They stopped chasing me when I got near home. The monster was still dangling on my line. Mom and Dad asked me what on earth was going on.

I said, "Look, look, I caught the monster."

Dad was serious when he said, "Beyond a doubt, this is the largest fish ever caught in Town Creek. It is called a sun perch."

I took oil cloth, lined a shoe box, and put ice in it from the ice box. I put another piece of oil cloth over the ice, and laid my fish on it. I put the lid on the shoe box, and put it in the refrigerator.

The next morning, the ice was melted so I put in more ice and took off for town with my fish in the box. I wanted to show the monster to Uncle Ed and Uncle Henley Crawford. They were calling everyone to come and look at the big fish I had caught in Town Creek. Everyone wondered how it got into the creek. They all agreed it was a sun perch, and the biggest fish ever caught in Town Creek.

The boys continued to fish the hole for some time, but no one ever got that kind of tug on their line again.

Our refrigerator is not large. Mother told me my shoebox was taking up too much room. She wanted me to throw out my fish. I begged her to please let me keep it another day or two. She had some little platters she had brought from the restaurant that she served hotdogs on. The platter was a little larger than my fish. I put my fish on one and cut a piece of oil cloth to lay over it. She said I could keep it one more day until J. Paul came from Kentucky. I wanted to show him the fish.

J. Paul came the next day, and I showed him the monster. Mother told me I had to throw the fish away. I have a dynamite box; it is a wooden box about the size of a footstool. I have played with it as long as I can remember.

Once, when Grannie Cearley came to visit, she put a cushion on top of it. She took some pretty material and put it over the cushion, and pleated a skirt all around the box. This made a pretty foot stool, and I sit on this stool a lot.

I left my fish on the platter, and hid it under the footstool. Whenever Mother comes into the room, I sit down on the footstool. When she is cleaning, I worry she will pick up the box, so I sit on it when she is cleaning the floor. I scoot the box around to stay out of her way. Mother asked me to stop scooting the box around because I was ruining the floors.

All was well until one afternoon, Dad came in the front door and said, "Carrie, what is that smell?"

As soon as Dad came in, I sat down on the footstool. Mother said she thought she had smelled something in the hallway.

They looked all over and Mother said, "Do you think a rat may have got in here and died?"

I waited until they got to the back of the house, and went to my room to get a cheap bottle of perfume. I poured it all over my fish, and then knew I had made a bad mistake. I knew they would wonder why that smell was all over the living room. I picked up a Progressive Farmer magazine and fanned and fanned. The smell just got worse. I opened both windows in the living room hoping that would help. I still couldn't bring myself to throw away the monster.

I knew I would have to get rid of him soon because he was looking a bit black in places. This is summertime and I am not in school, or Mother would have surely moved the box. I don't go outside to play much because I am afraid Mother will lift the box, and see where I keep the fish. Mother complains that Amelia and I must have spilled perfume in the living room.

Amelia and I decided to give the fish a funeral. We buried it behind our outdoor toilet which is still in our backyard. We placed a cross on the grave and marked it, "Here lies the monster."

MOLLY CRAWBOTTOM

There is a *Molly Crawbottom* hole in the creek down from our stables. Amelia and I go down below the pig pen to the creek and catch tad poles and molly crawbottoms with our minnow hooks. We have Mother's large fishbowl where we put our minnows. We decided to put our molly crawbottoms in the fish bowl. We now have five or six of them to put in the bowl. Mother told us she didn't know why we wanted to keep the ugly things. We put lacy fern we call fish food in the bowl. After we fill it with water, then we put them in. They all stayed in a circle on the bottom rim of the bowl. Mother had gold fish food that we fed them. It was thin clear wafers, but we don't know if they ate them or not.

One morning, Mother asked me to move the bowl. When I picked up the bowl, it came up without the bottom. The water and crawbottoms spilled everywhere. It seemed like the crawbottoms had cut around the bottom rim where they stayed all the time. The bowl had not leaked until I picked it up and dumped the crawbottoms. Mother was not too happy with us for ruining her bowl. We feel sure the crawbottoms cut the bowl.

THE MOUNTAINS AND THE MOON

In the evenings, after Polly is in her cage, covered up and asleep, I lie on the ground in the yard and look at the moon and stars. I try to see something moving on the moon. I am sure a lot of people do this. Many songs have been written about the moon. I know the moon brings in the tide and effects many things. The tales about werewolves and vampires have always centered on the full moon. Many people say they can't sleep well when the moon is full. I wonder if there is any way we could get to the moon.

When I was small, I looked at the mountains in the far distance; the further away they were, the bluer they looked. I thought they were like the moon, impossible to get to. I found out later that our trips to Athens were across mountains. We used to have to go across Neals Gap to get to Gainesville, Georgia. The drive over Neals Gap was scary to me. A little tar had been poured out and the edges of the road were very ragged, and it looked like you could go off the cliff any second.

Later, a road was built across the Unicoi Mountain. This road was much better, and people were happy to have it.

I was shocked when I found out I had been going across mountains all my life. They look different when you are on one than they look at a distance. I thought the blue ones were made out of stone. I now know they are trees and are green when you get near them. I think the moon may be the same way if we could get to it. I think it may look like something familiar if we could get there.

THE MOON

Betty Benedict

> I looked at the moon last night
> It's so soft and pale and yet so bright
> I wonder what is there
> I watched for movement but saw none
> It's so far away
> I don't suppose we'll ever know
> If it's made of stone or clay
> Are there people living there?
> I wish that I could know
> Maybe it's the home of God
> And the Angels make it glow

OYSTERS, SHRIMP, CHILI, DILL PICKLES, AND OTHER FOOD

When Mother had the restaurant, the Hackney Company from Murphy came to our restaurant with food. Oysters are in season in all of the months that have an R in their spelling. During these months, we would get fresh oysters from Hackney. Many people in town loved the oysters Mother served at the restaurant.

Dad had traveled to many places before he settled in Hayesville, and tells me about eating shrimp. We could not get shrimp in Hayesville. I don't know if they will ruin during shipment, or why we can get oysters but not shrimp. When I am in Kentucky with J. Paul, we cannot get shrimp there either. I look forward to eating shrimp someday. Dad has described them to me, and I believe I will know what they are if I see them.

One of my favorite things to eat is chili. Some mornings when I am not in school, I walk down to Mr. Matheson's store. I buy a can of chili, bring it back to the house, heat it, and eat it for breakfast. Mother fusses about this. I especially like to have cheese tidbits to go in it. If I don't have these, I just use saltine crackers.

I eat a dill pickle every night before I go to bed. I started this when I was very young, but I don't remember exactly when I first started eating them.

When I get home from school every afternoon, I check the inside pocket of Dads coat for my after school snack. Sometimes it is potted meat, Vienna sausage, or sardines, and something for desert. Desert is Almond Joys, Mounds, Three Musketeers, Paydays, or Nabs peanut butter crackers. There is always a surprise. Dad has a stash of all this stuff somewhere. If Amelia is with me, and she usually is, he has plenty for both of us. Many of my friends eat jelly biscuits when they get home from school. This is good for a change when I go home with them.

It seems that Mother brings up the perils of not drinking milk eighty times a day. She says I am going to have rickets, whatever that is, and beriberi, whatever that is. She buys all sorts of things to put in milk to make me drink it. I like hot chocolate very well. She bought some stuff called Ovaltine that was so horrible I had rather have plain milk. I sometimes put a teaspoon of sugar and a drop of vanilla flavoring in milk and choke it down. That is better than any of the other stuff.

TEMPTATION

Dad traded something for an old broken down 20-gauge shot gun that had seen better days. The stock was busted and was wired together. I wanted to shoot the gun, but Dad said I was too small. He said he had never shot the gun, and he sure didn't want me to. He said it would ruin my shoulder.

One afternoon, Mom and Dad were both gone, I was bored and kept thinking about shooting that shot gun. I got a tin can out of the trash barrel for a target, and set it up at the edge of the garden.

Betty with Rifle

I got the gun down from the closet and loaded it. I took it out in the yard. I took good aim and pulled the trigger. I have never heard such a roar. My ears stopped up. I went flying backwards, and it knocked the breath out of me. When I came to and got my breath, so I could get up, my head was still roaring. I thought I had lost my hearing forever.

I hadn't thought about how strong the powder would smell, and I worried how I could get the smell out of the barrel. I finally put the gun back in the closet, and hoped Dad would not pay any attention to it. I left the closet door open for a while. Every time I went into their bedroom, I could smell the powder. They haven't found out.

My arm is so sore I have never seen a bruise as bad as this. I have to be sure to cover it up. It is so sore I have to keep them from seeing that I cannot use it. I have to comb my hair with my left hand, and it is very hard to get my clothes on and off. I will never shoot the gun again.

Although I had the bad ordeal with Dad's old gun, I am still working on getting a rifle. Each time Ray writes, he sends me a dollar bill. It just seems I can never save enough to get the J. C. Higgins rifle in the Sears catalog. I think Dad would have bought me one, but Mother doesn't want me to have a gun. I have told her over and over that I will not be careless. I know I have to learn to shoot, but Dad can help me. None of my girl friends have any interest in guns. We all like to play cowboy and play with our toy pistols. Even Amelia is not interested in owning one.

SHOPPING FOR SCHOOL CLOTHES

Even though the TVA changed our roads, we still have nice stores around the Square. We are able to buy almost everything we need right here in town, but Mother takes me to Athens to get my school clothes if we don't find the things we need in Hayesville. Dad believes we should shop as much as possible with our home town merchants. I get a few clothes at Bob Tiger's store, but he never has boots or jodhpurs.

Betty Benedict, Mary Katherine Bradshaw, Joy Padgett

We go to Athens to get these, and if I need a winter coat we buy it there. Sometimes Mother and my aunts go to Atlanta to shop. I love to go in the stores there where they have revolving doors and escalators. They don't have these in Athens.

One of the neat things they do have in Athens is what they call fluoroscopes. They are in the large shoe stores. You step up on a platform and put your feet in the slot. You look through a screen on top and you can see your feet inside your shoes. The shoe salesman can look and tell exactly how much room your toes have in your shoes. This helps you get the correct fit. We kids think it is fun to see our feet in our shoes although we are not buying shoes.

I buy heavy snow shoes and wool socks. These keep my feet warm when I walk through the meadow to school. One time, my feet got so cold by the time I got home they were aching so bad I wanted to cry. Mother wasn't home when I got there. I didn't know better than to run hot water in a big pan and put my feet in.

And then it was awful, my feet started itching and burning so bad. I got them out of the water and started running up and down the hall to keep from crying. When Mother came home, she rubbed my feet between her hands and got the circulation back. I told my friends to never put their feet in hot water when they are cold. I wish someone had told me this.

(When X-rays were found to be harmful, fluoroscopes were outlawed in stores.)

NIGHTMARE ENDS—WAR IS OVER

Tommy Gray came by this morning, and we went down to try to dam up the creek. We work at this all summer long. It was a nice day and I wore Ray's swim trunks. They are black wool with a white stripe up the side. I always play in the creek with only Rays swim trunks. It never entered my mind that I needed to wear a top. I was twelve years old, but as twelve year olds we were still little children. As prim and proper as my Mother was, she had always let me play in the creek with the boys and girls without my top.

We had been playing for some time when all of a sudden we heard all the church bells start ringing. The sawmill whistle was blowing. Car horns were blowing, and it scared us.

Tommy said, "Something bad has happened."

Betty on her Schwin 1946

We took off running up the hill and out the road to town. Mother came out of the house and came running after us. She caught up with us, and put an apron around my shoulders. She was crying and said the war was over. We continued to run. People were out of their houses running with us. We wound up in the courthouse square under the flag pole. One of the pastors from one of the churches quieted the crowd, told us the war was over, to bow our heads, and give thanks to God. All of the tears that were shed were tears of joy; our loved ones will be coming home. This is the day that none of us there will ever forget.

BICYCLES

During the war with everything rationed the only bikes we could get were called Victory Bikes. They were tiny narrow bicycles that didn't take a lot of material to make. Some of my friends have these bicycles. Glenda Prater has one and one day we both were on it going down the sidewalk from my house toward town. The bicycle flipped with us, and sent us flying into a deep ditch. It was filled with blackberries bushes with large thorns.

I landed on the bottom with the bike on top of me, and Glenda on top of the bike. I got the breath knocked out of me. We were both scratched up, and our clothes were ripped by the briars.

Cordia Padgett

Dad said he would try to find me a used regular-sized bicycle. The only trouble is the one he found was a boy's bike. It was pretty much a wreck, but I rode it just the same. I had to get on the porch to get on it, but once I was on it I could manage to pedal the bike by leaning over to each side. I was too short for this boy's bicycle.

I was riding my bicycle one day when I saw the boys riding theirs across big roots that stuck out from the ground. The roots were from a big oak tree out on the corner from our house. I thought this looked like great fun, so I got up speed to hop over the roots and was thrown into the air. I came down on the rod across the bicycle and went to the ground. Everything was spinning round and round. I thought I was going to die. I ran home pulling the bicycle and was so sore I could hardly sit down.

A few days later, Dad pulled up in a truck and unloaded this brand new red and white girls Schwin bicycle. I was so thrilled. The hardware store had received their first bicycles since the war was over. They got one for girls and one for boys, both were of the same color. Dad bought me the girls, and Jimmy Palmer who works at Star's Drugstore bought the other one.

CUTTING MARY JO'S HAIR

I ride my bicycle everywhere I go. I was in town going past Mary Jo Chambers Beauty Shop. She came out and called for me to come in. I pulled my bicycle over and parked it, and went in to see what she wanted. Mary Jo had very long hair that went down below her waist. She has always worn it in a ball like bun at the back of her head. She told me she wanted me to cut her hair.

I said," Mary Jo, I do not know how to cut hair."

She said, "I will tell you what to do."

She told me she had plenty hair, and if we made a mistake we would just cut it again. I cut her hair, and told her I felt like she needed to get a permanent so the curls would hide some of the gap places I had made.

She said, "Do you want to do a permanent?"

She told me how to do the permanent, and it turned out pretty good. This is my first experience working in a beauty shop.

Mary Jo is a very tall, stately woman. I have always admired her long hair, and her beautiful silver bracelets. They are coin silver that the Cherokee Indians have made. Her sister teaches on the Cherokee Indian Reservation in Cherokee, North Carolina. Mary Jo wears her bracelets all the time.

(Mary Jo married Ralph Burch.)

BAPTISM IN LAKE CHATUGE

I accepted Jesus as my personal savior when I was nine years old. I had kept this a secret because I didn't want the older people saying I was too young and didn't know what I was doing. I am now thirteen, and I decided it was time I made this decision public. On Sunday morning at the Baptist Church, I went up when they had altar call. I told the pastor that I had given my heart to the Lord and I wanted to be baptized and join the church.

We don't have a Baptistery pool in our little wooden Baptist church. The pastor waits until there are several people to be baptized, and then we go up to the Lake Pavilion for the baptism.

The girls wear their Sunday dresses, and to keep their dresses from billowing up when they go into the water, they pin the dress between their legs with a big safety pin. When they walk out in the water, their dresses still billow up on each side like two big balloons. I thought it was ridiculous to get my dress all wet and messed up so I decided to wear Ray's swim trunks. I saw nothing wrong in doing this because I always play in the creek with just these swim trunks on and no top. I am thirteen years old, but I am still a child and I still look like a boy up top. I left my sash undone and buttoned one button at the top of my dress. Several people were baptized before me.

When it came my turn, I just unbuttoned the top button and my dress fell to my feet. I gracefully stepped out of it, and went walking down to the water. My mother came running after me telling me to put my dress back on. The preacher motioned to her to let me come on down. I knew I was in trouble, but I walked on out to the pastor and was baptized.

Mother was so mad. I think she thought my baptism was not going to work at all. I prayed all the way home that she would get over being so mad. She said I had disgraced my family by making such a spectacle of myself. We got home, and she would not even talk to me.

I thought I was ruined. I didn't dare mention how I felt to anyone and no one mentions it to me. I just keep praying that people would forget it and not hold it against me. I don't understand what the big deal is; she had let me go swimming for years with no top on.

Now when I play in the creek, I take my bathing suit down to the barn to put it on. I don't want her to see it, be reminded, and start fussing at me again. No one at our church ever mentioned this to me. I guess they know what a sore subject it is.

WAR IS OVER/WALLACE COMES HOME

Wallace Crawford, 1945

I went by Uncle Ed's and Uncle Henley's service station, and they were talking about what they would do when Uncle Ed's son, Wallace, comes home from the war. They are hoping that he will come to work for them. I look forward to Wallace Crawford coming home. He was my friend before I started school when he worked in Fred Pass's soda shop.

I am a little worried that things will change when he comes home. I borrow money from Uncle Ed and Uncle Henley when I need it. I try to pay it back with money I get from

Ray, or my money I get when I sing for Allen Bell. If I get too far behind, Dad pays them back. Of course, I still work sweeping the floors when I get off from school.

I don't know how much longer I will be able to sing for Allen Bell. Mother says I am getting too old to do this. She says I make a spectacle of myself. I told her it was a fifty-cent spectacle. Fifty cents is a lot of money.

It seems I need more money all the time. I get a quarter a week for my allowance. Mother says that should be enough because it allows me to have a coke every afternoon on school days.

The day has finally arrived and Wallace is home. Uncle Ed and Uncle Henley are pleased to have him join them as a partner at the station. Wallace was very glad to see me. Uncle Ed and Uncle Henley told him that I sometimes borrow money and they pay me to sweep the floors. He was okay with that, and I was happy that it all worked out.

MONEY

Betty Benedict

Money is the most elusive substance of all
It's all around us everywhere and yet so hard to get

What a marvelous game is played to try to own the stuff
Many people seem to lose yet others win it all
If you don't have it they call you poor
And if you do you are rich
Adjectives are often used like dirt poor and filthy rich

There are the poor white trash and the newly rich
You've heard about old money
That seems to be the best
There are certain virtues you get just from being poor
The preacher tells you about these and many, many more

He tells you how money is evil and will ruin your soul
Then he passes the collection plate to relieve you of your gold

I don't see that money is bad
You must have it to live
I think it's a wonderful game
And if you play it to the hilt
Money is the reward you get for using your effort well

Royal Hedden

Royal Hedden, Wallace's first cousin, is home from service, and he hangs out at the station a lot of the time. Royal is planning to teach school at Hayesville next year. He will be teaching the seventh grade, and he wants to get me in his room.

We are so relieved to know that our loved ones are home and not in danger. Ray plans to stay in the Navy, but we now know he will be safe.

One of the things I like to eat is country ham. Any time I ask Mother when we are cutting the ham, she says, "We will cut it when Ray comes home." Ray loves country ham and grits. He had never seen grits until Mother fixed grits after she and Dad married.

My brother Edwin is in the Army, and we look forward to having him visit us more. He does not plan to stay in service. Dad will be excited to have his whole family around him. Many people who do not know that Mother is Dad's third wife say that Ray looks just like her. They say Ed and I look more like Dad. It pleases Mother and Ray that people think they look alike.

Since gas is not rationed the service station has picked up in business. Even though Wallace is working full time, they need more help. My friend, David White, is working there now and I enjoy being able to see David more often. He brought his radio for me to put in my room. Ray had sent me a small radio, but it was too weak to bring in the stations.

My friends and I enjoy David's radio since we can get all the stations including Frank Sinatra on the "Hit Parade" every Saturday

Red, Carrie, Betty, Ray and Ed Benedict

night. Frank is a new star. Every radio station you turn on has something about Frank Sinatra. He is a skinny, ugly guy that wears a big bow tie, but he sure can sing. We try to learn all the new hit songs. If I want a new record, I have to buy it. Charles Higden no longer takes care of the juke boxes around town.

MOONSHINER'S PARADE

The moonshiners are still running the moonshine to Asheville, North Carolina, and other large cities. They will often come to town on Saturday in their large cars. The men dress in overalls, and in the summer time they wear them with no shirt. They take their young girls on trips with them to run the moonshine. The girls shop in the big city stores while the men take care of their moonshine business.

The girls come to town with them on Saturday. They wear semiformal dresses with sequins and beads all over them. They also wear high platform heels. We love to come to town and watch them parade around the square.

Every Saturday one of the men who wears overalls and does not wear shoes goes straight to Noogie Bell's drug store. He orders a niller (vanilla) ice cream cone. We follow him to watch and listen. He knows we do, and he enjoys putting on a show. He licks his ice cream cone, wiggles his bare toes and says in his mountain dialect, "I shor am bad atter at air niller ice crem!" The translation is "I sure am bad after that there vanilla ice cream."

We get a kick out of this and we copy his talk. If we like something, we say "I shor am bad atter at."

FIRST GIRL SCOUT TROOP

Hattie Jarrett came to Hayesville to be our County Home Demonstration Agent. We want to start a Girl Scout Troup. Miss

Jarrett has agreed to do this with the help of Sue Benson, the wife of our Methodist preacher Clark Benson. All of us girls are excited to have a scout troop. We have been reading about the scouts and look forward to camping.

The only worry we have about this is the threat of polio. Mother wouldn't let me go to the Baptist or Methodist youth camps this past summer because of many polio outbreaks. There have been outbreaks all over North Carolina. Many of the parents will not let their kids go swimming. We don't know what causes it, but there have been outbreaks where kids go swimming. Miss Jarrett has asked us to get a list of girls who would join the troop. We have worked at this and have more girls wanting to join than we had expected. Some of the girls wanting to join do not live in town. We will enjoy getting to be with them more often. We can meet in our little wooden Baptist Church to get organized. Miss Jarrett says we can meet in the scout's homes if we want to. I know it will be alright with Mother for us to meet at our house.

Joy Padgett   **Janet Palmer**

Our first meeting was a great success. We met in the Baptist Church. Those attending: Joy Padgett, Betty Frances Cherry, Janet Palmer, Frances Beal, Mary Janice White, Emogene Carringer, Amelia Standridge, Mary Katherine Bradshaw, Janet Kitchens, Gay

Nell Mingus, Regina Johnston, Cordia Padgett, Helen Herbert, and Betty Benedict. Miss Jarrett was very pleased with the turnout. We got our Scout Manuals, learned our Girl Scout Pledge, and planned our next meeting. It will be a cookout at the Methodist Parsonage, the home of Sue Benson. We plan to make Hungarian goulash. We were each assigned an item to bring for the stew.

We are looking forward to getting our uniforms and Girl Scout Pins. Each girl will get "The American Girl Magazine" every month. They have pictures of sterling silver Girl Scout rings in this magazine. We all want one of these too.

PRINTED FEED SACKS A FASHION BOOM

Buena Hedden

The feed sacks that Dad gets his livestock feed in have always been white with the company name printed on them. People bleach the printing out and use the white sacks for many things. They make sheets, pillow cases, gowns, pajamas, and under clothes from these. The feed companies have started putting their feed in pretty printed sacks. This has been a surprise and caused a lot of excitement. People who don't have any farm animals also want these sacks to make dresses. The farm families have found they can make extra income by selling their feed sacks. Even people who have money seem to want a feed sack dress. This has become the rage.

It takes four feed sacks to make a dress for the average person. Trading feed sacks has become a fad among the farm ladies to get four sacks of one pattern to make their dress. Dad gets only a few feed sacks because he has only a few animals. I usually have to buy or trade to get enough sacks for a dress.

I have always wanted to learn to sew. Beuna Brown, who works as one of the Home Demonstration Agents, married Royal Hedden after he came back from service. We call her Brownie. She said she would teach me to sew. She and Royal live at his parents' house. She invited me to go home with her to help me make a dress. I doubt Mother would buy material, but I have enough feed sacks to make one.

It only takes two feed sacks to make me a dress. Brownie let me cut out my dress by a pattern we bought. It took several days to get my dress made. Brownie said I a natural. She said it was easy to teach me to sew. We made a little two-piece dress with a separate skirt and top. She said I should enter the 4-H Clubs sewing contest, and I plan to. The 4-H Club is sponsored by the Home Demonstration Organization, which is a government-sponsored program for rural children.

MAKING PICTURES

Betty holding Frances

I usually have a camera that I borrow from Wallace Crawford or David White. My problem is most of the time I don't have money to buy the film. If I can buy the film, I don't have money to send them off to be developed. We are interested in trick photography so we bought a magazine that shows how to do trick photos. We did one picture that looks like you are standing in your friend's hand. We did another one that looks like we have thrown our own legs across our shoulders. Actually, it is a friend behind us with their legs over our shoulders.

Everyone has to send their film to "Jack Rabbit" in Spartanburg, South Carolina to be developed. When we send the film, we are excited to get our pictures back. I go to the Post Office every day looking for my pictures. Sometimes, Uncle Ed Mease will tell me my pictures didn't come. He then pulls them from behind his back, and gives them to me. I usually show him all of the pictures before I leave the post office.

(The following pages include many of our photo memories of the wonderful days gone by.)

Betty Benedict and Mary Katherine Bradshaw

Betty Benedict

Amelia Standridge and Janet Palmer

Betty Benedict and
Gay Nell Mingus

Amelia Standridge and Frances Beal

Betty Benedict and Mary Katherine Bradshaw

Frances Beal

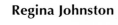

Regina Johnston

Betty Benedict

**Gay Nell Mingus, Joy Padgett,
Mary Janice White**

Betty Benedict and Carolyn Fincher

Cordia Padgett

Janet Palmer Joy Padgett and
Gay Nell Mingus

Betty Frances Cherry, Joy Padgett, Mary Katherine Bradshaw

Frances Beal

Mary Janice White

Mary Janice White and
Amelia Standridge

Betty Benedict

Betty Benedict and Frances Beal

Regina Johnston

Betty Benedict

Betty Benedict

Joy Padgett

Glenda Prater, Janet Palmer, Gay Nell Mingus, Betty Benedict

FIRST TRICK OR TREAT IN HAYESVILLE

Every Halloween in Hayesville is a nightmare for all the business and homeowners in town and surrounding areas. We all go out on Halloween and have a good time. Our parents tell us to never do anything destructive to people's property. The day after Halloween night the town is in shambles. Business windows are all soaped; there is toilet paper in trees everywhere. Rocking chairs are found in trees and on top of houses. One time a farmer's wagon was put on the roof of the high school gymnasium. Another time a cow was locked up in the principal's office. Pots of flowers were exchanged from one porch to another.

It is terrible, and every year, everyone has to go through it all over again. We have never heard of trick or treating; we just thought you tricked. This was not only in Hayesville, but in a lot of other places. I know that when visiting my relatives in other places I would have heard of trick or treating if it was done.

One Halloween a boy was visiting in town, and we were all getting ready to go out and do our tricks.

He said," Why don't you do trick or treat?"

We didn't know what that was so he explained it to us. We thought it sounded like a great idea. We went to the first door and knocked and said, "Trick or treat."

Of course the lady said, "What?"

We explained it to her. She thought this was a very good idea. She didn't have anything to give us, but she said she had made a cake.

She said, "Would you like a piece of cake?"

We said that was fine.

We went in, she cut each of us a piece of cake, put it on a dish, gave us a fork, and we all sat down and ate it. Her name was Mrs. Wily Vaught.

The lights were out at some of the homes. We went next door and had to explain it all over again. They gave us each an apple. We went inside, sat down, and ate them.

The next house was Velma Beam's. She told us she thought this was a great idea. She said she didn't have anything, but she could open some soup. We went in and sat at her kitchen and dining room tables. She fixed soup and served it to us.

Every home gave us some sort of food, and we thought we were supposed to go in and eat it. Its good we found out how to really do trick or treat because we were so full when we got home we were sick. That was the first trick or treating ever done in Hayesville.

(This became the thing to do, and little by little Halloween became less of a nightmare in town.)

TENT THEATER ON THE KNOLL

In the summertime, I usually go to visit my relatives. I spend part of my summer in Athens and part up in Kentucky. I love riding the train when I go to Kentucky. I often feel that I miss a lot by not being with my friends in Hayesville in summer. They go to Lake Chatuge, and swim up at the pavilion while I am gone.

This summer a large tent theater has come to Hayesville and is set up on the knoll. I have decided to stay home this year because I know all of my friends will be going to the tent theatre.

This theater travels to small towns where there are no theaters, and the tent is almost full every night. They have movies every night except on Sunday they only have a matinee. Most of the movies are the very latest to come out.

I am sure they feel they have struck a gold mine in Hayesville. They sell boxes of candy at intermission. The candy is terrible, but people buy it anyway to see what the prize is.

One night, I got a bottle of liquid hose as a prize. We put some on Amelia's leg, and it looked like brown shoe polish on her. I notice every night that many people got this same prize.

We still play in the creek and on the Kaolin mine, ride horses, and play paper dolls, but the movies have made the summer fly by.

FINALLY, I GOT MY RIFLE

I went home from the movie one night, walked in the parlor, and noticed Dad was acting strange. Mother didn't seem to be in the best mood. I ask them what was wrong.

Dad said, "Don't you see anything different?"

I started looking around, and finally I looked over by the piano in the corner. There was a 22 Winchester bolt action single-shot rifle. I have never been this excited. I have tried so hard, for so long to get one. This was the one thing I could never figure out how to get. Dad had a box of shells for it, and I went out in the yard and shot my rifle right then and there. I practice using diamond penny match boxes as a target. It is a problem to keep enough money to buy shells. They are seventy-eight cents a box. If I have shells I practice all the time.

I got to where it was no problem to hit the center of the diamond, and keep putting the bullets through the same hole. The hole would widen, but not very much. I guess anything you practice enough you get good at. Dad is so proud that I am a good shot; he says I am a natural and he brags about this in town. I have had several men ask to come out and target shoot against me. The only one I ever shot against was Sam Cox, and he is a very good shot. I held my own against him.

I have heard about people who can light a match with a shot. I have practiced and practiced to try to do this. So far I just snap the match heads off, and Dad says that it takes a good shot to do that. I will just keep trying. I would like to be a real good shot with a pistol; I don't have one.

RAINED OUT AT TURTLE POND

Mary Janice White

We have a new Girl Scout leader, and her husband is the Boy Scout leader. He is the Methodist pastor and she is his wife. Miss Jarrett, our former leader, had to give up her leadership, and the Bensons have been called to another church.

The Girl Scouts still take up a lot of our time. We enjoy our meetings and outings very much. We camped along with the Boy Scouts at Bobbie Waldroups farm on Qualla Road. We used pup tents and have learned to pitch our own tents.

We are planning to go to summer camp at a place called Turtle Pond which is part of the National Forest. It is located near Highlands, North Carolina. Wilbur Mingus said he would take us and all of our gear in one of his large trucks with a tarp. Dry Falls is near this camping area. We have had a rough time getting our parents to agree for us to go on this trip; however, we have finally worked it out.

This is not an organized camp, only our Girl Scouts and Boy Scouts and leaders will be there. The Boy Scouts camp will be a good distance from ours, but we will cook our meals on a campfire and eat together. We piled into Mr. Mingus truck with all our camping gear, clothing, food, and everything we need. We had a great time on the way there singing and cutting up with each other.

When we got there, Mr. Mingus helped us unload our stuff, took the boys to their camp site, unloaded their things and returned to Hayesville. He is to come back for us in a week. We saw no other people camping anywhere; it was just our group. The boys built a big campfire, and the girls cooked our first meal.

Otto McClure told us he had brought something for us to try. He said none of you have probably tasted it before. He said it was the best thing he had ever eaten. He got a can out of his jacket pocket, and it had a key on top. You put the key in a little tab and turn the key and a strip of metal winds around it. This opens the top of the can. The label on the can said Prem. Sure enough, we had never seen any. He cut it into little pieces, and we put it on a stick and held it over the fire. We browned it and took a taste and thought it was delicious. We couldn't wait to get back home and get some more.

We sang songs and told jokes around the campfire that night. It was a wonderful time and we all had a good nights rest. We got up early the next morning and fixed breakfast. We then took a hike to see how far the highway was from our camp. It was a nice long walk, and we noted many cars were passing by. We also saw a Greyhound Bus that had Highlands on the front to show its destination. The next day, we hiked to Dry Falls, and most of us walked under the falls. Some of the girls would not go under it.

The boys were all complaining about one particular boy's shoes that stunk so bad they were about to run him out of camp. They were on him constantly about his stinking shoes. He would take them off when he was at the campfire. They sure did stink.

It started raining the second afternoon we were in camp. We thought it would stop, but it never did. It went on and on, day in and day out. We put our food under a tarp, and did the best we could to keep it dry. It rained so much most of our food got wet and our cereal got wet and soggy. It was raining so hard we couldn't cook.

At breakfast, all we had to eat was wet cereal. Most of us managed to force some of the cereal down, but Mary Janice said she just couldn't eat hers.

Our new Girl Scout leader forced Mary Janice to eat the wet cereal. Mary Janice threw up all over the place. She, of course, made Mary Janice clean up the mess and would not let any of us help her.

By this time, the quilts in our pup tents were all soaked and were the biggest mess imaginable. We decided to go up to the road and catch a bus to Highlands so we could make a call for Mr. Mingus to come get us. Our leaders selected four of us to go to Highlands, and I was assigned to make the phone call. We had to stay up at the highway for several hours because we did not know when the bus would come by. We did not remember what time we had seen the bus. After a long wait, we decided the bus might not run that day. Maybe it just ran on certain days. When we were about to give up the bus came along, and we flagged it down.

We gave the bus driver our money and rode to Highlands, North Carolina. The pay phones were all busy at the bus station, but there was a drug store nearby that had pay phones. I made the call to Mr. Mingus from the drugstore, and he said if we could hold out one more night, he would come get us.

I told him that all our quilts were wet, and asked if he would please come to get us tonight. He said he would, and he asked if all the quilts were wet. I told him yes, that we had been trying to wring them out. He said to get the boys to wring them out as well as they could, and he would bring two trucks. One truck will come for us and one to haul the wet blankets.

We didn't know if a bus would go back to camp today, but we found out it did. Mr. Mingus came that evening and took us back home to Hayesville.

When I got home with all of my wet quilts, Mother said, "I think this is the last one of these trips you will make."

We were certainly glad to be home in our dry beds.

STAGE FRIGHT

There is talk of building a hospital in Hayesville. The ladies have cake sales and cake walks to raise money for the hospital. Bill

Standridge, Amelia's mother, and Miss Sue Haigler are planning a musical show to raise money. I have been asked to sing and I plan to sing, I'm always Chasing Rainbows. This is from a Betty Grable movie. Peggy Crawford will play the piano for me. We practice every day and soon, time arrived for us to have a dress rehearsal.

The afternoon before the rehearsal at the school house auditorium, we heard that Myrt Padgett was home. She is Andy and Eva Padgett's daughter. She is the older sister of Jerry and Cordia Padgett. She majored in music in college, and has a fabulous voice. They asked her if she would take over directing the show. She agreed, and I was very excited because as far back as I can remember Myrt has been my idol. Her dad calls me little Myrt because he says I look like her and people sometimes ask me if I am Myrt's sister. This is a thrill for me because I think she is very beautiful, and I like to look at her pictures when I visit Cordia and Jerry. She is as pretty as any movie star.

The afternoon of the rehearsal, Myrt told me she had a song she wanted me to sing. She said it was a new song that was just making the charts. The name of it is "I'm a Big Girl Now." I had never heard of this song and neither had anyone else. She had the words and music and gave me the sheet music to take to Peggy so I could practice.

Myrt will play for me on the night of the show which is the very next night. Here I have a song to sing that I have never heard, and I am going to have to practice with Peggy, who will not be playing for me at the show. Myrt also told me she wanted me to memorize the words, and I thought surely I could do this. I have sung many times before large crowds and never had stage fright.

I was in the operetta when I was only six years old, and I have never been frightened in front of a crowd. The song "I'm a Big Girl Now" has several long verses. Myrt wants me to wear a short skirt, and dress like a little girl wanting to be grown up. I have a taffeta skirt that has become too short for me, and it makes me look like a little girl. I put a big bow in my hair, and I wore lipstick, ear rings, some large bracelets, and shoes with high heels.

While singing, I have to dance back and forth across the stage. The night came, and I felt like I knew the words to the song, but I didn't feel as comfortable as I usually do. When I sang before, I always had the words in front of me.

Myrt was at the piano with the curtain drawn just so you could not see her. I started to sing:

> "I'm a big girl now,
> I want to be treated like a big girl now,
> I'm tired of wearing bobby socks like kiddies do,
> I want to wear some stockings and some high heel shoes.
> I want the boys to look at me and yell woo woo.
> I'm a big girl now."

When I got through singing the first verse, my whole mind went blank. I could not remember another word! A horrible feeling came over me. One minute I was hot, and one minute I was cold. My heart was pounding, and I was in a total panic. I went across the stage, and Myrt would tell me a few words. When I crossed the stage from her, I just whistled the tune. This has been the worst night of my life; I had never been in such a panic.

I ran off the stage, sat down on the steps, and cried. I could hear the audience applauding, but I felt like I was ruined. This was the first time I knew what stage fright felt like. I had heard of it, but I had no idea how terrible it was.

I told Dad I was never going to sing again. I was so ashamed, and I had made such a fool of myself. Dad told me that people may have thought it was supposed to be that way. I know better. Since that time, I never get up to sing without feeling some stage fright, and sometimes it is worse than others. When I told Dad I never wanted to sing again, he said, "It's just like riding a horse; you have to get back on."

SHE'LL BE COMING AROUND THE MOUNTAIN

I finally convinced Mom to let me go on another planned Girl Scout trip. We are going to Vogel State Park on Neals Gap Mountain just south of Blairsville, Georgia. The Boy Scouts plan to go to. Wilburn Mingus has agreed to take two trucks to carry our camping gear and bicycles.

We will rough it in pup tents again, but we will have a covered pavilion to cook and eat our meals. There is also a swimming pool with dressing rooms; however, these are not open to the public. The camp

Betty Frances Cherry

has been closed to the public for some time. We have permission to camp, and the boys will put chemicals in the pool so we can swim.

Betty Frances Cherry and I will be tenting together, and are excited over this trip. We are praying for the

Betty at 12

weather to be good. We had a very good time on our trip over to Vogel. We still have the Methodist Preacher and his wife who were our leaders last year. Mr. Wilbur Mingus helped us get our belongings and bicycles out of the trucks, and left us for a week.

We set up our pup tents and put up our food. We are tired, but having a wonderful time singing and telling stories around the campfire. The boys and girls are together during this time. There is a water fall down below our camp, and we can hear the water. Betty Frances and I have a tent on the outside circle near the woods. The others did not want this spot because they were afraid of snakes.

The same boy whose shoes smelled so bad last year is along on this trip. Some of the boys slipped his shoes out of his tent one night and threw them off the falls. He had to go barefoot for the rest of the time.

One night, some boys put a dead snake in a tent in our camp. When the girls pulled the cover back to go to bed, there was the snake curled up. There was wild screaming from both girls as they came running out of their tent. They were yelling there was a snake in their tent and this caused a big up roar. Our scout leader demanded that her husband find out who did the trick, but no one told on them. I know the two boys who did it, but I will not tell.

Everything was going fine, and we were having a wonderful time. The weather has been dry, but humid. We go swimming every day in the large pool and have a wonderful time. One very hot day, I went swimming, and forgot to take my pigtails down. I didn't think about my hair souring, but man did it stink.

I thought I could shampoo my hair in the pool. The scout leader told me I could not do this. I told her I would take a pan of water to the pavilion and shampoo it there. She told me she didn't want to hear any more about shampooing my hair. She said I should have known not to swim with my hair in pigtails and I should have taken my hair down after leaving the pool.

It was terrible smelling my soured hair all the time and feeling so dirty. Everyone I got near to complained, and didn't want me near them. I had to sleep in the pup tent with Betty Frances Cherry. It smelled bad enough to me in the small tent, and it was driving Betty Frances crazy.

I decided to ask our leader one more time if I could shampoo my hair. I told Betty Frances if she could make it through one more night I would ask our leader one more time. If she would not let me shampoo it, I have a plan. I went to the leader and asked her to please let me shampoo my hair. She got very mad, and told me she was not going to let me shampoo it. I made the mistake of asking her why. She told me she did not want any more trouble out of me and did not want to hear any more about it. It is now time for my plan.

There is a store at the top of the mountain above our camp that is owned by an old man who keeps bears in cages. My family often stops there on the way to Athens. I got on my bicycle with the rest of the kids, and we rode up the mountain to the old man's store.

I asked him, "What time does the mail truck run?"

He said, "About six thirty in the morning."

I plan to catch the mail truck and go home, but I wondered what to do with my new bicycle.

After dark, I took my bicycle up in the woods about halfway between the camp and the highway. I covered it with brush and left it there. Betty Francis wanted to know where I was going. I told her it was better she didn't know, but I would be back. One of the boy scouts stayed with me all night beside the road.

We saw the mail truck coming, and I took a white pillowcase and flagged him down; he said I could ride. I told him I didn't think he wanted me to ride up front with him since my hair smelled so bad. He went around to the back and opened the door and told me to hop in. I slept most of the way to Hayesville on the mailbags.

We got to Hayesville early. I asked him what time he goes back to Vogel. He said he would be driving back late that afternoon, and told me what time to meet him.

I walked from the post office to my house in West Hayesville. Mother saw me coming.

Mother said, "What on earth has happened? Why are you home?"

I told her my hair was soured, and our scout leader would not let me shampoo it.

Mother said, "How on earth did you get here?"

I answered, "I rode the mail truck. "

She said, "Well get in there and take a bath and shampoo your hair. You are not going back."

I said, "I have to go back because no one knows I have come home."

**Ed Mease—Hayesville
Post Office**

Mother said, "Why wouldn't she let you shampoo your hair?"

I said, "I don't know, but I was afraid to ask her if I could come home. I was afraid she would not let me."

I got my hair shampooed, dried, and braided back into pig tails. After a good bath, I felt much better. I went back to town and met the mail truck at the post office. I told him I could ride in the front seat now, and he said that was good. I told Uncle Ed Mease at the post office what had happened because he wondered why I showed up on the mail truck that morning. He just shook his head.

I got back to camp before dark. My leader was ripping mad. She said I had worried all of them to death. I doubt she was too worried. She probably would have liked it if I had not come back. I brought a clean pillow case back to put on my pillow, and Betty Frances and I enjoyed the remainder of the camp. My bicycle was like I left it; no one found it.

I doubt if Mother will ever let me go on another camping trip after this. We still have to worry about polio every summer. This fear is always over our heads. We keep hearing they are looking for a cure; I hope it will be soon.

SHOE SHOP SANDALS AND ROMANCE

Most of us girls have some boys paying us attention at school. Even in fifth grade, in Willie Roger's room, the boys and girls would pass notes. A bunch of us were playing down in Tommy Gray's yard. Everything was going as usual I thought. Everyone started going down to the Gray's barn and going up in the loft. Tommy said I couldn't go and I really didn't know why. I figured it out and decided the boys and girls were pairing up, and may be kissing. I stayed with Tommy and Edgar Duckworth down near the side walk. Finally, the lumber company whistle blew at five o'clock. They all came out of the barn to go home. (Probably they only kissed, and I thought no more of it.) All of us girls are still playing in the creek and playing paper dolls. However, sometimes our paper dolls get into more romantic situations than they used to.

Mr. Glen Martin has opened a shoe shop in Hayesville next door to Booth's Drug Store at Herbert Street on the square. He not only repairs shoes, he makes leather sandals for men, women and children. He has tan, dark brown, oxblood, and white leather. These sandals have become quite the rage.

I went to get a pair, but none of them fit. Mr. Martin measured my foot, and said he would make me a pair. He said he would make me a design that he had not made for anyone else. I told him I wanted tan sandals. These sandals are made so well that I think they will last forever. I love my sandals, and I have worn them all summer long. We all feel very much in style in our starched feed sack dresses and our shoe shop sandals.

DRUGSTORE HANGOUTS

Noogie Bell, Allen Bell's son, has opened a drugstore on the corner where the old Methodist Church used to be. He built a brick building with offices upstairs that are rented by the Clay County Health Department. Nurse Mac McGuire has her office upstairs in the building, and she is married to Garth Thompson. Dr. Leon Staton has his office there with his Nurse, Ellen Ledford. We also have a young dentist who has an office there. We are happy to have another drug store and soda shop.

Mary Catherine Bradshaw, Gay Nell Mingus, Joy Padgett, Janet Palmer, Glenda Prater, Amelia Standridge and Betty Benedict, 1947

Booth's gave up the Rexall Drugstore franchise. Now, Star has made it more like a gift shop, but still serves sandwiches, fountain cokes, and ice cream. I still eat lunch with Star and Sarah most school days.

When Noogie opened his drugstore this fall, he stocked it with games and different items to sell for Christmas gifts. Now, we go to Noogie's every afternoon from school. Some of the older kids have opened a lot of the games in the store. We play with these games at the tables and in the booths.

Mr. Herbert's pool room closed several years ago. Now, there is a new pool room under Noogie's Drug Store, and the boys go down there to play. We girls never go down there.

The jukebox in the drug store has all of the favorite tunes of the day. I have a slug that is actually a German coin that I can put into the jukebox and play five tunes. I meet the man who changes the records to get my German coin back. I tease with Noogie Bell and tell him if I do not get there when the man comes to be sure and get my coin back. He tells me if he gets it I will never see it again. He acts like he is mad, but he really doesn't care.

THE MUSE

Betty Benedict

The muse and I have
Cokes at Noogie's
He seems to like it here
He fills me with ideas,
And the Coca-Cola with great cheer.
The place is filled with people.
I don't think that they can see,
My companion here beside me,
Drinking Coke and talking to me.
They wonder how I sit alone,
And drink Cokes enough for two.
Or why I write and stare into space
Then write and drink some more
They think I'm doing important things,
They don't know I'm piddling about,
Just drinking my Coca-Cola
And letting my tensions out.

Things seem to be really changing. More and more the girls are talking about boys. The boys in town that we have played with all our lives do not hold much interest for us. We usually like the boys that do not live in town. June Swanson likes Amelia, and he has walked her home from the movies. She likes him too. Even though this change is taking place, we are still playing paper dolls.

BIRDS AND BEES

Betty Benedict

Do you suppose the birds and bees do it together
Or do they do it to each other
Or do they do it to people
When they don't even know it
Well—they may do it to people
But they've never done it to me

Why do people get so excited
About the birds and bees
Someone's always going to tell you about them
They constantly say they will
If anyone ever told it they certainly never told me
I don't care to hear about them
It just doesn't interest me
Why not talk about something different
Maybe cows and fleas

One afternoon, a group of us girls were down at Amelia's house playing paper dolls. One of the girls looked out the window and up the sidewalk. She saw June Swanson, and we knew he was coming to see Amelia. We grabbed our paper dolls, crammed them under sofa pillows and under the sofa. June came in, and we tried to act like grown-ups. After he left, we got our paper dolls out and tried to play. It just didn't seem to be as interesting as it used to be.

As I walked home that afternoon from Amelia's house, I had a very sad feeling come over me. I felt as if a wonderful time in my life was coming to an end.

(I think about the song Toyland that says, "When you cross its borders, you can never return again.")

FRIENDS

Betty Benedict

You are my friends and I love you
I need you when I skin my knee
Or bump my butt against the ground
When I am biting dust
You help me eat it
When I am happy
You are all happy too
When any of us are down and out
We call on each other
To be lifted up and made to fly once more
I know your greatness and your souls,
Far better than any of you

From here I can take a clearer look
Wherever the years take us.
Whatever we decide to do
Lets always count on each other
And know I am here for you

PART TWO

1947-1952

ENDING OF CHILDHOOD

This is an ending and a beginning. My childhood has been so wonderful. It has been made so by all of my friends who work and live around the square. I realize how fortunate I am to live in this warm wonderful town. All of my childhood has been spent playing adult and talking about what we will do when we grow up.

All of a sudden, I don't want to grow up. I do not want to cross over and find myself away from Toyland. When this happens, we have no choice; we have to keep going and growing. The sad thing to me is that I did not get to do this slowly. It just seemed to happen all at once. One minute, we were at Amelia's house playing paper dolls, and the next minute we were hiding them because we knew it was time to put them away.

Everything is going to be all right even though I am leaving childhood. I still have all my friends around the Square, and we will make this journey together. Come go with me as I continue *Winding Round the Square.*

Amelia Standridge, Janet Palmer, Gay Nell Mingus, Mary Catherine Bradshaw, Mary Janice White, Glenda Prater and Betty Benedict

Child in front Mike Prater

DAVIS BOYS COME TO TOWN

We have been invited to a party at Bobby Waldroup's farm and all of us go. He built a big bonfire. We roasted wieners and marshmallows and had a great time.

We have a new Methodist preacher whose name is Davis. Some of the girls have been talking about his cute boys. The party was the first time I had seen the Davis boys. They came with a group of other boys from town. Their hair was red as a carrot. The tall one is Joe Davis, and he is the oldest. His younger brother Billy is shorter. They both have wonderful personalities.

All of the girls are going wild over the Davis boys. We can't carry on a conversation without something coming up about them. After we ate, we started playing games I had never played before. We played a game called Spin the Bottle. One of the boys spins the bottle inside the circle of girls. When the bottle stops, the boy gets to kiss the girl the bottle is pointing to. Most of the kisses are little pecks, and everyone seems to think this is exciting. There were lots of giggles, squeals, and laughter.

We then played a game called tap hand. This is a game where the girls are in a circle, and the guys get to come and tap a girl they wish to take for a walk. Quenton Lyon kept tapping me.

Joe Davis kept tapping Gay Nell Mingus. Most of the girls let a boy take them home that night. Quenton asked to take me home, but I didn't let him. This was the night that most of my friends started dating. Amelia is going with June Swanson. Gay Nell is dating Joe Davis. Joy Padgett goes with Billy Davis, and on and on. My friends vary in age from three years older than me to two years younger. The reason I don't date is I don't know if Mother and Dad will let me. I hang out with my close boyfriends in town as I always have.

SECOND DATE

Bobbie Penland

We still spend the night with each other. Most of the talk is about boys, who are going out with whom, and who likes whom. It seems there isn't much choice for me. I have been too close a friend with most of the boys in town. It would seem like incest to date one of them.

Our group is known as the *town girls*. There are many boys out in the country who we think are cute, and would like to go out with. They think we are stuck up because we live in town. They will not ask us to go out on a date. We have talked about what we could do to let them know we like them. There seems to be no way of telling them without seeming forward.

We girls have a dating moral code we live by. I don't know how we got it, but you don't let boys touch your breast. You don't kiss a boy until the third date and so on. I have a close girlfriend, Bobbie Penland, whom I have gone home with from school since we were very young. We read the same books and always have something to talk about. It is always exciting to go to her house because they don't have electricity. They use big Aladdin lamps for lighting.

One of the exciting things is just getting to ride the school bus to her home. Sometimes she will come to my house to spend the night. She is dating a boy who lives in her community. When she comes to my house, her boyfriend usually comes over. Dad builds us a fire in the parlor fire place, and we enjoy his visits.

One day Bobbie was coming home with me from school and she said, "I am going to the movie with my boyfriend, but you have to come, too."

I said, "Well, okay."

She said, "He has a boy with him who wants to go with you to the movie."

I didn't want to go. She told me her mother would not let her go unless she double dated.

I said, "Well, I will go if Mother will let me."

I was sure Mother would say no. I asked Mother if I could go, and she said yes. All four of us got into the cab of a big log truck and went to the movie. That was my second date. I had my first date with Victor Bell when I was three years old.

After this second date, it was a good while before I had another one. I was only fourteen.

Cross Roads

Betty Benedict, 1947

There are things in life that are good and bad
There are things that are weak and strong
There are things that make your heart grow heavy
And things that give you a song
There are two roads my heart must decide
And they both seem rocky to me
I'm in love with life

But I wonder if real love was meant to be.
I pray to God and ask that his love will ever be my guide
And with his help
I'll choose the love who should be at my side

LUXURY IN THE HOSPITAL

I have a baby eye tooth that I have never lost. I went to the dentist the other day, and he pulled it. He said he thought my permanent tooth would come down if he pulled the tooth. He had pulled it before I knew what was going on. Here I am, fourteen years old, with a front tooth missing. When I went home and told Mother what had happened, she and Dad were upset. This dentist didn't have an X-ray machine. Mother said she should have taken me to Athens to the family dentist there because they have X-rays.

Mother took me to Athens two weeks later. The dentist found my permanent tooth lying up in my gums. It was pushing on the teeth next to it, and had made my teeth spread out at an angle. He scheduled me to go into Athens General Hospital to have the tooth removed. The problem was the tooth lying on the root of the next tooth. He was afraid when it was removed, that it would injure the tooth next to it and makes it turn dark. I asked him what I was going to do about the missing tooth. He said he would make me a bridge to replace the missing tooth, and it would be permanent.

They explained to us that my teeth needed to be straightened before the bridge was put in. He said I will need braces for several months to a year. I will need to come back to Athens regularly to get the braces adjusted.

My aunt has a beautiful ivory satin gown and negligee, and she let me take it to the hospital. When we got there, some sort of emergency had happened. All the rooms in the hospital were filled, and the one scheduled for me was taken. Dr. Talmadge, who operated on me for appendicitis, told us not to worry. He said he would pull some strings to get me a room.

I was put in room 300. A lady whose husband is chairman of the board has the room for her use only. It is her private room, and she could use it any time she wants. It does not look like a hospital room, but more like a princess's bedroom with all the French-style furniture. I am wearing this fabulous gown and negligee, and I felt like a princess.

The dental surgeon's young assistant evidently thinks I am a rich VIP. He came to visit and brought me flowers. Dr. Talmadge also sent flowers, and all the nurses seem very impressed. They are all doing flips to take care of me. I told Dad I may not have a front tooth, but I have never had so much attention. I think the dental assistant has a crush on me. He said he was going to be in the operating room, and he might possibly get to do some of the operation. I told him I would rather he tried his skills on someone else.

I think I will be in this room for about three days. I have a floor model radio and record player in my room with loads of classical music. I mentioned this to the dental assistant, and he brought me a record of "In the Mood." He also brought me magazines. Man this is the life. The only thing that mired my feeling of being rich was we forgot my house shoes. I have been wearing my green and white saddle oxfords when I get up to move about the room.

I was operated on and woke up looking like a freak. My lip was swollen, and it turned black and blue. It had gone down by the time we left to go back home. I will have to go back to Athens in three weeks to get my braces if I have healed well enough. This is going to take most of my summer going back and forth to Athens. I can go by myself on the bus, but I have to change buses in Gainesville, Georgia. I have an hour layover there, and I enjoy eating at a cafeteria called the Wisteria. The bus will let me off in front of my grandmother's on Prince Avenue just inside Athens's city limits. The Jefferson Highway becomes Prince Avenue at the city limits.

NEW BUSINESSES IN HAYESVILLE

We have a new movie theater in Hayesville. Roger Curtis built a brick building for the theater where our house on the Square used to be. It was sad when they tore our house down. Most all of the houses on the square are gone and replaced with brick store fronts. The theater is neat, and we enjoy it. We get some of the best movies. Most of my friends who date go to the theater and afterwards to Noogie Bell's drugstore.

J. Walter Moore has built a restaurant and motel in Hayesville, where Miss Flora Davis's home used to be. It is across from Dr. May's house where Mrs. May still lives. We still miss Dr. May. Mother is helping J. Walter get his restaurant open and operating. I have a job there waiting tables when I am not in Athens. I enjoy working there. The business has been good. I get good tips, but sometimes the busboy gets my tips and doesn't give them to me.

I go to Athens about every three weeks and stay a week. I have healed well, and they put the braces on my teeth. I have the braces which have tiny rubber bands that I have to stretch across my teeth. The dentist says I will probably only need the braces for six months before he makes the bridge for the new tooth. I must be the first person in Hayesville to have braces. People look at me and say, "Ooooh, what is that?" This doesn't bother me because I know I will look better when I get my tooth in.

ON A BET

After one of my trips back home from Athens, I was at Star Bristol's drinking cokes. Everyone was talking about the new boy in town and how good-looking he was. I asked what his name was and they told me. His family moved in to work in a new factory. They came from eastern North Carolina.

I didn't pay too much attention to what they were saying because the girls always go wild over any new boy in town. They said that he has dated most of the girls. He only goes with a girl once or twice, then moves on to someone else. "Billy Davis said he hasn't seen you before, he will be asking you for a date." I said I could go with him for a month. Billy said a month with him not going with anyone but you!

Billy said, "I will bet you five dollars you can't."

I am thinking this is a lot of money. "It's a bet," I said.

It wasn't thirty minutes until the boy came into the drugstore. I knew it was him, and he made a beeline for me. You could tell he was accustomed to a lot of attention. We talked, and he wanted to know why he had not seen me before. I explained I had been getting my teeth fixed in Athens. By this time, my braces only had to be adjusted once a month.

He asked me, "Would you like to go to the movies?"

I told him that I had just gotten home, and I needed to spend some time with my family. I told him to give me a call.

When he left the drugstore, Billy said, "Aren't we cool? I need to spend time with my family." I am still not worried about losing my five dollars.

I went home pleased with myself, but I am not sure Mother will let me go in the first place. As it happened, his family is attending the Baptist church, and Mother has met them. She thinks they are nice people.

He did call, and Mother said I could go with him to the movie. We started dating, and a month went by. I got my five dollars from Billy Davis.

Three months have gone by, and I enjoy going to the movies with him because most of my friends are now dating.

One night, I was getting ready go out with him. One of my friends called and told me that my boyfriend had found out about my bet with Billy. My friend said that the boy felt I had made a fool of him, so he was going to stand me up tonight. My friend told me to get out of the house, and go to town as soon as possible. It is considered a terrible put-down to be stood up.

I immediately called my friend Pede Williams, and asked him to come get me.

He asked, "What for?"

I hurriedly answered, "Never mind. Just come and get me. It is very important."

Pede is several years older than me and has a car. We have always run around together. I knew Mother wouldn't mind me going out with him. We went to Noogie's drugstore, and by the time my boyfriend came in, I was sitting there with Pede.

I said as loud as I could, "Oh, I had a date with you, didn't I? Oh, I'm so sorry, I forgot."

You talk about mad; he was so mad, his eyeballs were popping out because he had been taken to the cleaners.

FIRES CREEK BRISTOL CAMP

I was in the drugstore the other day when Star and Sarah Bristol were talking about when their family lived at the Bristol Camp on Fires Creek. This was located up in the mountains.

It was during the depression, and they could not sell their sheep. This was their main source of income that gave them food

Star and Sarah Bristol

and warmth through the winter months. Star, Sarah and their mother were at the camp and they were very worried because they hadn't sold their sheep. Winter was approaching and they had no money.

Star told me they didn't have many visitors there in the mountains. One day, a big truck drove up in front of the camp, and they were wondering who in the world had come up there to see them. The three of them were afraid because they were alone, and they saw this tall thin man get out of his truck and approach the house. Her mother opened the door just enough to find out what he wanted. He asked her if the sheep were for sale. She said it was all they could do to keep from showing how excited they were.

He asked them how many head of sheep they had, and Mrs. Bristol told him the approximate amount. Star said they were still trying not to show their excitement. He told them he would give them the fair market price and named the amount. Mrs. Bristol told him that sounded fair enough. He told them he could take all the truck would hold that day, and would return for the remainder the next day.

She told me their eyes got as big as saucers when he pulled out a big roll of money to pay them for the sheep. He counted out the money, gave it to Mrs. Bristol, and left to load the sheep. Her mother closed the door, and laid all the money on the kitchen table. They joined hands, and danced around the table rejoicing that they would be able to get through another cold winter.

Dad continued to buy sheep from them as long as they lived at the Bristol Camp.

Star said, "Many people in the county had their lives made easier that terrible winter because your Dad bought their sheep and shipped them to market."

Dad and J. Paul bought not only sheep; they bought tobacco and shipped it to market. This was an annual event that went on for years.

Star said, "That is why I love your Dad, the man who bought our sheep."

THE LITTLE STRAY LAMB—BUCK

One year after sheep-buying time, someone told us that one of the little lambs had been left in a barn that Dad had rented to house the sheep. Dad and I went down to the barn, and found this little lamb that was so young it could hardly stand on its spindly legs. On our way home with the little lamb we bought baby bottles to feed it. We took it home, and I wrapped it in blankets and took care of it. It was such a sweet little thing. The lamb became our family pet, and my little dog Trixie loved it. She would lie down against it, and they would both take a nap.

We named our lamb Buck. He grew and grew into a huge sheep. Mother was perturbed because we let Buck run around so freely. When he would come on the front porch, it would sound like he was tearing the house down. Mother kept complaining to us about this. When we played in the yard, he would chase me as if he was going to butt me and knock me down. When he got near me, he would slow up and only tap me with his head.

When sheep-buying time came the next year, Buck disappeared. It was sad, but Buck had become so big we were afraid he would hurt someone. Dad never seemed to be attached enough to anything that he wouldn't sell. Mother said Dad would have sold us long ago if anyone would have us.

Dad said, "Now, Good Woman, I wouldn't trade you for a horse and a brand new red wagon." The way Dad trades this is certainly a compliment.

Dad once told me that Mother told him years ago, not long after they were married, that she was going to leave him.

Dad said he told her, "Wait a minute, and I will get my hat and go with you." He said that was the last time he ever heard of her going to leave.

SKIPPING SCHOOL AT LUNCHTIME

Ever since I started school, we could go home, or leave the school grounds at lunchtime. It was alright to leave as long as we returned promptly after lunch. I eat lunch at Star's drugstore every day. For some reason, our principal, Mr. Scott Beal, decided we could not leave the school grounds at lunchtime any more. This new rule really upset me.

At this time, I was dating a boy who had graduated a year before and was no longer in school. I would usually meet him at Noogie Bell's for a coke after I had my lunch at Stars. Mr. Beal had told us that we would be punished if he caught anyone leaving the school ground during school hours.

I got tired of eating at the lunchroom, and I decided that I could slip off and get by with it. I left the school ground, went to Stars, then went to Noogie's as usual. I was sitting in a booth with my boyfriend and had my back to the door. My boyfriend was seated across from me, and he could see the front door. We were in the back booth.

My boyfriend said, "Here comes Scott Beal and Allen Bell."

Mr. Allen Bell is the school superintendent. I was wishing that I could have gone under the booth. I sat there afraid to breathe. They came back and sat down in the booth next to ours. Mr. Beal had his back to my back and Mr. Bell was on the other side of their table facing the back of my head.

They ordered coffee; I could hardly breathe. I knew I was caught. It seemed they stayed there forever. We did not talk at all, but they carried on a normal conversation that we could hear. They finally got up to leave, and I thought, "Maybe they haven't recognized me."

As Mr. Bell walked up toward the front, he started singing at the top of his lungs "Did You Ever Go Sailing?"

I knew then that he had known I was sitting there. I dreaded going back to school, but I did. If Scott Beal saw me, he never said a word about it.

This stopped my going off-campus to lunch for some time. Temptation finally got the best of me; Louise Cloer and I would go

Louise Cloer

to town to eat lunch, anyway. We never got caught although almost every day, someone did. I don't feel bad about doing this because I could never understand what it hurt. We were not missing any classes.

Next month will be the last time I have to go to Athens for my braces. They are planning to take them off, and do the impression for my bridge. I am looking forward to getting my bridge. It will be nice not to have a missing tooth. I enjoy going to Athens, but it would be nice to go and not have a dental appointment.

I have been reading "Gone with the Wind" this summer. I have been surprised that some parts of the book are so different from the movie.

My fifteenth birthday is coming next spring, and it will be on Saturday, May 6, 1948. J. Paul has promised to take me to the Kentucky Derby, and it will be on my birthday. This will be a very exciting time for me. J. Paul knows several of the race owners whose horses will run. Ironically, I was born on Derby Day.

AUTUMN

I am looking forward to fall here in Hayesville. I love this time of year when the leaves turn and the air becomes nippy. I get out my turtle neck and flannel shirts. These are the clothes I like to wear most with my jeans. Some of my girlfriends think that fall is a sad time of year. It does have a different feel, but I love it. I like all the changing seasons here in Hayesville.

I love this place, and I am so glad that Mom and Dad moved here and stayed. Dad had worked everywhere, and would move anywhere he could make a dime. For some reason, he loved it here, too, and this is the place they decided to call home. Dad loves the people here, and says he never lived anywhere else where the people are so generous, friendly, and freely giving of their lives to each other.

He always says, "The people of Clay County are the salt of the earth. They are more honest and have higher morals than in any place I have ever lived."

From the time I was a small child, I was taught to love this place in the mountains called Clay County. I realize that someday I will have to leave for a while. Almost everyone does, but I will never leave for long. I know this in my heart.

HOME

Betty Benedict

By shady brooks
In whispering pines
In hay lofts and stable walls
A porch where moonlight sheds its beams
A bedroom filled pleasant dreams
There is a place in the midst of space
Where time will stand still for me
And all the dreams I've dreamed in quiet
Will live for all to see

Clay County Courthouse

MY CLAY COUNTY ROOTS

Betty Benedict, 1947

I am so human
So small and frail
I walk in a land made by God
I know that my strength
However weak it may be
Is rooted in red clay sod
I'll go forth into the world
To make my mark upon it
I'll never get the red clay off my foot
No matter how I stomp it.

JERRY PADGETT'S BIRTHDAY PARTY

Jerry Padgett

It is hog-killing time again. You would think after all these years it would not be as exciting as it was when we were small. We have the same excitement. The weather is nice and cool. Fall is here, and we have all the wonderful fresh meat to eat once again.

Joy and I have been invited by Mrs. Eva Padgett for Jerry's birthday dinner at the Padgett home. The only people there will be Jerry, the guest of honor, Joy, Joe Thornburg, and me.

Mother has cooked a big pot of the mixed meat and a big pot of rice, and Joy and I cannot stay out of the pot. We keep going back, taking off the lid, finding what we want and eating a small amount. Mother keeps telling us we are going to be so full that we will not be able to eat Mrs. Eva's good food. We keep telling Mother we are just eating a little bit.

By the time we got to the Padgetts's, we were wondering how we were going to eat anything. We walked there and thought this would help get our appetite back. I told Joy, maybe Mrs. Padgett would not have dinner ready when we got there, but it wasn't long until she called us to the table. We tried our best to eat, but were so full we couldn't eat much.

A few days after the party was over, Mrs. Padgett saw Mother and told her that we didn't seem to like anything she had cooked for the party. Mother explained to Mrs. Padgett what had happened. I hope Mrs. Padgett has forgiven us. We enjoyed being there for Jerry's party, and she is a wonderful cook.

SWINDLED

Betty, 14 Years

We have no photographer's studio in Hayesville so when I was a baby and a small child, Mother would take me to Murphy to have my picture made about once a year. Every once in a while, a traveling photographer will come through Hayesville and visit homes and businesses.

Wily McGlamery built a brick building on the corner for a restaurant and hotel that is also used for a bus stop. We received a mail out that a photographer was coming to town and would be making professional pictures upstairs over the restaurant.

Jerry Padgett and I got permission to leave school early and walked up to the hotel to have our pictures made. The photographer was there with his camera. He posed us in different ways and made several pictures. We had to pay him for them before we left.

We never did get the pictures, and now I am sure he did not have film in his camera. Dad and Andy Padgett tried every way they knew to get in touch with this man. The fake photographer had used the name of a legitimate studio, and when Dad contacted the studio they were very upset. They sent someone to make our pictures free of charge.

CASTE SYSTEM OF HAYESVILLE

Even before I studied, about the caste system of India in geography. I realized there was one in Hayesville. I was quite young when a little girl's mother, who lived out of town, deserted her family. Her father told Dad what grief the little girl was going through, and Dad told him to bring her to town to play with me. She was a very cute little girl, and I enjoyed playing with her. I did my best to make her happy. One of my friend's mother told her that she could not play with me when the little girl was at my house. She said the little girl was not from what they considered to be a good family.

I was puzzled by this, and as time went on I noticed more and more that people in our county had a definite place. I think this is just as bad as the caste system in India. I played with the little girl, anyway. One day, I wrote this poem to express my frustrations.

THE WAY IT IS

Betty Benedict

Where are you in the cast system of Hayesville
Where are you on the totem pole
I could make a list of names
And tell you exactly where you go
Oh I've heard about old man so and so
And the lady whats-her-name
Who's not quite up to snuff
Of one thing we don't have to worry
We all have our definite place
If you're born at the top don't worry
You never can fall from grace
There are certain names that don't get it
There are certain names that do
I sure am glad I'm not whats-her-name
There couldn't be anything worse
I know God created the people
But I don't know who made the list
It could have been a great big joke
When someone up and got pissed

MY DAD, THE THIEF

Dad and all his cronies in town still keep on with all their foolishness. An old man from Tusquittee was visiting Dad down at his stable, and said, "Red, are you actually a Jew?"

Dad told him, "By reputation only."

The man asked, "Well, what kind of a name is Benedict, anyway?"

Dad replied, "It is just a good old Kentucky name."

The man asked, "Well, that's something else I don't understand. Why did you come here to this little town?"

Dad lowered his voice and answered, "What I am going to tell you, I would appreciate you not telling anyone. I came here because I needed a place to hide. You know I had those stores, and I had stolen everything in them. You know, everything went along good for a while, but they finally caught up with me, and the law was after me when I came to Hayesville. The last year I was in business, my stock got so low, I had to steal from Bob Tiger's store to keep my business going."

The man's eyes got bigger and bigger, and he asked, "Did Bob Tiger ever know about this?"

Dad said, "Lord, no, and don't you tell him, I'd just have to run again."

"Don't you feel bad about stealing?"

"No, it's just always been a way of life for me."

The man said, "Does your wife know this?"

"Goodness, no. And don't you tell anybody, especially her," Dad replied.

The man said, "I wouldn't tell this to anyone."

Acting relieved, Dad told the man, "It is wonderful to have someone like you to talk to. I have a loft full of wonderful suits and ties. You can have anything you want. "

The old man said, "I can't do that. I have never worn a suit in my life; everyone would know something was wrong if I start wearing a suit and necktie."

Dad said, "Well, if you ever change your mind, just let me know. If I don't have the correct size, I will go to Tiger's and get the size you need."

Dad couldn't wait to get to Tiger's store to tell Mr. Tiger what had happened. Later the man went to Mr. Tiger's store and asked.

"Bob, have you been missing anything lately?"

"No what do you mean? What are you talking about?"

"Mr. Tiger, there is someone stealing you blind. You need to keep your eyes open. Bob, do you not keep a check on your inventory?"

"No, why should I?"

"Mr. Tiger, I am just trying to tell you what is going on, and you are too dumb to hear me. There is someone right here in town stealing you blind. He has a whole barn loft of your clothes, and he offered to give me some. I did not take them. I'll give you a little hint. He used to have a store, and everything he had in it was stolen. He told me when his merchandise got low, he stayed in business for about a year selling stuff he stole from you. Bob, you are going broke if you don't start paying attention to what goes on in your store. "

"I know who you are talking about. You may as well have called his name. He is a friend of mine, and I don't believe he would steal. You have just got it all mixed up."

The frustrated man told him, "Bob Tiger, you're dumber than hell. I am not going to tell you anything else, but you better open your eyes and pay attention to what is going on."

About a week later, Dad saw the man go into Tiger's store and followed him. Dad went over and when the man was watching, he took a tie off the rack, and put it inside his suit coat pocket. The man immediately went over to Mr. Tiger and said, "Bob, did you see that?"

"See what?"

The man answered, "If you are not going to watch him, he is just going to steal you blind."

The old man and Dad left the store at the same time. When they were outside, Dad pulled the tie out of his pocket and said, "Do you want a tie?"

The old man said, "I don't want a tie. I don't wear one, and you are going to get caught."

One morning, just about daylight, the old man came to our door. When Dad answered the door, the old man asked "Have you seen my mule?"

Dad said, "No, I haven't."

He continued with his questions.

Dad asked "Do you think I stole your mule?"

"No, I don't think you would steal from me!"

Dad said, "Well, you are welcome to go down to the barn and look."

The man said, "Well, I have already been down there! He's not there."

Dad said, "I've got to eat breakfast, but you are welcome to go over in my woods to see if he is there."

I am sure the old man's mule must have turned up back at home because we didn't hear any more about it. The old man would tell people in town that he felt so sorry for the nice woman and poor little girl that had to put up with that thief.

Mother says, "I can't understand anyone getting enjoyment out of people thinking they are a thief."

One day, the old man was in Booth's Drug Store. Booth said, "I have been missing quite a few things around here."

The old man said, "It is good enough for you and Bob Tiger if you can't take care of your business and can't see what is going on right under your own nose."

This went on for several years. All of Dad's friends in town went along with him. Any time Dad's friends wore anything new, the old man would think Dad had given it to them. This was carried on longer than any of the other prank episodes and entertained everyone for years.

Junior Benedict

TRAIN RIDE TO MURPHY

My visits to Kentucky were interrupted because of my trips to Athens to go to the dentist. Since I finally have my bridge I can go back now. I love to ride the train when I go to Kentucky and I often travel by myself. We have a train that comes to Murphy, but Dad always buys my ticket from Blue Ridge, Georgia.

The train goes through Chattanooga and Knoxville Tennessee. I usually have a layover in Chattanooga and I go to the restroom and wash up. When you travel by train, your skin

Christine Benedict on Hayesville Square

gets coal dust on it. You don't look like you have it on your face, but when you wash you get it on the washcloth. When you board the train in Blue Ridge, they come around selling candy bars, fruit, potato chips, and things like this. The further along we get, the better the food becomes, and after you leave Chattanooga, you can go to a dining car. They have pretty starched white tablecloths, and serve you on nice china. Your food is brought on platters covered with silver domes. Your water and drinks are served in crystal goblets. You are treated like royalty, and I feel like I am in the movies.

I have wondered why I don't get to catch the train at Murphy instead of Blue Ridge. I know they have passenger cars. I asked Dad why we couldn't go to Murphy and catch the train. He said, "Oh, you don't

J. Paul's Home in Kentucky

want to do that."

I have gone to Kentucky on the train since I was quiet small. When I was younger and traveled alone, the conductor would take me to the next train when I had to change. He would take me to the dining car. I always loved the train rides.

Uncle Al and my cousin, Junior Benedict, met me at the station in Kentucky. I went to visit them on their large dairy farm near Lebanon, Kentucky. My cousin Christine and I always look forward to seeing each other. They have a beautiful home sitting back on rolling land and have ponds scattered about over the pastures for their dairy cows to get water. They have one pond near the house that has a sandy beach, tables, and chairs with umbrellas where we go swimming.

The pond is just like a big swimming pool, but instead of concrete or tile there is dirt in the bottom with a sandy beach on the sides.

My cousin Ed has a restaurant in Lebanon called the Snappy Grill, and another cousin has a Putt-Putt golf course. Cousin Junior has a road house for teenagers called the House of Blue Lights.

Being on their dairy farm is fun. Most of their cows are milked with electric milkers. One of the cows will not let them put the electric milkers on her so someone must milk her by hand. She lets me milk her, but you don't have to know what you are doing. You just touch her, and the milk comes down. They spend a lot of time cleaning the milking machines, and they keep the dairy barn very clean.

They have large trucks to haul the milk to market. Sometimes I ride on the truck to deliver the milk to the creamery. On the way back we stop at a restaurant for breakfast. It is made in the shape of a large coffee pot. They serve breakfast all day and all night. I am fascinated by its shape.

I go to Cousin Ed's restaurant and work on the weekends; it is very busy. His hamburgers and hot dogs are delicious, and he uses my mother's recipe for chili. I often have young boys ask me for dates while working at the Snappy Grill, but I don't have time for this. I have too many other fun things to do with my relatives.

J. Paul came to get me, and I went to Danville, Kentucky for a week.

Betty Ray Benedict

While there we go to see many horse shows around Lexington. J. Paul wanted to enter a couple of his horses in shows. He said he would take me and get me fitted for some riding clothes. I told him I didn't know anything about riding in horse shows.

He said, "I know Uncle Red has taught you to ride."

I said, "J. Paul, you have seen me ride before.

I got on one of his horses; he was trying to tell me what to do. I made a perfect mess. He said, "What on earth is it with you? Has Uncle Red never taught you anything?"

I said, "J. Paul, I know how to post and ride English-style; I know nothing about riding in horse shows. We do not have horse shows in North Carolina. I am sure if my Dad was here, it would not take him long to get me ready for a show. He is not here, and I can see you don't know how to do it."

J. Paul went snorting off mumbling about Dad not teaching me to ride and what a waste it was. We went to the show, but J. Paul didn't enter his horse. I couldn't help, but wish that I had learned to ride better. Dad had always been disappointed that I wanted to ride western because of liking to play cowboy as I grew up. People in Hayesville ride quarter horses, and I have never heard of anyone riding English-style. When you ride in Kentucky, it is a totally different style of riding. Of course, Dad grew up in Kentucky and learned the English style.

When Christine and I were planning our return trip back to Hayesville, I had told her we would get our tickets to ride the train all the way to Murphy.

When it was time to leave Uncle Al's, we got on the train and had a wonderful time. We ate in the dining car all dressed up and feeling like movie stars. Things were going well, we were enjoying our trip. We arrived in Blue Ridge, Georgia. When we told the conductor we needed to find the train going to Murphy, North Carolina, he looked rather alarmed. He showed us where the train would pull in. We waited and the train finally came for us to board for Murphy.

I have never seen such a bunch of raggedy looking men scurrying around. They looked like they did not know what they were doing. They told us we would have to wait a minute, and they would take care of everything. They seemed anxious and very excited.

"Do you think something is wrong?" Christine asked.

I said, "I don't know."

We were all dressed up in very nice clothes. They finally came and got us, and told us we could board. They had cleared a seat in the passenger car. The rest of the seats were taken up with open, wooden chicken coops with big red chickens in them. They were called *Rhode Island Reds*. It was the dustiest place we had ever seen. The men had spread out some dirty towels over the old dusty velour seats for us to sit on.

I asked, the poor man trying to make us comfortable, "Is this a passenger car?"

He said, "Yes, young lady it is, but we haven't had a passenger to Murphy in years."

I started to tell him we would probably be his last ones for years. There was no air conditioning in the car, and we joggled along burning up.

Christine keeps asking, "How much further is it?"

I told her, "It is not far we will soon be in Murphy."

After a little while we came to a big high trestle. I said, "We are here."

As soon as I had said that, the train stalled on the trestle. All we could see was straight down into the water. We sat there for some time; it felt like hours.

They finally got the train started, and we crept into Murphy as slowly as a snail. We got a taxi, and went on to Hayesville. I told Christine not to mention what an ordeal we had. I will not be riding the train to Murphy again from Kentucky!

MR. LEE PENLAND'S SPEAKING CONTEST

Lee Penland

I am in Mr. Lee Penland's room this year in eighth grade, and he is a very good teacher. His daughter, Virginia, dates my friend Wallace Crawford, and they live near Bobbie Penland. Bobbie thinks they will get married soon. Mr. Lee Penland has a speaking contest each year for his eighth grade students. You do not have to enter, but he likes for you to be interested enough to enter his contest. I want to enter, but I don't know what to recite. Everyone chooses a poem written by a famous author. I want something different that no one else has done.

I asked Velma Beam if she would help me find something. We selected a poem that I had never heard before called the "Little Rose" written by Noel Flaubert. It was a long poem about a young girl who had been invited to her first grown up party. It tells about her trying to dress up, and all the snooping around she did in her sister's room. It is a comical poem that lends itself well to acting out the funny calamities she gets into. I practiced and practiced this poem with the help of Velma Beam.

Most of my life, when practicing for a performance, I never seem to get into it very well until I have an audience. Mr. Penland was upset with me being so nonchalant about this program. He told me he felt there was no need for me to continue if I couldn't take it seriously. I told him I did not want to drop out; it was very special to me and I would do well that night.

He said, "Betty, you will have to prove it to me."

The night arrived, and I had my usual bout of stage fright. When it was my turn, I went out and gave it my all. I could see Mr. Penland down near the front with a pleased look on his face. He was nodding in approval of me. This gave me encouragement as I continued with my poem. He told me later he was very pleased that I did so well. I won three silver dollars for the performance. I owe a great deal to Velma Beam for the help and encouragement she gave to me.

MY TRIXIE

Pomeranian

Trixie

Our little Pomeranian, Trixie, has been a wonderful part of our family, and loves all of us very much. She helps Dad bring cattle in from the pastures. We have found that Pomeranians are used as sheep dogs in other countries. When I was smaller and playing dolls, I would dress Trixie with doll clothes. She would ride in my doll carriage lying on her back with her front paws held up. My friends and I played like she was our baby, and she enjoys our attention.

I could hold one of her front paws in my hand, and she would walk beside me on her hind legs.

When Dad goes to town, we tie Trixie up to keep her from following him. If we untie her she immediately goes to town to find him. She first stops at Uncle Henley Crawford's filling station to get a treat.

He says, "Trixie may visit many places in town, but she always stops here first." She continues going into the stores until she finds Dad.

People in town often say, "Red, your dog is looking for you."

Head of the Road—First Train

When I go to school, she doesn't try to follow me, but about the time for me to come home, she will sit at the end of our front walkway waiting for me. Mother seldom goes out of town, but once she went to Athens to visit her family. Dad and I stayed home, and we could not get Trixie to eat a bite of anything while Mother was gone. As soon as she came back Trixie was so happy, she started eating again.

One fall morning, Dad left in a wagon. We had tied Trixie up, but somehow she got loose. She overtook Dad at Boice Supply at the head of the road. She jumped up in the wagon, and rode for a while up Tusquittee Road. For some reason, she jumped off the wagon and a car hit her. Dad brought her back home immediately. She didn't seem to be in pain, and would wag her tail when we talked to her. Howard, Whittie, White was delivering papers in the neighborhood; he stopped, got off his bike, and sat there with us until Trixie died. I was always glad that we got to talk to her, and tell her how much we loved her. Dad made a wooden box, Mother lined it with a blanket, and we buried her across the road deep in the grove. We put up a cross and placed flowers on the grave.

TRIXIE WITH LOVE

I am sad, but tears don't come
Our house is filled with grief
Oh to never see her again
Or have her run to me
Dad and I buried her today in a box
Beneath the old oak tree
Mother with tears gave me a blanket
To cushion the resting place of Trixie
The companion we loved so much
I'll see her wag her tail
And walk on her hind feet
I'll see her run around the house
I'll see her in my dreams
I'll never lose these memories
Though time goes passing by
I'm very glad we had her and I'm not going to cry

J. PAUL BENEDICT

I sometimes get lonesome and want to see my cousin J. Paul. He often comes to Hayesville, but when he hasn't been here in a while, I begin to miss him. I go over to the central telephone office, call him and ask him to come get me. I don't call from our house because Mother gets irritated with me.

She said, "J. Paul has things to do besides running up and down the highway to take you to Kentucky."

Another reason I like for J. Paul to come and get me is that it takes less hassle than going on the train. The best reason is that J. Paul lets me drive, but we don't tell this to anyone because I am only fourteen.

Sometimes J. Paul and I go by the Indian Reservation at Cherokee and cross the Smoky Mountains to Gatlinburg, Tennessee. We stop in Gatlinburg and eat at this cute restaurant and then I shop. J. Paul doesn't mind. I always have some money with me, but I won't spend it on jewelry. I love to look at all the Indian jewelry they have in the cute shops. I tried on bracelets, but didn't buy anything.

We left Gatlinburg and drove for several miles. I looked down, and I had a narrow silver bracelet on my arm.

I said, "J. Paul, we have to go back. "

He said, "Why?"

I said, "I have this bracelet on my arm. We have to take it back; I didn't pay for it."

J. Paul said, "Don't worry, we will stop when I take you back home, and pay the lady for the bracelet."

We did stop on the way back and the lady thanked us and said she had not missed it. I am sure she was glad we were honest.

Chalk Dog

When I was much younger J. Paul, Mom, Dad and I went to Kentucky to visit Uncle Bob Benedict. We went across a place called *Halls Gap*. There was a place on the mountain that sold all kinds of chalk figurines. I begged Dad for a large chalk dog and he bought it. Mother did not want me to have it.

She said, "It was tacky."

I carried it on my lap all the way to Uncle Bob's and back home to Hayesville. When we moved to West Hayesville, I always kept the dog next to the French doors in the entrance hall.

(This dog now sits in my foyer, next to the French doors at my home in Social Circle. I think my dog cost seventy-five cents.)

DAD'S ADVICE ON MONEY

Many evenings after dinner, Dad and I sit out in the yard under a tree and talk. We have always spent a lot of time together talking, even when I was very small. Dad always says that he is teaching me how to do business. I never grow tired of talking to him, and getting his advice about things that are happening to me at school or with my friends. Dad always seems to know how to make me think, and come up with my own solutions. Many times when things come up at school, I will remember something he has said that fits the situation. My friends, especially Amelia, ask his advice about things that are happening in their lives.

One of the things that Dad talks to me about is taking care of my money. He says, "It isn't so much not spending money, as it is being careful how you spend it." He has preached to me every since I can remember to not buy anything that has no resale value.

His motto is, "Never buy anything that you can't sell later if you need to."

Dad often says that he worries about his boys, but he will never have to worry about me because he said "I'm not gullible." I hope I can live up to his expectations.

Most of our families have businesses of their own. I know that someday I will go into business, but I don't know what I would like to do. Mother and Dad expect me to go to college, but at this point I have no idea what I would want to study. I don't feel like I would ever want to teach school, even though I admire many of my teachers.

(When I became older and had a home of my own, Dad's advice on money was embedded in me. I would joke, and tell people how I hated to buy toilet paper and paper towels. Of course, these are necessities, and they serve a purpose. With indoor toilets, we can't flush pages from the Sears Roebuck catalog.)

BROTHER ED

My brother Ed Benedict is a race car driver, and I get to see him when I go with J. Paul to Kentucky. Ed comes to our house at Hayesville when he is not racing, or when he is going through North Carolina with his racing. This year he finished in the top ten at the Darlington race in South Carolina. Ed started his racing career in Miamisburg, Ohio, and has done very well. When Worth Palmer was in service he attended several of Ed's races. Worth didn't realize it was my brother until he told me about a Benedict that he had seen racing. Dad worries about Ed racing, but we are very proud of him.

LEAVING GRAMMAR SCHOOL

My year in Mr. Lee Penland's room is flying by. He is a wonderful teacher, and makes his students feel like he cares about their success in life. We not only study and learn new things, we also have fun and sing songs on Friday mornings. He has me lead our songs.

Most of my friends are involved with boys, but I don't have anyone whom I care about. This is our last year in grammar school. At the end of this year, we will have a graduation ceremony before going into high school. We will leave the rock school building, and go over to the two-storey brick high school building. It will seem strange to have a teacher for each subject. We will change rooms each time the bell rings. We look forward to this change, and yet it is sad. Time keeps moving on.

My hair now is shoulder-length; I was born with a big cowlick on the right front side. When we were small most of my friends had bangs. Whenever Grady Palmer cut my hair, I would ask, "Please, Mr. Grady, can you cut me some bangs?"

He would then tell me that having this cowlick would make my bangs stick straight up. My friends and I look at movie magazines, and try to wear our hair like the movie stars. Many of the stars have shoulder length hair, and they have bangs with curls in them. I decided that having curls like this would solve my problem with the cowlick. I cut my bangs, put pin curls in them, and sat out in the sun until they were dry. I took the pin curls out, combed it, and I was so pleased. It looked wonderful, just like the pictures in the movie magazines.

Tomorrow night is graduation, and I have a nice little white suit with matching shoes to wear. Viola Gray will help me make my corsage with flowers from Mother's yard. She grows beautiful hyacinths and tulips, and we turn the leaves of the tulips back making them look like orchids. We add asparagus fern and tie it all with a pretty ribbon. We then pin it on our dress with a large hat pin. I am so thrilled with my bangs, and excited about our graduation ceremony. I decided to go to town and visit Star's to see if any of the girls were hanging out there. I just couldn't wait for them to see my hair.

By the time I had walked to town, I had perspired and my bangs became straight as a stick. I just turned around and went back home knowing I had really messed up. I could see my bangs bouncing up and down with every step I took. When I got home, I walked over to the sewing box, got the scissors, gathered all my bangs up in my hand, and cut them off. I had no sooner done this when I began to cry.

Mother came in about this time, saw what I had done, and really pitched a fit. She called Louise Moore's Beauty Salon which is located in a can house in her backyard. Mother asked her if she could fix my hair. Louise took one look at me, and burst out laughing.

She called her sister Tootsie and said, "Tootsie, come here and see what Betty has done to her hair."

They did the best they could, which wasn't much, to repair the damage. I graduated into high school looking like a skinned onion. Mother said she wasted her money on my beautiful dress. The thing about it is that no one is as mad at me as I am at myself. Again, I do not know why I did it.

KENTUCKY DERBY

J. Paul promised me that on my fifteenth birthday he would take me to the Kentucky Derby. I have looked forward to this for several years. The Derby is held at Churchill Downs Track in Kentucky. J. Paul knows many people in the horse racing world, and goes there almost every year. He says we will sit in a wonderful box that belongs to some of his friends.

When J. Paul came to get me he was dismayed to see my hair all cut off in front. Sometimes J. Paul has a tendency to stutter, and he couldn't get his words straightened out after taking one look at my hair. I reminded him that all of the ladies wear hats at the Derby, and I told him I thought I was old enough to wear one too.

We stopped in Danville, Kentucky, and he bought me a very pretty floppy brimmed straw hat. I will wear a pretty dress with a round low neck and puffed sleeves made of powder puff muslin. It is ivory with little sprigs of flowers in pink and lilac on it. Pauline Bryan made it for me. I have black patent leather shoes with little heels, short white cotton gloves and a black patent leather clutch bag. I am wearing hose for the first time, and I hope I can keep the seams straight. Mother had to buy me a garter belt to help keep up my hose. I feel so glamorous and grown-up. (This was before any pantyhose came out in the market.)

Citation

J. Paul said he was very proud to take me to the derby especially since it is also my birthday. I think beyond a doubt that I have never been more excited in all my life. The people at the derby are so glamorous with all the ladies dressed in the latest fashions, and excitement is everywhere.

I was surprised to see the grounds around the derby filled with pickup trucks with families eating off the back of them. I don't know how they can see the derby from the great distance where they are parked. I listen to the derby every year on the radio, but it is amazing to actually be here and see it.

J. Paul introduced me to all of the people in the box. They have cold drinks, and anything we want to snack on, and there is a man who is cooking hot dogs and hamburgers for everyone. At last they start playing "My Old Kentucky Home", and I bet you there is not a dry eye in the crowd.

Before starting the race, the horses parade around the track and are then put in their starting gate. Then, the race is on. It seems like the race is over in a flash, and Citation has won the Derby and takes home the roses. (Citation went on to win the Triple Crown that year. He was sired by Calumet Farms where my Dad worked in his youth. It was twenty five years before another horse, Secretariat, won the Triple Crown.)

SUMMER AFTER GRADE SCHOOL

Summer seems to be passing by fast. I have made my usual trips to Kentucky and Athens. My Aunt Bob made me a pretty sun dress out of brown checked gingham with a little cape that buttons on the straps. We went to Michaels in Athens to pick out our material, and bought a cute pair of sandals to match.

Grandmother Cearley believes I am old enough, and should be doing some needlework. She helped me pick out some dish towels; one for each day of the week. They have pictures on them of sun bonnet girls doing housework. She taught me how to embroider them, and it looks like a lot of work to me. I agreed to have this done by this time next year. (I did finish them, and Mother displayed them in her kitchen for several years.)

Everything that has happened this summer seems boring compared to the excitement of going to the Derby. I have a big picture of Citation hanging on the wall in my bedroom. I feel so fortunate that I got to see a Triple Crown winner in the Derby on my birthday. I like to think that it was good luck for me and good luck for Citation. Dad has been so excited for me getting to go to the derby.

I am looking forward to school starting more than usual since I will be in high school with my friends Amelia, Frances, Gay Nell, and Mary Janice.

Guy Padgett, Joy's Dad, has opened a furniture store in the old building Dad had his store in on Main Street just before Tuesquittee Street. Mr. Padgett lets us young people dance there when business hours are over. Someone has an old crank record player we have been using. We also have dances in the spillway up at Chatuge Dam using this record player. With all the room this is a great place to square dance. I am sure no one got permission from the TVA; we just go there and dance. There was never anything said about our dancing as far as I know. When the lake is full the lower part of the spillway is full of water for us to swim. When the lake is down and not leaking, the spillway is dry, and we can dance.

I am still reading "Gone with the Wind," and with everything going on I have many more pages to read. This is the thickest book I have ever seen. I have to read it very carefully because there are a lot of things in the book that are not in the movie.

Another thing we continue to enjoy doing is sleeping in the barn loft. We girls take sandwiches and sodas for treats. We have quilts and blankets to make things comfortable on the hay. Usually Amelia, Joy, Gay Nell, Frances, Regina, Mary Catherine, Glenda and I are there and we talk most of the nights. We have every copy of Life Magazine tied in neat bundles of ten in the order they came. We enjoy reading them, and Mother doesn't mind as long as we put them back in the order we found them.

(One winter, these magazines were stolen from our barn loft. This remains a mystery because there was no way a truck could have gone down to the barn without us knowing. Someone had to carry them out a few bundles at a time. All were gone. They also stole all our quilts. I guess with fall coming they wanted something to read through the winter, and quilts to keep them warm. Mother never let us sleep in the loft after this incident. She was very upset about the theft of her precious magazines and quilts. If someone knows who stole them I would like to know.)

HIGH SCHOOL

**Janet, Joy and Gay Nell
In their Jackets called Toppers**

The awaited day has come. Regina, Tommy, and I are high school freshmen. Regina, and I have new clothes. She got a black turtle neck T shirt in, Asheville, when she went to visit her cousin Willa Jean McGlamery. I love her T-shirt. I went to Athens, but could not find one anywhere.

We have a new store in town owned by Cut Worm Phillips, and Mr. Moore, called the Peoples Store on the square. I was surprised when I found turtleneck T-shirts for sale in their store. I bought three T-shirts, one black, one white, and one Yellow-Jacket gold. Our school colors are black and gold because our mascot is the Yellow Jacket.

The fashion rage this year is jeans, circle skirts, or very straight skirts with a slit up the front or back. The skirts are long, not quite to our ankle. We wear school sweaters and I have a gold one that has Ray's letter from football on the pocket. We wear Bobbie socks with our saddle oxford shoes.

Gene Waldroup

I have Mr. Gene Waldroup as my math teacher, and he makes math very interesting. I have never liked math, but I enjoy his idea of trying to spend a million dollars. He says every Friday we will work on spending our million. We are each supposed to think of wonderful things we would like to have, and research the cost of these things, and come into class with our list on Friday. He does not think we will be able to spend a million dollars before school is out for the summer.

We looked up the cost of vacations all over the world, priced automobiles, yachts, and everything else we could think we wanted. We never did spend our million dollars. This gave me such a feeling about spending a million dollars that I thought about it a great deal. I wondered how one could possibly make a million dollars and not be able to spend it. I wanted to make a million, but it just seemed outrageous and beyond anyone's reach.

When all of those people like the Gettys, the Rockefellers, the Vanderbilts and the Carnegies made all of that money they didn't have to pay one penny of income tax. This is another thing that boggles my mind. (How did our country make it with people paying no income tax?)

I mentioned to Dad about how out of reach a million dollars seemed.

He said, "Money is very elusive, and is very hard for people to make, especially during a depression."

We talked about people who lost everything they had after being wealthy, making bad investments, and having their money in banks that were not insured.

Dad said, "In order for you to understand what a million dollars is, we need to start counting a million dollars every day."

I looked at him and asked, "Where on earth are we going to get a million dollars?"

"We will just pretend."

I said, "If we couldn't spend a million dollars in a whole year in class, I don't think we can count a million in a day."

"You know you helped me count money when we were in the restaurant, and you were very small. You know what a stack of fifty one-dollar bills look like? Can't you picture a stack of them right now?"

I said, "Yeah, I can see a stack of fifty ones stacked and banded."

He said, "Pretend that each bill is a thousand-dollar bill."

I said, "Okay, I see a stack of fifty-thousand-dollar bills banded."

He said, "Okay, if you have twenty stacks of these, you have one million dollars."

Confused I said, "That cannot be true because we can lay that right here on the table. Mr. Waldroup says we can't spend that in a year, and yet I can see that lying here on the table."

Just seeing that example has helped me to understand what a million dollars is. Then Dad asked me whose picture is on a thousand dollar bill. He told me I needed to find that out. I asked everyone I knew, including my teacher, and no one knew. We went to the bank at Hiawassee, and they didn't even know. Dad told me the picture is President Grover Cleveland.

GREETINGS, I'M DRAFTED

Eighteen-year-old boys are being drafted to go into the Army for the Korean War. I went to the post office one morning to pick up the mail, and there were more people there than usual. I asked for the mail, got our stack, and without looking at it, walked out the door. I noticed everyone was staring at me and acting really weird. When I left, several of them ran down the street following me. I noticed Myrt Plemmons, who works at the draft board, was in the group.

Someone hollered, "Betty, aren't you going to open your mail?"

I stopped when they caught up with me. I looked through the mail, and I had a letter from the draft board addressed to me.

Someone said, "Open it, open it."

I opened the letter from the draft board. It said, "Greetings, you have been drafted to serve your country." I have been drafted into the Army!

Everyone was dying laughing at my puzzled look. Myrt Plemmons explained to me, they went over to the courtouse to get all the birth certificates of the eighteen-year-old males. When she got back to the office and found that my birth certificate listed me as being a male, it was too great a joke not go on and draft me.

(Mother later checked into this and I am registered in Washington as a female. I felt sure with all the commotion about the drafting that they changed my certificate, however I am still listed as a male in the Clay County courthouse.)

IN LOVE

Betty Benedict at Sixteen

Almost everywhere I go on the school grounds, I see a certain boy that I like very much. I don't mention this to any of my girl friends. We have always talked about the boys we like, and the ones we think are cute. For some reason, I just want to keep this to myself. I think he must like me because everywhere I go I see him. He is older than me and plays football. Some of the other girls think he is cute, too.

This is the first time I have liked a boy this much. I still run around with all the boys in town. I have no interest in any of them, and they have no interest in me. One of my town boy friends, and I tried to date one time, it just didn't work out. I look forward to going to school every day because I think that he might ask me for a date.

I know a lot of times boys from out of town don't think the town girls would go with them. I don't understand the reason for this. Most all of my friends would like to date boys that don't live in town. Many of the boys who live out of town have their family truck or car they can drive. Most of the town boys do not have a car.

(Many years later Julia Wheeler, Sarah's daughter and I were talking about how many people did not have cars when we were growing up.

Julia said, "Well, we didn't need one; we were already here.")

It is more exciting going to school every day, since I like someone. I love going to the football games to see him play. It just doesn't seem like he will ever ask me to go out. One day, I was getting a drink at the water fountain. He came by with a group of his buddies and said, "Look, that's her, boys."

I walked around with my head in a cloud for days. I often think about talking to some of my girlfriends to see if I might do something that is not too forward to get him to ask me for a date.

The days and weeks and months drag on, and I see him everywhere I go on the school grounds. It seems like he always follows me, but I don't think he is ever going to ask me out. I wish there was someone else that I could date because it would make me feel more a part of my group. A whole carload of my friends, boys and girls, will go to Murphy to a movie or we will go to the new theater in Hayesville.

Pede Williams and I go to church dinners out in the country on Sunday. Sometimes there are a group of us, but most times it is Pede and me. I don't know how Pede finds out where there is going to be an outdoor dinner, but he always knows. He loves to dress up, and tells me what fancy dress to wear to impress the people at the dinners. He tells me to go around with him, and just get the food he chooses because he knows who cooks well.

We drive his dad's car, and cut up all the time. The car has a city horn, a country horn and more. Pede is a lot older than our crowd, but he isn't married. He is still home with his parents who go to our church. Mother always knows I am in good hands with Pede.

I call Pede when I am bored, and all of my friends are with their dates. He usually comes to get me driving his Austin Healy. He comes to most of the singings if I am going to sing. He stands in the back and makes faces at me and tries to make me laugh. I told him he was just wasting his time because I don't think he is funny. I am sure the real reason he goes to the singings is to hear the Ritter Quartet sing. He is no different than anyone else; he loves to hear them sing. (When I get to Heaven, I hope I will hear them once more.}

We play shuffle board and ping-pong in the basement of the Methodist Church. This has been a hang out for us for several years. Since we now like boys, it has become more and more a place for boys and girls to meet. One night, the boy I liked showed up in the basement of the church with a group of other boys. We didn't talk to each other the whole time we were playing games.

It came time for me to go home and I started to leave. As I was leaving, he bounded up the steps, and asked if he could take me home. We walked home to my house and sat on the steps of the front porch for a long time talking. He asked me if I would wear his class ring; I was thrilled.

Quenton Lyon

The end of school came all too soon, and he graduated from high school and left for the Air Force. When he was in basic training and finally was allowed to go shopping he sent me a present. I was so thrilled with it. Christmas came, and he sent me a watch which was the nicest thing a boy could do for you. All of my friends are very envious, and yet thrilled for me to have such a thoughtful boyfriend. I get letters every day, and sometimes two a day. Uncle Ed Mease at the post office was teasing me about all the mail from my boyfriend.

On a leave in August of 1950, my boyfriend is home; I am very happy and think everything is fine. We double date with Gay Nell Mingus and her boyfriend. It didn't take me long to figure out that something was troubling him. I started hearing all these rumors that he was going out with other girls after taking me home at night. He vowed this was not true, but I was unsure of this. I was not comfortable with what was going on and I could tell his attitude toward me had changed.

Gay Nell, her boyfriend, and the two of us were parked at the spillway. This is a favorite parking place for lovers. Gay Nell and her friend walked off. We also got out of the car, and I was stewing about all the things I had heard. I got up and walked back to the car.

The next day, he left before his leave was up, and went back to the base without telling me goodbye. I was unaware that he had been told that I was dating other people while he was away. I had only one letter from him after he left, and it was very cool and impersonal. That was the end of our romance, and I was heartbroken. The pain was almost unbearable, and I grieved for my loss.

Another boy one year older than me started asking me out. I started going with him. By this time, I was in the eleventh grade, and he started asking me to marry him. I didn't want to get married, but being a silly teenager, I finally told him I would. We set a date. I couldn't sleep at night from worrying about getting married. One night, I woke up in a sweat and thought, "I don't have to marry and tomorrow I am going to tell him I am not going to."

The next day I told him I was not going through with it.

Several months passed, and he started asking me again to marry him. I finally told him I would if we could keep it a secret until I graduated from high school. He agreed that we could do that. We set the date for April 28, 1951. This was just a week before I finished my eleventh grade. I told him I absolutely had to finish school, and he said that was fine with him. When I told some of my girlfriends what I was going to do, they said they thought it was very romantic.

One of my friends at school is Claude Scroggs; we call him Froggy. We went in the auditorium and sat down on one of the backseats. I told him I needed to talk to him, and I asked him what he thought I should do. It took him by surprise; I don't think he knew what to say. I think I was just trying to get someone to tell me not to get married. He said he didn't know what to tell me.

April 28 rolled around and my friend Harold Byers and a girl who is my boyfriend's first cousin went with us. We went to Blue Ridge, Georgia, got our blood test, and were waiting for the results. My boyfriend and Harold went into an ice cream place. I told his cousin, "I don't think I can do this."

She replied, "Oh, Betty, you have to, you have already backed out one time."

We got married and went back to Hayesville. I thought it would be kept a secret until I graduated, but one of my girlfriend's mother found out. She called me to her house, and told me if I didn't tell my mother, she was going to. That really upset my plans.

I had to go tell Mother and Dad, and I cannot describe what an ordeal that was. The news was out of the bag, and soon everyone in town knew. Needless to say, everyone was very disappointed in me.

(This marriage was to Quenton Lyon. It lasted for forty-seven and a half years until he passed away in October 1998.)

MR BEAL TO THE RESCUE

I had to go back to school, and face the music with my teachers and classmates. School was over except for finals. All of my teachers were very upset with me. The fortunate thing was there was no rule against married people going to high school in Hayesville.

I had passed every subject except French, and I failed the final exam. I had passed French the year before, and you must have two years of French to get credit. If you fail the second year it cancels out the year

Scott Beal

before. Without this credit I did not have enough points to graduate. This made it impossible for me to graduate the next year. Needless to say, I was extremely upset.

I talked to several friends who were in my French class and asked them to go see our French teacher, Mrs. Laura McGlamery, and ask to see their tests. We divided up the test questions so each person could copy five questions each from the test. We were afraid Mrs. McGlamery would not let them see their tests, but she did. She told them she was pleased they were interested in their scores. I eventually had the complete test with all the correct answers.

Laura McGlamery

One of my friends said, "Betty, this may be one you don't pull off."

I went into the principal's office while all my friends were waiting outside to see what would happen. I didn't knock; I just pulled open the principal's door and went in crying at the top of my lungs.

Mr. Beal said, "Betty, Betty, what on earth is wrong?"

I said, "Oh, Mr. Beal, I have failed my French class and I must graduate next year. Oh, Mr. Beal, what on earth am I going to do?"

He said, "Betty, Betty, quit that crying, let me get your record out." He went over to the cabinet and pulled out my French file and said, "Betty, this is not good."

I said, "Oh, Mr. Beal, you must help me. I have to graduate next year. You must help me."

He said, "Betty, just sit down over there and stop crying. I will go see Mrs. Mac and be back shortly."

I went over to the chair and sat down and put my head in my hands. He came back in a few minutes and said, "Mrs. Mac will give you the test over again."

I said, "Mr. Beal, thank you so much."

I went out praying that Mrs. Mac would give me the same test again. When I came out I let my friends know that all was well. I went up to Mrs. Mac's office, and told her that I appreciated her giving me the test over.

She said, "Betty, you go home and study, and be in here tomorrow to take the test."

I studied that test and memorized every bit of it. I went back the next day, and Mrs. Mac sat in the desk with me while I took the test. I passed with flying colors and Mrs. Mac said, "Betty, this makes me so mad; you could have been one of my best students."

If it had not been for the good heart of Mr. Scott Beal, I could not graduate the next year.

At the end of summer vacation in 1951, Quenton left to go into the Air Force. I got a job selling popcorn at the Hayesville Movie Theater, and my friend Louise Cloer was selling tickets in the box office. School starts again and I am a senior in the twelfth grade. The old brick high school building was torn down over the summer, and the new school building is partially finished. My last year of high school began in a building of concrete blocks that were unfinished. I am very sad not to be in our old brick building, and I wish it could have been left standing for me to graduate.

HIGH SCHOOL IN SAVANNAH

Quenton is out of basic training and has been stationed at Hunter Field in Savannah Georgia. He started begging me to come to Savannah. His cousin, Juanita Lovin and her husband Bill Stanley are living in Savannah, and David Ledford is also stationed there. I told Quenton that I would come if I could go to high school in Savannah. He rented an apartment for us in the Godley Mansion at 2108 Bull Street. Juanita and Bill lived in an apartment within walking distance on Montgomery Street.

David Ledford was in Hayesville on leave and took my luggage to Savannah. I rode the bus to Savannah, where Quenton and Juanita were to meet me. When I got there, I waited and waited, but they didn't show up. I had them paged and finally gave up, so I called a cab to take me to Bill and Juanita's home. Soon after I got out of the cab at their home, David pulled up in his car with my luggage. No one was home at Juanita's so we sat on the steps and waited. We finally went next door to a service station, and I called the bus station and had them paged again. About that time, we saw them pull up in a cab. David took us over to our apartment on Bull Street.

The next morning, I got up early. I had a list of high schools I had gotten from the phone book. I called a taxi and went out Victory Drive to Savannah High School on Washington Avenue. I went into the office and asked to speak to the principal. I told him my situation, and asked to transfer to his school.

He said, "I am very sorry, but we do not allow married students to go to school here."

I called a cab and left his office. I went to every high school in Savannah, and not one would take me because I was married. I talked to Quenton and told him, that it looked like I was going to have to go back to Hayesville.

He said there was no need for me to finish high school.

I said, "You may not see any need, but I am going to finish."

I went out early the next morning and walked to Savannah High School which was a thirty minute walk. I went to the office and asked to see Mr. Varnadow, the principal. The secretary went to his door and told him the girl who was here to see you yesterday is back again.

She came back and said, "There is no need seeing him."

I immediately went over, opened his door, and went into his office. I didn't give him a chance to say anything. I told him I had to go to school. He said he had already explained to me that the school does not take married people.

I said, "Please, I am begging you to let me go Mr. Varnadow. Why will you not let me go?"

He kept easing me toward the door, and I put my back against it and begged him all the harder. He said once again the reason I cannot let you go is the policy that does not allow married people to attend.

I said, "Is this a state policy?"

He said, "No"

I said, "Is it a county policy?"

He said, "No"

I said, "Is it just your policy?"

He said, "Well, yes, and all schools in Savannah have the same policy."

I said, "Then, you can change your policy. Please let me go."

He said, "I must be losing my mind, because I am going to let you go."

He said, "If finishing school means this much to you, I will let you go, but you listen to me and you listen well. If I hear of you talking sex to any of these young students, you are out of here. I want you to promise me that if you get pregnant, you will come and tell me, and you will have to leave school."

I said, "Mr. Varnadow you need not worry about any of this, I will not get pregnant."

Of course, he never forgot my face, and would always speak to me and call me by name when he saw me in the hall. Several of the girls I met in school became my very good friends. One of the girls was working in the lunchroom, and I asked Mr. Varnadow how I could get a job there, and he got me one. My last class before lunch was home economics, and they let us out ten minutes early so we could get to the lunchroom before the rush.

My job was punching a hole in the top of the paper milk bottle tops. My friend Barbara would put the straw in the hole. We took turns about doing these jobs. The line moved fast so we were busy punching holes and putting in straws. We got no pay, but we could eat all we wanted and whatever we liked. This included all kinds of ice cream. They had the most delicious food that you could find anywhere.

For the first time in my entire life, I saw shrimp. They had made a dish called shrimp creole. You spooned rice on your plate, and then put the shrimp on top, then put tomato sauce over it. Dad had told me about shrimp and had described it to me so many times I immediately knew what it was. I fell in love with shrimp. I had deviled crab for the first time, and we had wonderful fried shrimp a few weeks later. They had yeast bread that was absolutely delicious.

I really buckled down and studied very hard, and I made very good grades, including math. I tried my best to be a model student, and not disappoint Mr. Varnadow. The friendships that I made in the school lasted for many years. My friend Barbara Covington was the closest friend I made there.

The Navy Band came to Savannah High to put on a show. A young singer named Julius La Rosa was the star of the show. A group of the seniors went out to Tybee Beach because they knew the band was going there. La Rosa took a special liking for Barbara. That night at the concert he sent her a note telling how much he enjoyed talking with her at Tybee. He told her that he was going to be a regular on the Arthur Godfrey show. He signed the note "Julie." We got a kick out of this. We thought he was making up the part about the Arthur Godfrey show just to impress Barbara.

We got television in Savannah not too long afterwards, and were very surprised to see Julius on Arthur Godfrey's show every time it came on the air.

I became very homesick for my home in Hayesville and wanted very much to graduate from Hayesville High School. I didn't feel good about graduating from any other school even though I enjoyed my time at Savannah High. Quenton got notice that he was being sent to Stillwater, Oklahoma, to go to school at Oklahoma A & M. (It is now Oklahoma State University.)

I returned to Hayesville to finish high school with my classmates. I have my job back at the theater selling popcorn in the evenings. I don't make much but have plenty of popcorn and movies are free.

CHOOSING CHINA AND SILVER

Star Bristol

Star sells Haviland China and Reed & Barton and Alvin sterling flatware. Star says it is time for me to choose a pattern in each for my formal dinnerware.

She said, "Several people have come in and asked if you have picked a pattern. The old man Haviland who owns the company has a favorite pattern of china called Roseland, and if you choose this pattern it will never go off open stock. The company will always make it."

This is also the pattern Star selected. I told her I liked the pattern, and that was a good idea for the selection. She gave me a large chop plate, and I said, "Star, do you think I should go for service for eight or a service for twelve." Star said in her colorful way of talking, "Hell, don't go for service for twelve, anybody is a damn fool that will have more than eight people for dinner at one time."

(I have never had over eight people at my house for dinner that I haven't thought about her advice. I also chose Star's personal pattern of silver flatware Chateau Rose. She advised me to get dinner size rather than the luncheon size.)

BUS RIDE TO STILLWATER OKLAHOMA

School is going great, and I am studying hard. I really want Mr. Beal to be proud of me. Easter holidays were coming up, and I decided I would like to see Oklahoma. I called Quenton, and told him I wanted to come out for the holidays. He said it was a very long bus ride.

We had always played cowboy, and in my mind Oklahoma was cowboy and Indian territory. No one wanted me to go, but I was determined to make the trip. In order to make the long trip, I will have to miss some days at school. I went along with my plans and somehow Mr. Beal heard about it. He called me in the office and set in on me about missing school.

He said, "You have already missed too many days transferring to Savannah and back to Hayesville. I am telling you that you should not go on this wild trip."

I said, "Mr. Beal, Quenton may be sent overseas."

He said, "Don't start trying to pull that stuff on me. I happen to know that Quenton is in school out there. You are going to mess around and miss so many days of school that you will fail."

I said, "Mr. Beal, I have been studying very hard, and I have been making good grades."

He said, "Yes, I realize that, but I am not impressed. You could have been making this kind of effort long before now."

He said, "Just let the hammer fall where it will, and don't come crying to me. There will be no help from me this time around."

I told him I was not going to fail, and I was going to study so hard they could not fail me. With me being a silly teenager, I felt like I had to go to Oklahoma while I had the chance.

I went to Murphy to the bus terminal to get a ticket to Stillwater, Oklahoma. This threw them for a loop. I have never seen such scurrying around trying to find maps to figure out where I was going. It was going to take some time for them to prepare the tickets for the trip. They asked me if I could go home and come back the next day. The ticket would then be ready.

When I went back the next day, the ticket was ready, and it was just short of two yards long. It was rolled up, and I asked them if I had to change buses at every one of those stops. She said I did. I was scheduled to get to Stillwater at four o'clock in the afternoon two nights after I left Murphy. It seemed like it took me forever just to get to Memphis, Tennessee.

When I got to Memphis, I had to walk from one bus station to another to catch the bus. When I got to the station, I went in to find how long it would be before I could get on the bus. I handed the lady my ticket and she said, "Oh, my goodness, who on earth made this ticket for you?"

I replied, "I got it in Murphy, North Carolina."

She said, "You have been routed so far out of your way. I can change this, and you will get a sizeable refund, and get there in the morning at four o'clock." This was twelve hours earlier than before.

I was so tired that this sounded wonderful to me; she took the ticket and scheduled a much shorter route. I still had to change buses several times and I had a hard time remembering the names of the towns. Most of the changes I had to make were in towns with unusual Indian names.

My last bus change was in Okmulgee, Oklahoma, at two o'clock in the morning. I was feeling good thinking I had only two more hours to go. I got off the bus and went to get on my bus to Stillwater. The bus driver was sitting in the bus with three Mexican men. I did not get alarmed because I thought more people would get on, but the bus driver just closed the door, and we departed.

I didn't feel one bit good about this. The men kept talking in a language I couldn't understand, and kept looking at me. I tried to relax, but I didn't dare go to sleep. We drove for two hours, and came into this place that looked like a little town that was deserted. There were no streetlights or any lights anywhere. We pulled up to a bus station that was closed. I was really getting nervous.

The three men got off and stood in front of the station talking and looking back at me.

I asked the bus driver, "What time does this bus station open?"

He said, "In the morning at about seven."

I said, "I need to use a telephone. Where is there a telephone?"

He said, "Well, I have a key to the bus station, and I can open it and let you use the phone."

I said, "Well, that would be good."

He opened the station, and we went inside. I called the switchboard at the college to ask if they could get Quenton Lyon to come to the phone.

He said, "No, I can't do that. I will get in trouble if I leave the phone and go down to his room in the dorm."

I told him what a predicament I was in. I told him I was at the bus station, it was closed, and I was supposed to go to our friend's house when I arrived. I was twelve hours early. They were going to meet me at the bus station, and I had no phone number or address for their apartment.

The boy had mercy on me, and left his post and brought Quenton back to the phone. Quenton said for me to get a taxi and go to the Stillwater Hotel. I explained to him that there was no taxi or any activity there. I asked him to stay on the phone and wait just a minute. I called to the bus driver, and asked him if there was any way I could get a taxi to the Stillwater Hotel.

He said, "Yes I have a taxi out back that I drive, and I can take you."

I told Quenton that I could go to the hotel since the bus driver was also a taxi driver.

The bus driver went around back, and pulled his taxi up in front and loaded my suitcase in the trunk. I got in the back seat to go to the hotel. We were going through the little town, and he tells me that he is running late to pick up a man that he takes to the oil fields every night.

He said, "As soon as we get back from taking him to work, I will take you to the hotel."

I felt sure we passed by the hotel on the way to pick up the man. I thought for sure that this would be my last night on earth. I didn't know what to do. I tried to decide if I had anything I could use for a weapon in my pocketbook. All I had was a small pearl handle knife. I opened the knife and kept it in my hand inside my pocketbook. We rode and rode through the most desolate desert land that I had ever seen. We were on a dusty dirt road that seemed to go on forever. I prayed and asked God to please save me.

About that time, in the distance, I could see a little house with a man standing out in front. As we got closer, I could see he had a metal dinner bucket in his hand. Relief flooded over me, but I still did not feel completely safe because he could have taken me to the hotel when we passed it in town.

He pulled over and apologized to the man for being late, and explained he had to open the bus station for me to make a phone call. We drove several miles before we came to an oil field with all the towers and oil pumping. We let the man out, and started on our journey back to Stillwater. I was still concerned, and did not feel safe with this man. It seemed like forever to get back to town. We pulled up in front of an old building that had outside stairs going up to the hotel. He got out and carried my bags upstairs to the dark hotel. He knocked on the door and an old man in a night shirt came to answer it.

The bus driver told him that I needed a room.

The old man said, "Young lady, if you are by yourself that will be fifty cents. If you have someone else with you, that is a quarter more."

I said, "In other words, it is seventy-five cents."

I gave him fifty cents, and he took me down the hall, pointed out the bath at the end of it that everyone used. He opened the door to my room, it was very clean. I was so tired and so relieved, it looked like heaven to me. I had a lavatory on the wall inside the room, and I was getting settled when a knock came on the door.

The old man said, "You've got company." It was Quenton.

The keeper kept taping me on the shoulder saying, "That's a quarter more, that's a quarter more."

Quenton reached into his pocket and gave the old man a quarter to get rid of him. Quenton had to slip back on campus that night to prevent trouble.

The next night Quenton came to spend the night, and the old man told us it would only be fifty cents since Quenton didn't stay the night before.

Stillwater was an interesting place because their native Indians were so different from the ones in North Carolina. The country was so flat with hardly any vegetation, and everything was very dusty. There were just a few little shops and a restaurant in a straight row on the only street through town. My stay ended with the Easter holidays and I started my trip back to Hayesville. I dreaded the long trip of two days and two nights, but I made the return trip just fine.

I am back in school and studying very hard. My high school days are coming to an end and I don't know what to do.

I have always known when summer ended; I would be back in school when fall comes. Looking back on all of it, it has been a wonderful journey. Although there have been ups and downs, I have enjoyed most of it. I dread not knowing what to do. I am sure Mom and Dad are disappointed that I married, and won't have the future they had planned for me. This is not mentioned except they remind me that I can still go to college, it is not too late. They have told me this many times. I want to take this summer to try and figure out what I need to do with my life.

GRADUATION FROM HIGH SCHOOL

Allen Bell

Graduation night is here and I have made it through to graduate. Regina Johnston and Claude Wimpey are the two shortest in our class so they will march in the lead to get our diplomas. Jerry Crawford and I are the next couple. Allen Bell is our superintendent of schools, and he always presents the diplomas. Regina and Claude were called first to the podium. Next, when my name was called, I walked out on the stage, Mr. Bell handed me my diploma. Then, holding my hand so I would not go on past, he said in a low voice, "Betty, I'll give you fifty cents if you will sing 'Did You ever go Sailing' for me."

I said, "I will."

He laughed and said, "I know you would! Get off this stage."

After the ceremony everyone was asking what Mr. Bell and I were talking about for so long.

(Allen Bell died in 1956, and I did not see him again after the graduation ceremony. I didn't know that May of 1952, at my graduation ceremony, would be the last time he would ask me to sing "Did You Ever go Sailing Down the River of Memories.")

Like most of my classmates, after graduation we leave Hayesville, but most of us return. There seems to be a pull on everyone raised in these mountains that brings us back like a magnet. We may stay away for many years, but we are all eventually drawn back to our roots. There could have been no better place in the world to grow up and go to school. Where else could I have made so many friends, and had so many people love me? I in turn loved everyone I have told about in this story.

Dad gave me the name for my book. Often, people would come into the restaurant, look around, and say, "Where is Betty?" Referring to my daily visits to the people who lived and worked around our Hayesville Courthouse Square, he would tell them, "Oh, she is probably out"

"WINDING ROUND THE SQUARE."

THE END

TRIBUTES

BILL STANDRIDGE

Earl Standridge

Bill Standridge

I walk along the sidewalks in Hayesville, I feel very good and all warm inside. I am nine years old, and I know lots and lots of things that you probably would know if you stopped to think. Then again you may not have been to Hayesville, or even heard about it. I'll tell you this, you have missed a lot. You have missed the music that is such a part of our lives, and has made our lives special. I know this is true because I tell people about the plays and operettas we have at our school. People from other places say they never had all these at their schools. I tell them the reason they never had these things is because they didn't have Bill Standridge.

The reason they don't have her is because they don't have Earl Standridge. You see, he was born here in Hayesville. He married Bill somewhere in South Georgia, and brought her here to live. She made our town special because she brought us her music. She gives us her time and love, and she has us doing musicals and having a great time.

You have never heard a piano played until you hear her play. When she sings "Back to Bethel" at church, I cry a little because it touches me inside.

Yes, our town would be almost like any other town if it hadn't been for Earl Standridge marrying Bill. With her doing all this for us, I am going to tell her so.

(I went to see the Lick Log Players, and I thought how wonderful it is, that the town is still special. I know somehow it all goes back to Bill, whether anyone remembers her contributions to the community or not.)

WILLIE ROGERS, MY FIFTH-GRADE TEACHER

Willie Rogers

For taking extra time and interest in me to teach me better penmanship. She has beautiful handwriting, and she filled out the diplomas for all students graduating to high school. She realized my penmanship was below par and took special time to teach me. When I finished fifth grade, the improvement of my handwriting was astounding. Mrs. Willie Rogers would tell me that I learned to write just like her.

JULIA JAMES BUCKNER

When I was small, Mother had a pretty young girl work for her and sometimes stay with me at night. Her name was Julia James Buckner. Her father brought his family to Clay County not long before Julia came to work for Mother. Her father's name was Deck James, and he was a horse trader who often traded livestock with Dad. Mother thought a lot of Julia and said she was one of the best helpers she ever had.

Julia James married Joe Buckner who had a large farm on lower Tusquittee. They had several children. She and Joe worked very hard to keep their farm going in order to pay their mortgage. Joe died when the children were young, and left Julia with the big farm to pay for. Everyone said Julia would never make it. She worked, took care of all the animals, raised crops, and took care of her children. Of course, when the children were old enough, they all helped. It is hard to imagine any woman who could do what Julia did. It is hard to think of all the hard work it took to keep that farm going.

Mother said, "If anyone was ever a superwoman, Julia was it."

Mother worried about Julia, knowing all the work she had to do on the farm. Julia would come to visit Mother from time to time. Her children all grew up and made her proud. There is a road through her property named for Julia, but the biggest tribute to her is her son Joe who teaches school at Hayesville and is active in community affairs.

WILLIAM WILSON HANCOCK, 1787-1863

This book would not be complete without a tribute to William Hancock. Clay County was established in 1861 after breaking off from Cherokee County. The new officials were looking for a site for the county seat. Several sites were being considered, Mr. Hancock made an offer to donate twenty acres of his land to build the town of Hayesville. Down town Hayesville now sets on these twenty acres. The Hancock family moved to this community from Tennessee in the early 1800s. Mr. Hancock owned many acres of farmland. His daughter married a Sanderson, another prominent family in Hayesville at the time. Mr. Hancock died in 1863 shortly after the county was formed. His wife and four sons sold their property and moved back to Tennessee.

Other prominent names that have passed from the county are Standridge, Winchester, Ketron, Hunt, Mingus, and Pass.

MOST OF ALL I PAY TRIBUTE TO MY FRIENDS

Joy Padgett

Amelia Standridge

Mary Janice White

Emogene Carringer

Betty Benedict

Glenda Prater

Frances Beal

Cordia Padgett

Gay Nell Mingus

Regina Johnston

Helen Herbert

Janet Palmer

Mary K Bradshaw

Evelyn Winchester

Hayesville

Betty Frances Cherry

Janet Kitchens

THE WHOLE TOWN GANG

EARLY LITTLE FRIENDS ON THE SQUARE

THESE ARE THE FIVE FRIENDS THAT PLAYED WITH ME AT A VERY EARLY AGE ON THE SQUARE

Amelia Standridge		Mary Janice White
Joy Padgett	Glenda Prater	Emogene Carringer

Three of my close friends are no longer with us. I miss them very much—Amelia Standridge, Regina Johnston, and Evelyn Winchester. They remain in our hearts.

I have many other friends whom I met in school that became very dear to me. The friends listed here are the ones who lived on the Square or in the area just off the Square.

DAD ALWAYS AND FOREVER

Betty Benedict

I stoop to touch the earth I love
I rise to sniff the air
I breathe the smells of long ago-
The same dreams come back now
The earth was here
The sky was too
The girl stands here as then
So much is gone
So much has past
But to my heart returns
I must go now
I've much to do
A promise still to keep
To reach our dreams of long ago
I'll have no time to weep
I touch the earth for strength
You gave all this to me
And every word and every smile
They will not leave my heart
But light my path
And guide me on
You will not leave me ever

(July 10 1965. Hayesville NC. The day Dad was buried.)

ABOUT THE AUTHOR TODAY

No matter where her life took her after graduation from high school, she never felt a belonging anywhere and never called anywhere home except Hayesville, North Carolina. Even after her mom and dad both died and she had no relatives living in Clay County, she never stopped going back home regularly. She purchased the Hyatt House in West Hayesville in 1996 and goes there as often as she can. She has a home in Social Circle, Georgia on the main street, built just like the old Sanderson house she lived in on the Square in Hayesville. The Social Circle house was built in 1850 before the Civil War and is registered on the national list of Historic Places as *Dr. Brown's Towne House*.

Before retiring in 1994, she owned and operated a cosmetology school. She opened the business before she was thirty years old. She operated the DeKalb Beauty College for thirty-two years. This school grew to have the largest enrollment of any cosmetology school in Georgia and was the third largest in the nation. The school was accredited by the Southern Association of Colleges and Schools. The DeKalb County Chamber of Commerce nominated Betty for Business Man of the year in 1972. They said she had affected the economy of the county more than any individual owning a business.

She was the first woman to be awarded Georgia's Business Man of the year in 1972 and 1973. Jimmy Carter proclaimed a week in her honor when he was Governor. She was the first woman to be named deputy sheriff in DeKalb County by Sherriff Lamar Martin in 1966. WSB Radio Station awarded her the "Busy Beaver" award in 1973. She served four years as the Georgia Cosmetology Schools Association Vice-President. Two pictures of her appear in Georgia's Senator Max Cleland's best-seller, "Strong at the Broken Places."

Betty was active in DeKalb politics and lobbied at the Georgia State Capitol during most of the legislative sessions from 1962 through 1993. After selling her business and retiring in 1994, she started her own interior design business with her daughter Alisa. She serves on the Board of Social Circle Historic Preservation Society.

DOWN TOWN MAP INDEX

A=BOB TIGER'S STORE
B=COMMERCIAL HOTEL
C=PEARL AND LIZZY
   SCROGGS
D=OMAR LEE ANDERSON
E=FRANK HERBERTS
F=FRANK HERBERTS POOL
   ROOM
G=ANGELS SHOE SHOP
H=DR. MAYS OFFICE
   UPSTAIRS
I=FURNITURE STORE
J=PASSMORE BEER JOINT
K=METHODIST
   CHURCH—OLD
L=SANDERSON—CURTIS—
   BENEDICT
M=BARBER SHOP
N=THOMPSON'S STORE
O=CURTIS HOUSE-FOOD
P=EARLY ANDERSON
Q=EARLY ANDERSON STORE
R=RED BENEDICT STORE
S=DUCKWORTH
T=GRANNIE WHITE

U=PASS HOTEL
V=BAPTIST CHURCH
W=CARRIES RESTAURANT
X=CANTRELLS DRUG STORE
Y=WALTER MOORE
   HARDWARE
Z=FRED PASS DRUG STORE
a=MASONIC TEMPLE
   UPSTAIRS
b=CENTRAL OFFICE
   UPSTAIRS
c=POST OFFICE 1937
d=MARY JO'S BEAUTY SHOP
e=CRAWFORDS SERVICE
   STATIO
f=CRAWFORDS TEN CENT
   STORE
1=BOOTHS DRUG STORE
2=PASS-HUNT SERVICE
   STATION
3=MARTIN SHOE SHOP
4=BASS DUVAL BEER JOINT
5=FLORA DAVIS HOME
6=MCGLAMERY BEER JOINT
7=EVERETT-JULIETT
   CRAWFORD
9=METHODIST
   CHURCH-NEW

DOWN TOWN HAYESVILLE

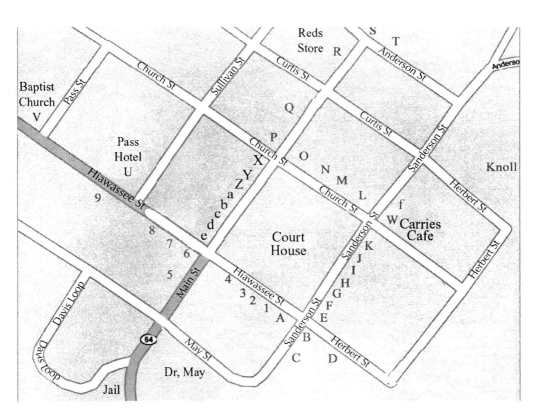

WEST HAYESVILLE MAP

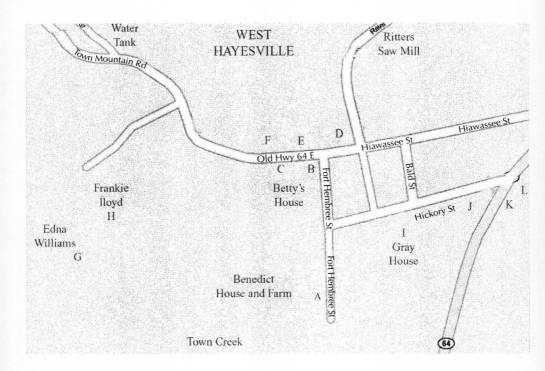

WEST HAYESVILLE MAP INDEX

A = BENEDICT HOME—WEST HAYESVILLE
B = LUTHER MATHESON HOME
C = BETTY BENEDICT HOME (HYATT HOUSE)
D = MISS ELLEN SCROGGS HOME
E = FRED WHITE HOME
F = WILBURN MINGUS HOME
G = EDNA AND OTIS WILLIAMS HOME
H = FRANK AND FRANKIE LLOYD HOME
I = TOM GRAY HOME
J = LUTHER MATHESON STORE
K = AMELIA STANDRIDGE HOME
L = MARY CATHERINE BRADSHAW HOME

INDEX

INDEX OF POEMS—
FIRST LINES

W

When the saints go marching in,
     80
Where are you in the cast system
     of Hayesville? 223
Whoop-se-Daisy, I sure feel lazy,
     112

Y

You are my friends and I love you,
     206

CPSIA information can be obtained at www.ICGtesting.com
Printed in the USA
243596LV00003B/1/P